Opium, Empire and the Global Political Economy

What is the link between opium, imperialism and capitalism? Was the British Empire built on opium? And what can the nineteenth-century drug trade tell us about the Asian heroin traffic of today?

Carl A. Trocki answers all these questions in his fascinating history of the great imperial drug trade of the nineteenth century: the British–Indian opium trade. The book brings together for the first time nearly fifty years of scholarship and research on opium trafficking, addiction, and other studies on drugs, the economy and human society. *Opium, Empire and the Global Political Economy* raises provocative questions about the historical relationship between opium, capitalism and European imperialism in Asia.

Opium needs to be considered in its role as an economic commodity, and seen in the context of other "drug" trades, including sugar, tea, alcohol and tobacco. Trocki's evidence convincingly suggests that European imperialism, and the creation of a global economy, relied heavily on these great drug trades. All reoriented labor, land and capital in the service of commodity production and usually involved "industrial" modes of production. In order to serve these trades, systems of international exchange – such as shipping lines and banking – were brought into existence. They created the first great mass consumer markets, first in Europe and then, with opium, in Asia. Opium, Trocki argues, facilitated important elements in the European imperial advance through Asia, and was equally a fiscal support for virtually all of the new Asian states.

Carl A. Trocki is well known for his work in this area. He is the author of *Prince of Pirates: The Temengongs and the Development of Johor* and *Opium and Empire: Chinese Society in Colonial Singapore 1800–1910,* and is Professor of Asian Studies and Director of the Centre for Community and Cross-Cultural Studies at the Queensland University of Technology.

Asia's transformations
Edited by Mark Selden
Binghamton and Cornell Universities

The books in this series explore the political, social, economic and cultural consequences of Asia's twentieth-century transformations and look toward their impact on the twenty-first century. The series emphasizes the tumultuous interplay of local, national, regional, and global forces as Asia bids to become the hub of the world economy. While focusing on the contemporary, it also looks back to analyse the antecedents of Asia's contested rise.

This series comprises two strands:

Asia's Transformations aims to address the needs of students and teachers as well as scholars, and the titles will be published in hardback and paperback. Titles include:

Debating Human Rights
Critical essays from the United States and Asia
Edited by Peter Van Ness

Hong Kong's History
State and society under colonial rule
Edited by Tak-Wing Ngo

Opium, Empire and the Global Political Economy
A study of the Asian opium trade 1750–1950
Carl A. Trocki

Routledge Studies in Asia's Transformations is a forum for innovative new research intended for a high-level specialist readership, and the titles will be available in hardback only. Titles include:

1. The American Occupation of Japan and Okinawa
Literature and memory
Michael Molasky

Opium, Empire and the Global Political Economy

A study of the Asian opium trade 1750–1950

Carl A. Trocki

London and New York

First published 1999
by Routledge
2 Park Square, Milton Park, Abingdon, Oxon, OX14 4RN

Simultaneously published in the USA and Canada
by Routledge
270 Madison Ave, New York NY 10016

Routledge is an imprint of the Taylor & Francis Group

Transferred to Digital Printing 2005

© 1999 Carl A. Trocki

Typeset in Baskerville by Keystroke, Jacaranda Lodge, Wolverhampton

British Library Cataloguing in Publication Data
A catalogue record for this book is available from the British Library

Library of Congress Cataloging in Publication Data
Trocki, Carl A.
    Opium, empire and the global political economy: a study of the
Asian opium trade 1750–1950 / Carl A. Trocki.
        p.   cm. – (Asia's transformations)
    Includes bibliographical references and index.
    1. Opium trade–Asia–History. 2. Drug traffic–Political
aspects–Asia. 3. Narcotics, Control of–Asia. I. Title.
II. Series.
    HV5840. A74T76 1999   99–22499
    363. 45'095–dc21

ISBN 0–415–19918–2 (hbk)
ISBN 0–415–21500–5 (pbk)
Printed and bound by Antony Rowe Ltd, Eastbourne

Contents

List of figures	vii
List of tables	viii
Acknowledgments	ix
Weights and measures	x
Introduction	xi

1	The dream of empire	1
2	All the drowsy syrups of the world	13
3	Cleverer than alchemists	33
4	In compassion to mankind	58
5	The most gentlemanlike speculation	88
6	In the hands of Jews and Armenians	109
7	A matter of considerably greater solicitude	137
8	The most long-continued and systematic international crime	160

Appendix 1 The literature of the opium trade	174
Appendix 2 A comment on the Jardine Matheson "Opium Circulars"	179
Appendix 3 Englebert Kaempfer's comments on opium from his "Amoenitatum Exoticarum"	181
Appendix 4 The economics of Malwa opium cultivation	183
Glossary	184
Notes	186
Bibliography	192
Index	203

Figures

2.1 Neolithic and Bronze Age sites in Europe and the Eastern
     Mediterranean Sea associated with poppy fossils and early opium
     use   15
3.1 India, Southeast Asia and China showing approximate sailing
     routes between Bombay and Calcutta and Guangzhou used by
     the Country Traders   38
3.2 Shah 'Alam (Mughal Emperor, 1759–1806) conveying the Grant
     of Diwani to Lord Clive, August, 1765   45
4.1 Warren Hastings, first Governor-General of India, 1773–1785   63
4.2 Marquis Charles Cornwallis, Governor-General of India,
     1785–1793 and July–Oct. 1805   64
4.3 The opium-producing areas of Benares (Varanasi) and Bihar
     States in Eastern India   69
4.4 Weighing of opium in the 1880s   71
4.5 Examination of opium in the 1880s   72
4.6 Drying balls of opium at the Sudder Factory in Patna, c. 1851   73
5.1 The clipper ships Ariel and Taepeng in a "tea race" near the British
     Isles   105
6.1 Opium exports from British India, 1829–1906   111
6.2 Hong Kong opium prices, 1860–1870   113
6.3 Overland trade routes in Southern China between the
     opium-producing areas of Yunnan and the southern coast   122
6.4 A Chinese opium den in Calcutta, 1946   127
8.1 Opium smokers in Sinjiang province, China, 1873   168
8.2 A Kachin woman of northern Burma tapping opium in the 1920s   172

Tables

4.1 Calcutta auction: opium prices (1787–1822)   65
4.2 Opium market report from *Calcutta Overland Price Current*, 1856   73
4.3 Malwa poppy cultivation districts, ca. 1820   77
4.4 Prices of opium per chest, in Spanish dollars as given in Canton,
     Macau or Hong Kong   81–2
5.1 Opium shipments to Canton and expenditures, 1800–39   95
5.2 All British India's exports, ca. 1836   97

Acknowledgments

This book was initiated through the support of a Luce Summer Fellowship at Cornell University in 1992 and was completed with support of a New Professor Grant from Queensland University of Technology. In addition to these sources of financial aid, I am grateful for the support of Georgetown University and my colleagues there in the history department, where I was employed when I began this project, and to the Queensland University of Technology, and in particular my colleagues in the School of Humanities.

Research was carried out in the Kroch Collection at Cornell University, the Library of the University of California at Berkeley, the Alcohol Research Group in Berkeley, California, the United States National Archives, the Library of Congress, the National University of Singapore Library, the National Library of Singapore, the Singapore National Archives, the National Archives of India, the Library of the School of Oriental and African Studies, University of London, the Public Record Office, the India Office Library, and the British Library. I am grateful to all the librarians, archivists and others who have labored to make these collections available to researchers. I am especially grateful to Matheson and Co., London for permission to use the Jardine Matheson Archive at the University of Cambridge Library.

Numerous individuals in the United States, Great Britain, India, Singapore, Malaysia and Australia have aided me in ways too numerous to count. I am grateful for the many acts of hospitality, for the advice, for the information and for the forebearance of those who listened while I bored them with yet another idea or afterthought. I must thank especially Benedict Anderson, Anthony Reid, John Sidel and my son Carl, who read and commented on portions of the manuscript at various stages in its composition.

I must also thank my sister Karen for her hospitality and many kindnesses while I was in California and for introducing me to the Alcohol Research Group and the work of alcohol researchers. My brother David translated the passages from Englebert Kaempfer as well as reading and commenting on the manuscript. I wish to thank my other siblings and my mother for their many kindnesses while I was at work on this book, and finally my wife, Orrawin, and my children, Rebecca and Carl, for their tolerance and assistance.

Weights and Measures

Currencies

Most currencies are quoted in Spanish or Mexican dollars. Unless otherwise stated, the $ signifies Spanish dollars. Spanish $ = 4s 2d, but in China was figured at 4s 6d.

Indian weights and currency

1 Chest (Caisse) of Bengal (Bihar or Benares) opium, about 2 maunds = 140 lbs (about 60–72 kg).
1 Maund = 40 seers = 76–80 lb (about 40 kg).
1 Seer = 1.9–2 lb (about 1 kg).
1 Vis (opium ball) about 3 lb (1.6 kg to 1.8 kg).
1 Bigha = 2/3 acre (about 2700 m^2).
1 Sicca (new) Rupee = 2 shillings (until 1872–3; it was devalued to 1s 1d in 1899)

Chinese weights and currency

Chinese Catty = 1.33 lb (about 605 g)
          = 16 Tahil (liang or tael).
1 Tahil = 10 Chee (chandu measures)
          = 100 Hoon (fen).
100 Catty = 1 Pikul, or 133.33 lb (60.5 kg).
1 Tael (silver) = 4s 6d (monetary). Ideally a tael = 1000 copper cash, but this could fluctuate.

Metric equivalents

One ball of opium =   1.6 to 1.8 kg.
Caisse (chest)   60–72 kg.
Pikul 60–62.6 kg.
Tahil 37.6 g.
Chee 3.76 g.
Hoon (Fen) 0.376 g.

Introduction

This book re-examines the British Indian opium trade to China and Southeast Asia. In the past half-century, much research has been done and many books and articles have been written on various aspects of the opium trade. Outside of David E. Owen's account, written in the 1930s, there have been few studies which look at the entire commerce. It is one aim of this study to provide an overview of the opium trade that would include much of the more recent literature on opium, the opium trade and drugs in general. Beyond this, the study seeks in particular to probe the role of the drug trade in laying the foundation for European colonial structures in Asia, both economic and administrative. The intention is to place opium in the same context with other important commercial enterprises which were also based on drugs, or drug-like products, including tobacco, alcohol and tea. So far as I am aware, this has not really been done before.

The study is informed by a number of assumptions about the relationship between drugs and human society. The first of these is that drugs are a "natural" part of human life. It recognizes that since human life evolved we have regularly made use of certain naturally occurring chemical substances for their mind- or mood-altering properties. Almost every human culture has found a place for some drug, including opium. Their use has often been associated with some sort of religious practice, social ritual, or spirit medicine, not to mention everyday physical medicine. Whether it has been opium, cannabis, coca, tobacco, alcohol, coffee, tea, betel, kutch, or one of the many other vegetable products, human beings have regularly had recourse to some selection of them so as to "doctor" their bodies or their minds.

Almost all of these substances can be considered, and have been placed, in the dangerous category. Inappropriate or excessive use of any of them may cause illness, physical or mental damage, addiction or even death. Most cultures have found ways to control the use of their native drugs, thus all human societies have their own "drug cultures." From a systemic point of view, I propose that drugs became social problems only when they were moved out of their "original" contexts to populations or nations which had not been habituated to their use, or when the availability, production or distribution of them was drastically changed. This, at least, is the historical process which I hope to demonstrate here. We have come to call such events "drug epidemics" or "drug plagues." They occur when a society is suddenly swept by a wave of use, and abuse, of a newly introduced addictive drug. Large numbers of people are affected and the phenomenon usually attracts considerable attention and comment from other sectors of society, who normally view it as a sign of social decay or even collapse.

It is clear that many drugs are "dangerous." That is, they are poisons that can kill or at least seriously impair our health. Many possess the additional property of being addictive. Without being scientifically exact at this point, addiction can be defined as the process by which an individual develops a physiological or psychological dependence upon a chemical substance that is not otherwise a necessity of life. Addicts thus require a regular and often continually increasing supply of the substance. At some point where use of the drug becomes habitual, they usually suffer ill-health, loss of wealth, an apparent loss of "free will" and some even lose their lives. Drugs, nevertheless, offer psychological compensations and comforts that appear, at least for a time, to make all the ills they bring worthwhile. These attractions are so strong that today, despite fairly strict legal, moral and social sanctions, people are willing to risk fines, imprisonment and even execution to procure drugs for their own consumption or to supply them to others.

It seems that there is one key ingredient necessary to create a true drug "epidemic." In addition to exotic introduction and changes in production, the commercialization of drug production, trade and marketing seem to have been crucial. This links these drugs with the development of capitalism. The commercialization of a drug has radically altered the established relationship between human society and a particular substance. This process has been associated with a number of fundamental transformations in human life, one of which has been the appearance of large plantations, or similar agricultural establishments, worked by some form of slave or unfree labor, where a drug is produced for sale at some distant location. The trade in such drugs usually results in some form of monopoly which not only centralizes the drug traffic, but also restructures much of the affiliated social and economic terrain in the process. In particular two major effects are the creation of mass markets and the generation of enormous, in fact unprecedented, cash flows. The existence of monopoly results in the concentrated accumulation of vast pools of wealth. The accumulations of wealth created by a succession of historic drug trades have been among the primary foundations of global capitalism and the modern nation-state itself. Indeed, it may be argued that the entire rise of the west, from 1500 to 1900, depended on a series of drug trades.

This book looks at the long-term historical transformation of opium, from an exotic chemical largely used as a medicine or occasional narcotic to an intensively produced and widely marketed commodity. It traces the creation of a new and pernicious drug culture in Southeast Asia and China where opium came to be "smoked" by increasing numbers of users. There is an attempt to look at its importance not only in human terms, but also in the administrative and economic structures of India, Southeast Asia and China. In particular, the focus is on the relationship of the drug trade to the rise and fall of the European, especially the British, empire in Asia.

In focusing on the British Empire, I wish to make indelibly clear the intimate historical link between the British enterprise in Asia-East-of-Suez and this phase of the international drug trade. Recent years have seen an upsurge of literature romanticizing the Raj, from Paul Scott's *Raj Quartet* to the novels of James G. Farrell and the virtual cottage industry of British books about Singapore before and during the Pacific War. Some glorify the endeavor, others find reason to criticize the people or the age, but most studiously avoid the topic of opium, unless to gloss over it as an "oriental" vice. While it is true that Asians used the drug, it is also true that Europeans became the most prominent producers and purveyors. Foremost among them were the British East India Company, its successor the British colonial government of India, and the community of British merchants who laid the economic foundation of the imperial economy. I argue here that without the drug, there probably would have been no British Empire. Admittedly, this is difficult to prove, and I am sure that my contentions will find critics. Nevertheless, if we try to subtract opium income and opium profits from the Indian budgets, from the merchants' balance sheets, from the other colonial fiscal structures, I believe we need to ask how else the superstructures of the European enterprise would have been financed.

There are a number of conclusions from the study. The first is that the nineteenth-century opium trade not only destroyed the integrity of social and political structures in China and Southeast Asia, but it also helped to build and to finance the creation of new and alternative structures. In Southeast Asia these were the colonial states, most of which were supported by opium revenues. In China, particularly after 1860, opium revenues became an important part of regional revenue regimes, which drew strength from the drug trade while the central government declined. Moreover, in the years following the collapse of the dynasty, opium became the fiscal mainstay of virtually all of the warlord and republican regimes that dominated China in the period before 1950.

At the end of the nineteenth century opium was thoroughly embedded in the political economies of every Asian state east of Suez. If it was not grown locally and sold to the population, it was imported from some other place where it was grown for export. While it is difficult to argue intent, it is clear that the structure of European imperial control and the capitalist structures which were built upon it were intimately tied to opium.

This book introduces the image of the "opium empire," a metaphor first offered by Joseph Conrad. It takes up the early history of opium and other "traditional drugs" such as tobacco and sugar and develops the paradigm of commercialized drug trades and ties that to the growth of European colonialism in the Americas and Asia in the second chapter. The third and fourth chapters look at the Asian opium trade of Britain, first as it grew in India and then as it affected Southeast Asia and China. The fifth and sixth chapters look at opium in China in the nineteenth and twentieth centuries, focusing not only on the spread of the opium trade but also on the evolving political economy of the drug as it came to affect Chinese political development. The seventh chapter focuses on the political economy of opium revenue farming systems in Southeast Asia, connecting them to the growth of colonial regimes and fiscal systems, while at the same time linking them to the growth of capitalist enterprises in the European-dominated territories.

Chapter 8 reviews the international movements at the beginning of the twentieth century to ban the traffic in narcotics and examines some of the repercussions of that development. This chapter also looks at the relationship between the nineteenth-century drug trades and the twentieth-century heroin traffic. An important theme here is the change in consciousness regarding the new drug cultures being created. This chapter also suggests a number of the lessons which the "imperial drug trade," as Joshua Rowntree styled it, have to teach the west as it enters the twenty-first century.

Throughout, the study is concerned with the links between drug trades, European colonial expansion, the creation of the global capitalist system and the creation of the modern state. Drug trades destabilized existing societies not merely because they destroyed individual human beings but also, and perhaps more importantly, because they have the power to undercut the existing political economy of any state. They have created new forms of capital; and they have redistributed wealth in radically new ways. As such, they have been the incubators of capitalism. Their production has enslaved or otherwise entrapped labor forces, their traffic has fed the exchange systems and the "brokers" who are the propagators of the system, and their distribution has lubricated the mass markets necessary for the establishment of capitalism. What sugar, alcohol and tobacco did for the Americas and Africa, opium did for Asia.

In looking at modern-day anti-drug policies and comparing those policies with the attitudes and projects of the years before World War I, there seems some cause for irony. Modern-day power holders may or may not realize that drug economies have been vital to the construction of the modern state; that they have been the stepping stones of the capitalist political economy. At the same time, nevertheless, they do realize that drugs, and more specifically drug economies, have the power to destroy or seriously undermine an existing political order. The question that we might continue to ponder, however, is whether the problem is in the drug or in the economy.

Carl A. Trocki
Shorncliffe, Queensland
September, 1998

1 The dream of empire

> I perceived that the pilgrim ship episode was a good starting-point for a free and wandering tale; that it was an event, too, which could conceivably colour the whole "sentiment of existence" in a simple and sensitive character.
>
> Joseph Conrad, 1917 Introduction to *Lord Jim*

At the beginning of the twentieth century, Europeans were generally proud of their imperial possessions. There was a consciousness that the peoples of western Europe, in particular, had a natural duty to bring the gifts of civilization to the lesser races of the world. Whether this meant Christianity, law and order, the end of slavery, material progress or merely free trade; whether it was called a *mission civilisatrice*, or seen as a white man's burden (every colonial power had its term): there was a sense that they were agents of a higher good.

Joseph Conrad, however, the great novelist of that era, saw no virtue in empire. His greatest novels are all, in one way or another, attacks on imperialism, and contain within them a thorough and systematic critique of Europe's, particularly Britain's, imperial adventure. He was one of the few, at that early date, who understood that imperial rule was not only a crime against the captive peoples, but also destroyed and corrupted even the best of the imperial peoples. It polluted everything it touched. I believe he saw opium as a metaphor for those pollutants, and it may be useful to probe his critique of Britain's "dream of empire."

In *Lord Jim*, the young Jim abandoned a ship full of Muslim pilgrims. This moral lapse set in motion the chain of events that makes up the plot. It was Jim's great crime. He was a ship's officer and in a time of danger he literally jumped ship, abandoning eight hundred people to what seemed certain death. Ironically, the ship did not sink, but drifted along until rescued by a passing French naval vessel. Later, in an effort to redeem himself, Jim isolated himself from European society in the fictitious Malay community of Patusan and gave up his life, heroically, but almost senselessly it seems, rather than betray his word.

The *Patna* episode, for that was the ship's name, introduces the novel. Conrad intended the episode to "colour the whole 'sentiment of existence.'" As such, we should expect to find there most of his main themes. This part of the story has thus attracted the attention of a number of Conrad scholars and there is a significant critical literature on it. I was ultimately drawn to this literature, because I wondered why Conrad chose the name *Patna*, and I wanted to see what the experts had to say on the subject of the *Patna*. As a historian of nineteenth-century Asia, I had my own ideas about the significance of the term.

Patna is one of India's most ancient cities. Formerly the site of Pataliputra, the Mauryan capital in the third century BC, by the nineteenth century Patna had long been an integral part of British holdings in the territories of Bihar/Bengal. These circumstances alone would have made it a likely choice for an exotic sounding name, but in the nineteenth century Patna meant something more. The word had a special status in the British Empire. Its significance was in its connection to the Englishman's other great contribution to Asia, the opium trade. In fact, we might look upon Patna as the unofficial capital of the opium empire that the British had created.

For nearly 150 years, Patna had been virtually synonymous with the opium trade. "Patna" was literally a brand name for one of the major types of British–Indian opium that was traded at Calcutta, Singapore, Hong Kong, Canton, and in every major port of Asia. Wherever one went east of Suez, on any day he could pick up the local English language newspaper to discover the daily quotations for the prices of "Patna" or "Benares" opium;[1] whether in the market at Singapore, or at the monthly auctions in Calcutta, or at any of the major ports of South and Southeast Asia or the China coast. Patna opium was as much a part of the every-day environment of maritime commerce in the region as tea, pepper, gambier, copra or tin. Almost without exception, Patna opium was carried on virtually every vessel that traded at Singapore, Hong Kong and Shanghai. Whether packed in chests as it came from Calcutta; or whether in individual balls, as taken from the chests; or whether as smokeable *chandu* packed in tubes or "pots"; Patna opium was as omnipresent as silver dollars and "native" coolies in the white man's empire.

The American merchant William C. Hunter repeats a bit of doggerel penned by one of his countrymen in Canton during the 1830s as a parody of the Byron poem, "Know'st thou the Land":

> Know'st thou the land where the drug in its glory
> With cotton and betel nut govern the day
> Where Patna or Malwa's the theme of each story
> The life of each anecdote, solemn or gay?
>   (Hunter 1882, pp. 111–12)

It seems fitting, if Conrad wished to make an ironic statement about the morality of imperialism, that he would make Jim the mate of a ship named for an addictive drug that deprived people of their sense of duty and morality. A drug that offered pipe dreams in exchange for dismal reality. It seems likely that a person of Conrad's background, one conversant with the day-to-day language and usage of Asian maritime commerce, would immediately associate the word "Patna" with opium. Most of the critics agree that the book has a strong anti-imperialist message, and Conrad scholars such as Jan Verleun see significance in the "dreamlike" quality of the *Patna* episode. It is a message that signals moral lapse and false consciousness about the grim and dirty work of empire which had been cloaked in light adventure novels and smug dreams of peace and order. It only seems sensible to link those themes to the very source of dreamlike delusion itself, opium; however, I admit that neither Conrad nor other Conrad scholars have made such a link.

I would thus suggest that for Conrad the *Patna* episode was a sort of parable of European imperialism. Like the empire the tale is filled with ironies and ambiguities. As the first mate aboard the floating death trap that was the *Patna*, Jim may be seen as the representative of the Good. He was, as Marlow, Conrad's narrator, describes him, the best kind of Englishman: "one of us." But, even here there is something ironic about this characterization.

> All the time I had before me these blue, boyish eyes looking straight into mine, this young face, these capable shoulders, the open bronzed forehead with a white line under the roots of clustering fair hair, this appearance appealing at sight to all my sympathies; this frank aspect the artless smile, the youthful seriousness. He was of the right sort; he was one of us. He talked soberly, with a sort of composed unreserve, and with a quiet bearing that might have been the outcome of manly self-control, of impudence, of callousness, of a colossal unconsciousness, of a gigantic deception. Who can tell!
>
> (Conrad 1986 [henceforth *LJ*], p. 100)

The passage ends with an interesting twist. Was Jim a sincere, open and appealing individual, or was he simply a clever liar, or even more troubling, was his quiet bearing and manliness the result of a "colossal unconsciousness?" Conrad seems to be playing with the reader here and he gives us several possible interpretations of Jim's character. In the final analysis, his intention seems to have been for us to choose "unconsciousness" as the fundamental problem. Jim is the English everyman, and like the rest of us, he is confused and misled in his own mind. Perhaps that delusion was shared by most of his contemporaries.

The romantic adventure of the *Patna's* voyage nearly turns into a tragedy and emerges as humiliation. Jim's dream is the source of the problem. He is shown as if in some kind of trance, or dream, or torpor; like a man who has taken a puff of opium. On the voyage aboard the *Patna*, the weather, the very universe seemed pervaded by a vast and profound calm. To speak of Jim being "penetrated by the great certitude of unbounded safety and peace" (*LJ*, p. 17) conjures up the image of someone under the influence of that most soporific of drugs:

> his joints cracked with a leisurely twist of the body, in the very excess of well-being; and, as if made audacious by the invincible aspect of the peace, he felt he cared for nothing that could happen to him to the end of his days.
>
> (*LJ*, pp. 19–20)

In those peaceful days, he dreamed

> his thoughts would be full of valorous deeds: he loved these dreams and the success of his imaginary achievements. They were the best parts of life, its secret truth, its hidden reality. They had a gorgeous virility, the charm of vagueness, they passed before him with a heroic tread; they carried his soul away with them and made it drunk with the divine philtre of an unbounded confidence in itself. There was nothing he could not face.
>
> (*LJ*, p. 20)

Jan Verleun remarks on Jim's psychic state, "Jim's sensibilities before the *Patna* incident are atrophied; he is too pleasurably languid and too intoxicated with imaginary successes to dislike actively his fellow officers, that is to perceive them even with any vividness" (Verleun 1979, p. 199, n. 6). The vile and corrupt captain, the opium-soaked chief engineer and whimpering second engineer were sad company for a "gentleman" of his quality. Nevertheless, Jim could pretend he did not share the same space with them.

> those men did not belong to the world of heroic adventure; they weren't bad chaps though. Even the skipper himself . . . His gorge rose at the mass of panting flesh from which issued gurgling mutters, a cloudy trickle of filthy expressions; but he was too pleasurably languid to dislike actively this or any other thing. The quality of these men did not matter; he rubbed shoulders with them, but they could not touch him; he shared the air they breathed but he was different.
>
> (*LJ*, pp. 24–5)

Jim's moral senses were anesthetized. Fundamental to Jim's delusion was his failure to recognize the evil around him. If Conrad placed such stress upon delusion and corruption, and if he took pains to associate these themes with the *Patna*, it seems sensible to look more closely as the word itself.

Jim's delusion is very much like that of someone like Thomas Stamford Raffles (the founder of Singapore) and other high-minded English liberals who attempted to establish systems of order and purity, to remake the world according to the rational principles of the Enlightenment and the best impulses of European civilization. They brought the gifts of free trade, economic and personal freedom, adherence to the rule of law, personal integrity and duty. They opposed slavery, feudalism, superstition, piracy and oppression. And yet, as we know, the European empires were exploitative, racist, violent and fundamentally pernicious. This reality made the "dream" a dangerous delusion, both for the English as well as their subjects.

Conrad was not a prisoner of the British rhetoric that justified their empire. Despite his debt to Britain and to the empire, which took him in, gave him a living, gave him a *life*, and recognized his genius, Conrad could never forget that he was also Teodor Josef Korzeniowski, the child of a country which had literally ceased to exist under imperial rule. To Conrad, an outcast, orphaned Pole, whose father had died in a Russian prison, whose uncles had been executed by the Czar, there were no "good" imperialists. Just as there were no good rapists. The evil was in the act itself, and the ends did not justify the means. Many of Conrad's most profound tales carry this message.

This was Conrad's paradox. According to Cedric Watts:

> The novel offers a general verdict on imperialism by showing that even those Europeans who, like him [Jim], attempt to be benevolently paternalistic to their subject peoples may, in the long term, do more harm than good, and it offers a general verdict on the romantic conception of personal honour by showing that the more it resembles exalted egoism, the higher may be the price that others have to pay for it.
>
> (*LJ*, p. 23)

The European adventure in Asia was as ethically confused as was Jim's experience aboard the *Patna*. Deeply involved, as it was, in one of the most pernicious, yet well-organized and profitable drug trades that has ever existed, the empire was rotten at its heart. Moreover, by the beginning of the twentieth century, it was like the *Patna*, rusted, decrepit and ready to collapse in the smallest crisis. How could a system based on the trade in this product, acknowledged even then as an evil, be morally squared with the ideals of the "best" of the empire builders? If I may give my own meaning to Conrad's metaphor, Jim in abandoning the *Patna*, and leaving a shipload of Asians to their doom, was the same as the European traders and colonial governments that left millions of their subjects, as well as Chinese non-subjects, to be carried to ruin by the opium habit, while they reaped a profit from the sale of the drug.

Like their subjects, Europeans were caught in the sense-dulling inducements of the drug. They too, were lost on their own Lethe of moral forgetfulness. For many of them, greed for profit and power were their own drugs. Conrad claimed that unlike Kipling, whom he said, wrote *about* the English, he himself wrote *for* the English.[2] His aim was to enlighten them about themselves, and the nature of their empire. He aimed to penetrate the false consciousness of high imperial complacency. He may also have had another audience in mind when he styled Jim as "one of us." The timing of the book is significant, *Lord Jim* was written between September 1899 and July 1900, this was not long after the American intervention in the Philippines (August 1898). It was published soon after Rudyard Kipling's "White Man's Burden" which was addressed to the "The United States and the Philippine Islands." Kipling wished to encourage Britain's American cousins to assume their place in the great work of European imperialism in Asia:

> Take up the white man's burden –
> Send forth the best ye breed –
> Go, bind your sons to exile
> To serve the captives' need;

> To wait in heavy harness
> On fluttered folk and wild –
> Your new-caught sullen peoples,
> Half-devil and half-child.
>
> Rudyard Kipling,
> "The White Man's Burden" 1898

This sounds a lot like Jim's "dream" of his mission in Patusan. It is possible that Conrad's purpose was to warn off the Americans from imperial adventures in Asia.

Opium had been the partner of British colonialism since the days when Robert Clive defeated the Nawab of Bengal at Plassey in 1757, and it remained so in the days when Mohandas K. Gandhi was raising the standard of revolt against the Raj under Lord Curzon. Oddly enough, by 1900, opium was generally not seen as a British, or European problem. It was an Asian problem. Even David Edward Owen, whose pioneering study first laid bare the trail that the British opium trade had cut through Asia, still saw opium as the "Orient's distinctive vice" (Owen 1934, p. 2). In some ways this was true. When European merchants and conquerors first came to Asia, the drug was already an item of commerce. It had first been brought to India by Arabs and was taken on to China where reports of its use date from the eighth century. When Albuquerque arrived in India in 1509, the trade was well-established, with Arab and Indian merchants selling it in Burma, the Malay Peninsula and China. He recommended to his ruler that Portugal begin producing it:

> If your Highness would believe me, I would order poppies . . . to be sown in all the fields of Portugal and command afyam to be made, which is the best merchandise that obtains in these places . . . the people of India are lost without it, if they do not eat it . . .
>
> (Owen 1934, p. 2)

By the end of the seventeenth century, however, Europeans had changed the nature of the trade. Opium was no longer only a medicinal drug or a buffer against stress, but had become a drug used primarily for pleasure. This shift came as Chinese and Southeast Asian users began to smoke it. This manner of use remained more or less restricted to Asian users until the twentieth century and gave it a peculiarly Asian association.

The dream of total control over the opium trade seemed to come true as hundreds of avid Englishmen fell upon the wealth of Bengal in the aftermath of Plassey. By 1760 the free-lancing "servants" of the English East India Company had arrogated to themselves the profits from most of the productive enterprises of Bengal. Among these, the most lucrative proved to be opium, which was so profitable that the Company itself eventually appropriated the monopoly on its cultivation. Government control continued throughout the nineteenth century. Owen takes at face value the somewhat bemused attitude with which many Victorian Englishmen seemed to regard the trade. It was really an aberration:

That roughly one-seventh of the revenue of British India should have been drawn from the subjects of another state as payment for a habit forming drug is, in the words of a British official, 'one of the most unique facts that the history of finance affords.' And when it is recalled that a large share of the opium sent to China was produced under the aegis of a state-administered monopoly which existed principally for supplying that market, the picture appears still more grotesque.

(Owen 1934, p. vii)

Indeed, it may have been grotesque, but we may question whether or not it was unique or really that unusual. I argue that the opium trade was not simply an aberration of the British Empire. It was a crucial component of it. The British Empire, the opium trade, and the rise of global capitalism all occurred together. That the rise of the three phenomena was simultaneous, is not proof of causality; it does however, suggest a relationship, and what I wish to do in this book is to explore that relationship.

The economics of empire

The last two decades have seen the production of a large number of specialized studies on various aspects of the opium trade. My first aim then is to attempt a new overview of the subject which would incorporate as many as possible of the findings of these efforts, most of which remain scattered in doctoral dissertations, journal articles and monographs under a wide variety of other headings. We have learned much about the opium trade in recent years and an update seems justified. I should also like to take the opportunity to point out some of the many remaining gaps in our knowledge of this era.

My second purpose stems largely from the changed perspective we must have of the Asian drug trade at the end of the twentieth century. Since Owen wrote, the United States and Europe have fallen victim to epidemics of drug use which in many ways resemble the experience of nineteenth-century China. The West as well as much of the developing world, today perceive themselves in the midst of a drug crisis. The phenomenon of wide-scale recreational drug use and abuse is no longer peculiarly Asian.

The late-twentieth-century observer is forced to adopt a radically different perspective on the history of drug use than those who wrote about opium before the 1960s. The drug "plagues" that now appear almost endemic in the Americas and in Europe, bear a striking resemblance to the drug plague that swept Asia, and particularly China in the nineteenth century. Despite this, little serious comparative study has been done to link the two phenomena. From that point of view, perhaps we can learn something about our own drug problems by studying that of the Chinese. While I cannot offer such a comparison here, I do hope to present the Asian drug crisis in a context that may facilitate such a comparison.

I find Conrad's metaphor of the *Patna* such a compelling one because opium was an important, if not vital aspect of European domination in Asia. The re-examination of the progress of the drug epidemic that swept Asia (from Turkey and Persia to India, to Southeast Asia and China) during the nineteenth century, should not only provide a clearer understanding of the advance of imperialism and capitalism in that region, but should also give a deeper understanding of the role of drugs in the modern world in general.

Finally, I wish to offer a somewhat different approach to the study of drugs. I think that opium needs to be understood as simply a commodity among many others. It is, however, a unique commodity, and its uniqueness is shared with other drugs, therefore we need to study the opium trade as we have studied the trade in other commodities and in particular other drug commodities. In this category, I include tobacco, coffee, tea, chocolate, sugar, and of course, alcohol. Too often, scholars and economic historians are prone to divide drugs between those which happen to be legal and those which are not. (Braudel 1979a; Braudel 1979b; Braudel 1984; Hobhouse 1985, pp. 115–20; Walvin 1997).[3] This may make sense from a law-enforcement or social policy point of view, but it makes bad history and worse economics. We have very little understanding of drugs-as-commodities, because they are rarely studied without prejudice by economists. Drugs ought to be seen as major actors in the economic history of the world. Drugs and drug trades, from tobacco to opium, from the sixteenth century to the twentieth, have been crucial elements in the course of European expansion. Opium was just the last in a series of imperial drug trades. It also had a crucial role in the formation of the British Empire and in the creation of a global capitalist economy.

Europeans first went to Asia in their quest for spices. All of the subsequent empires that they built in Asia were simply modified versions of the initial venture. The exact "spice" varied over time, but there was always one exotic chemical or another that became the object of European trading monopolies – first it was nutmeg and cloves; later it was pepper, coffee, cacao, and sugar; still later it was tea and finally it was opium. In most cases, the aim was to monopolize the delivery of the desired substance to the European market. For three centuries, European trade with Asia was marked by this one-way flow of exotic chemicals. Opium was the exception. Even though it was an "Asian" chemical, it was marketed primarily in Asia. It was thus essential in changing the balance of economic, and by extension, political relations between east and west.

The trade balance between the two halves of Eurasia was maintained during most of those three centuries between 1500 and 1800 by the reverse flow of precious metals from Europe to Asia; or, perhaps more precisely, from the Americas, via European agency, to Asia. Whether the gold and silver crossed the Atlantic or the Pacific, it ultimately found its way to Asia (east of Suez) to purchase the "riches of the East" and to allow the otherwise deprived inhabitants of the northwest Eurasian peninsula to share in the fabled Oriental splendors. The trade "imbalance," or bullion deficit, was compounded by the European demand for the manufactured luxuries of the east as well as its exotic chemicals: Indian cottons and Chinese silks and ceramics in particular. Well before the eighteenth century, the Spanish silver dollar (minted in Mexico) became the standard currency of the trading communities around the South China and Java Seas.

Opium was the first product that made it possible for the balance to be tipped in the other direction. As with American precious metals, the source was not in Europe but "agency" was. By the eighteenth century, Europeans dominated the flow of opium from India to China and had created in China something entirely new under the Eastern sun, a veritable "drug plague." Also, for the first time in history, western traders had something besides silver to offer for the riches of Asia. This shift in circumstances, in itself, made all the difference.

This was not the only circumstance that was changed by opium. A related and perennial problem with European empires in the India–Pacific region, had always been that of financing their establishments in Asia. Sooner or later every imperial structure became too big and too expensive for its own creators to maintain. In particular, the cost of defending colonies ultimately became prohibitive. The Portuguese empire fell to unencumbered Dutch mariners because of poor finances, manpower shortages, and the Spanish conquest of the homeland. The Spanish had neither the will nor the power to maintain Portugal's Asian colonies against the Dutch. Spain kept the Philippines because no one else really wanted the islands (except the natives). The Dutch VOC did quite well for a century and a half, but then it too grew too fat to support itself and went bankrupt at the end of the eighteenth century.

European empires all depended on what Fernand Braudel has styled "super-profits" that came from monopolizing long-distance trade. (Braudel 1979, pp. 405–8). So long as an imperial cabal could reap exclusive profits at a consistently high level, with a limited overhead, then the enterprise was considered worth protecting with state power. Such enormous profit-margins were, however, too tempting; and if the state lost its pre-eminent power, then others could take the profits for themselves. Even if they did not, the very servants of the "interests" could hardly refrain from lining their own pockets while they enriched their employers. Monopoly carried within it the seeds of its own destruction. Sooner or later all such enterprises collapsed under their own overhead.

Even the British found it possible to spend their East India Company into debt despite its opium profits. Nevertheless, opium paid a significant part of the cost of colonial administration. The East India Company and its successor, the British Indian government, reaped significant profits both from producing and exporting the drug, and also by selling it to their own colonial subjects. Opium came to be an essential element, indeed the cash cow, in the finances of every Asian state structure during the nineteenth century and even during the first part of the twentieth.

Opium was important to the development of both European and Asian capitalism. For the European merchants in Asia, the opium trade created their first major accumulations of capital – without which none of the rest that followed would have been possible. The great British merchant houses, the banks and the insurance companies that had their roots in the Asian trade, all had a start in opium. The drug was an important element in the process of commercialization. It was one of the first fully commercialized products in the trade of Asia and it was, like other drugs, a commodity that created other commodities. Land, labor, fiscal relations, and even the state itself were commercialized by opium.

Nor were Europeans the only ones to gain from the drug, but several groups of Asian merchants, particularly some Chinese, grew wealthy through opium. Opium made it possible for them to establish capitalist modes of production in Asia. This process included not only the opium which was bought and sold as the object of speculation, but also that which was directly marketed to colonial subjects, coolies, peasants and others through the opium revenue farms. We are just beginning to understand this aspect of the opium trade.

Other aspects of the opium trade, particularly as it applied to China, would seem to have been quite well studied. However, only certain, rather restricted aspects of it have come under truly close scrutiny. No end of books and articles have been written on the difficulties of the East India Company in China at the end of the eighteenth century, and about the growth of the opium trade into the 1830s, and of the Opium War of 1839–42, and there have been some that go further and look at the "Second Opium War" of 1857–60. Little, however, has been written until recently on the internal trade in opium. Virtually nothing has been written about the incredible expansion of the trade which took place after 1840. There has been some attention paid to the anti-opium movement which saw the colonial drug trade greatly curtailed. Not much attention, however, has been paid to the exact relationship between imperialism throughout the nineteenth century and the drug. At the same time, not much serious study has been done of the overall impact of the drug on the political economies of Asia, let alone the West. I hope that this book can fill a few of these holes.

The structure of this study

It is, in the sense of the economy of drugs that the study of opium is most lacking. Partly because it always has been seen as an aberration, rather than as something typical, or at least as a historical phenomenon with some precedent, its more general significance has been neglected. I would like to propose here, three hypotheses regarding the opium economy of the nineteenth century. The first, one which I suggested in my earlier study of Singapore which perhaps needs some reiteration, is that opium was crucial to the expansion of the British Empire during the late eighteenth and early nineteenth century, and without it, there may have been no empire at all. There were two reasons for this. The first is that it paid the bills and provided a regular source of high-quality revenue that made it possible for the Indian empire to continue. Secondly, the opium business also created a concentration of capitalists, in Canton and Hong Kong, in Calcutta and Bombay and finally in London, who profited from the trade, and whose influence buttressed the imperial lobby throughout the nineteenth century.

A second hypothesis, which flows from the first, is that the opium trade laid the foundation for the global capitalist structure, both in its nurturing of European imperial capital and its international merchant class, and also by providing a foundation for the development of indigenous capitalist groups in India, Southeast Asia and in China itself. It may have been that capitalism would have developed in Asia on its own without opium, but the fact is that it did not. At every stage of development, opium was crucial, first in the obliteration of "traditionalist" obstacles to the market, second in the process of commodification and third in the creation of a class of consumers, and most of all, in the creation of the market itself.

In a rather perverse way, we should take at face value all the voices who supported the continuation of the opium trade. Perhaps they were right in their warnings that imperial finances depended on opium. When the opium trade was ended, the empire began to collapse. This occurred only after the Chinese had developed an appetite for opium and then developed an indigenous productive capacity which far surpassed the British–Indian cultivation. Indeed, its decline was already well advanced by the time Conrad wrote of the pathetic *Patna*, dreaming its way through history, burdened with hapless Asians and run by deluded Europeans either too corrupt or too idealistic to understand the predicament they had created. The corollary of this proposition is that economic empires, at least in the age of European expansion, have, to some extent, depended on drug trades and drug economies in their initial stages and that capitalism was always intimately tied to drug economies. With the rise of industrialism, European capitalism seems to have freed itself from the drug trades, though this may only be a temporary phase. As a system, capitalism has now moved onto other, perhaps more useful areas of endeavor, but this has not entirely eliminated the impact of legal and illegal drug trades on the global economy.

It is appropriate to think of all of nineteenth-century Asia, east of Suez, (with some qualifications about Japan) as simply the "European empire." Admittedly, it was subdivided into various spheres, controlled by different Western powers such as British India, Burma and Malaya, French Indochina, the Netherlands East Indies, the Spanish and then American Philippines, and some regions were technically autonomous like China and Siam. Despite these specificities, there was an underlying economic unity and even a great deal of administrative and political interaction on certain significant levels that should be understood better than it currently is. A key to this commonality was opium.

It is also important to look at least generally at the nature of the change, if that is indeed the case, in European and Asian consciousness about drugs. In the latter part of the nineteenth century, Americans and Britons moved to control the use of opiates and other "narcotics" in their own societies. By the early twentieth century, a coordinated movement was underway among most European powers to ban or at least control the international trade in drugs altogether. At the same time, China itself embarked on a large-scale anti-drug campaign, that enjoyed a considerable degree of success for a short period of time. These developments all had an important impact on the place of opium, and "narcotics" in general, in twentieth-century life.

Another point of study will be the manner in which Europeans came to change their thinking about drugs in their own societies and ultimately in their empires. These changes had a major impact on the development of more recent attitudes towards drugs. These have colored our understanding of the past as well as affecting our means of dealing with the present. Opium in particular seems to be at the bottom of that grab-bag of attitudes, prejudices and assumptions that Edward Said has called "orientalism," at least as it applies to monsoon Asia.

Finally, we need to see drugs as among the most powerful of social or cultural substances. It is true that some people are drug addicts, but others are equally addicted: some to the profits of drug trade, still others to the moral superiority gained from condemning drug use by others, and finally some cannot live without the political and social power gained over society through the mechanisms of controlling drug use. As Timothy Leary has suggested in *The Politics of Ecstasy* (1970), the control of drugs has far deeper ramifications than simple concern for health on the part of political forces in every society. Because drugs are so universally delusive, we need to study them quite carefully if we are to fully appreciate their true impact on society and on general historical change in modern times.

2 All the drowsy syrups of the world

Opium in pre-historic times

Before looking at the origins of opium use and the opium trade, it seems useful to raise the question of the role of drugs in human society in a more general way. Human beings have, it seems, always taken drugs of some kind for reasons beyond the purely medicinal. Opium has never been as widespread or as commonly used as drugs like tobacco or alcohol. Despite this, opium conforms to the general pattern of most drugs. Brian Inglis has suggested four major patterns of drug use among pre-modern peoples.

The first and perhaps most transparent use for drugs has been for healing, or at least to remedy or alleviate some physical distress. Perhaps this one use may cover all other possible uses, however, once we move beyond the cure of some definite physical disorder, the picture is less clear: it seems sensible to be more specific. The next area of usage, and one which is often overlooked involves what we might call the "work drugs": those substances which kill pain, increase stamina and dull hunger while one labors, travels, hunts or engages in warfare. Such substances as alcohol, coca, betel, tobacco and opium have been, and in some cases, continue to be used in this manner, along with coffee, tea, amphetamines and other stimulants. A third type of drug use involves the "healing" of the spirit, or at least changes our perceptions of "reality" and thus moves us to an "altered state." Many tribal cultures have, at some point, used drugs as ceremonial intoxicants to make it possible for the users, usually a shaman and perhaps other celebrants, to enter trance states and see visions, foretell the future, cast or remove spells as well as to achieve other "ritual" purposes. Closely related to this is the use of a drug by individuals in order to attain self knowledge. This too could be considered a sort of a "religious" application and might often have been done under some supervision, either by a shaman or within some ritual context. (Inglis 1975, p. 12) Finally, is the aim of pure enjoyment, indulgence or recreational intoxication. In this case, we use drugs for "play." We may use, and perhaps abuse, the same drugs we take in the medicinal or ritual contexts, but with no "serious" intent. We want to feel different, sometimes happier, sometimes more comfortable, more talkative, less apprehensive, more energetic, calmer, wiser, whatever. We know today that drugs like this mimic, or approximate the chemicals that our brain releases to give us similar feelings. While people have not always understood the physiological mechanisms involved in these processes, they have grasped the effects readily enough and at a fairly early stage in our evolutionary development.

It seems that every culture has had an intoxicant of some kind. Whether it was alcohol (beer or wine), tobacco, cannabis, coffee, coca, cacao, tea, psilocybin, mescalin, or betel, the substance was incorporated into the ritual and ceremony of special occasions and often found a place in everyday life. Partly because of availability, partly because of conscious cultural choices, various societies have developed historical preferences for specific drugs, often to the exclusion of others. Europeans very early cultivated a taste for beer and wine. Braudel notes the economic and cultural significance of the division of Europe into the traditionally wine-producing and wine-drinking areas of the Mediterranean basin, and the beer-producing and beer-drinking areas of the north (Braudel 1979a, pp. 232–3 and 238-9). Tea, rice wine and millet beer were popular in China. Muslims have eschewed alcohol and favored coffee, tobacco, cannabis and even opium. Likewise, in pre-modern times, betel nut was the ceremonial drug of choice throughout Southeast Asia (Reid 1988). At one time, it was chewed by almost everyone and on a regular basis. It also found a place in rituals such as marriage, coronations and welcoming; and specific vessels, tools and implements were created to store, prepare and present the leaves, the nut, and the lime paste that made up the betel quid. Similar substances were in common use in South Asia and throughout Africa. Coca and tobacco were widely used in the Americas, along with psilocybin and peyotl – depending on availability. Over time, most cultures have diversified and developed a repertoire of intoxicants. Moreover, the same drug may be used in a variety of circumstances: to heal, to sustain labor, to transport and to divert.

In historical times, opium does not seem to have been the dominant drug of any pre-modern society. On the other hand, it is one of the few drugs that has been used for all of the above purposes. Its use may have been somewhat restricted, nevertheless, opium was well-known throughout the ancient European and Mediterranean world and had a place in the repertoire of many early cultures. Mark David Merlin's study of the archaeological evidence and early literary references show that opium was already being used in the Neolithic and early metal ages.

The earliest evidence of opium usage dates from around 3100 BC. The fossilized remains of the seeds and seed capsules of *Papaver somniferum* (the opium poppy) were discovered in ancient lake beds in the Alpine region of western Europe. There is a cluster of sites dating from late Neolithic and early Bronze Age in parts of what are today Switzerland, France, and Germany (Figure 2.1). In these places, archaeologists have found fossilized poppy seeds, poppy seed cake and poppy capsules. The sites are associated with settlements of lake-dwellers variously identified as the Michelsburg, Cortaillod, Horgen, Lagozza and Pfyn cultures, which flourished between 3000 BC and 2500 BC (Merlin 1983, pp. 135–45).

There is no conclusive proof that these people were using the seeds or seed capsules for their psychoactive properties. Poppy seeds are edible and also can be

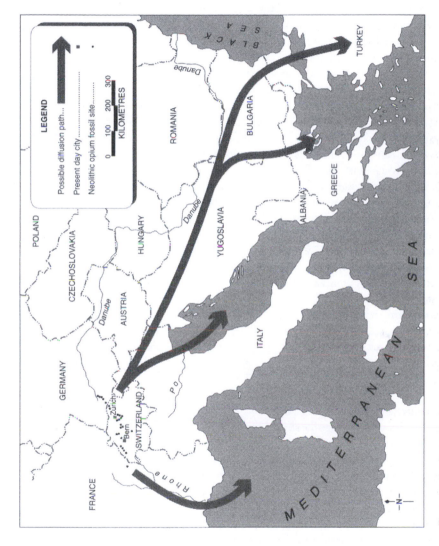

Figure 2.1 Neolithic and Bronze Age sites in Europe and the Eastern Mediterranean Sea associated with poppy fossils and early opium use. The possible paths of diffusion of the opium poppy into the Mediterranean Basin are shown

Source: Merlin 1983

used as a source of oil. The presence, however, of the capsules in a number of these sites suggests an awareness of the plant's mind-altering properties. There are few other uses for green poppy capsules. These are the source of the sap from which all opiates are made. It thus seems reasonable to assume that these lake-dwellers were making use of the alkaloids produced by the opium poppy. It is possible that these lake-dwellers not only used opium, but they may even have been the ones who developed the plant.

Merlin maintains there are no truly wild varieties of *Papaver somniferum*. All known varieties are cultivars, and while there are many semi-wild and self-sown, or "feral" varieties, the wild ancestor of this plant either no longer exists or else subsequent genetic alterations have totally obscured the plant's origins. Even those feral types of the opium poppy are usually found near cultivated or arable land, and there are no varieties found in natural or semi-natural vegetation complexes. This suggests that the plant is the product of an extensive and sophisticated process of primitive "genetic engineering" that was accomplished almost five millennia ago. The opium poppy has thus been associated with human beings for a very long time and can be considered to be dependent on human beings for its very existence (Merlin 1983, pp. 53–4).[1] The same is true, by the way, of other drug plants such as the coca plant and *Nicotiana tabacum*. Only our most basic food plants also show evidence of this kind of genetic tinkering at such an early period in human technological development.

In any case, these facts suggest two things about the relationship between human beings and drugs. The first is that historically, we have been extremely interested in perfecting our drug plants; at least as much as our food plants. The second, is that the possession of psychoactive properties in a plant is more likely to be the result of artifice than of nature. That is, any part of any plant, in any stage of its development, that offered even the slightest "buzz," was not only sure to be harvested and cultivated by our most ancient predecessors, but that these properties were also sure to be enhanced, developed and increased by whatever means were available to these individuals.

It is a paradox that the plant, which is today so firmly associated with Asia was probably transmitted from Europe to Asia. Its cultivation or use in western Europe seems to have declined significantly after the disappearance of the lake-dwellers. Before that happened however, Merlin indicates that the knowledge of the plant's uses had spread, apparently along the Neolithic trade routes, through the Alps and into the Mediterranean basin. Since the opium poppy will grow in a wide range of climatic and soil conditions, its cultivation spread as well. It appeared among the early Greeks during the Mycenaean period, sometime after 2000 BC. The drug was introduced by shamanistic cults which spread its use among the Greeks and other peoples of the Mediterranean. Merlin disputes the assumption by other scholars that the drug was known to the Egyptians and Sumerians prior to this period. All remains associated with opium, or with poppy use, in the Fertile Crescent date from the second millennium (Merlin 1983, pp. 247–9). The drug's route of travel seems to have been from northwest to southeast, and the plant continued in this direction in the following centuries (see Figure 2.1).

Opium and civilization

Opium played an important role in Greek fertility cults, particularly those of the Mother Goddess.[2] Here there seems little room for doubt that the hallucinogenic properties of the poppy were well-understood and exploited. Greek iconography has many images of Demeter and her daughter, Persephone, with poppy capsules. For instance the fifth-century BC statue of Demeter from the Athenian agora shows the goddess with branches of wheat and poppies together in her hand. The poem "Idylls to the Temple of Demeter Alois" says that Demeter "smiles on us, sheaves and poppies in either hand." Merlin writes:

> The agricultural cult of Demeter, and the "mysteries" surrounding it, were among the most important features of ancient Greek ritual. In the Homeric Hymn to Demeter, this great cult and its association with life, death, and rebirth are presented in allegorical terms. The central theme involves the abduction of Demeter's daughter, Persephone, by Hades, the God of the Underworld or the Dead. After Demeter realized that her daughter had been seized, she set out in an attempt to find the maiden. According to at least one interpretation, following a long, unsuccessful quest for Persephone . . . the gods caused poppies to spring beneath [Demeter's] feet. She knelt to look at them and their breath caused her to fall asleep. Thus she obtained rest for her weary limbs.
>
> (Merlin 1983, pp. 220–1)

In another image, Persephone is shown rising from the ground with sheaves of grain, lilies and poppy capsules in each hand and with snakes around her arms. The existence of the Cretan "poppy" goddesses, images crowned with poppy heads, are further indications that the psychoactive uses of the drug – particularly the use of the poppy capsule – had found a role in the religious practices of the ancient Greeks.

It is possible that the Greeks also may have used opium mixed with wine. Carl Ruck commented on the manner in which the Greeks drank wine. It was "a variable infusion of herbal toxins in a vinous liquid. Unguents, spices, and herbs, all with recognized psychotropic properties, could be added to the wine at the ceremony of its dilution with water" (Wasson *et al.* 1978, p. 42). In the *Odyssey*, Helen mixed the "euphoric nepenthes" with the wine to help the warriors forget the passions and traumas of the Trojan War. Merlin speculates that the active ingredient in nepenthes may well have been opium, although it may not have been the sole ingredient. Opium had thus already taken on a range of medical, religious and psychic associations. It was at once the bringer of sleep, death and resurrection, of dreams, visions, healing rest, and comfort for the sorrowful and depressed. Later on, it appears as an essential element in Greek materia medica. The recipe for Claudius Galen's (ca. 130–200 AD) *theriaca*, or sovereign cure-all and antidote, included 24 oz. of opium along with many other ingredients to be mixed with 960 oz of honey (Merlin 1983, pp. 216–17).

By the third century BC, opium use among the Greeks had changed signifi-cantly. Neither the city-state priesthoods nor those of Christianity or Islam looked kindly upon shamanism and on the encouragement of individual, ecstatic encounters with the godhead, especially not through drug-induced trances. Inglis draws attention to the status of shamans and drug trances among tribal peoples:

> By 1871, when Edward Tylor published his Primitive Culture – the first serious attempt at a comparative survey of tribal life and lore – a mass of such information had become available, and it was remarkably consistent. Almost all communities, in every part of the world, had their medicine men, witch doctors, or shamans, selected mainly on account of their ability to communicate with the spirits. To visit the spirit world, the medicine man had to be able to enter a state of trance; and this was frequently attained with the help of drugs. In this state he behaved as if he were drunk, or in a kind of fit; but he would be able to recall his visions when he recovered. Or he might appear to be possessed, describing what he was seeing (or hearing) in a voice not his own. Either way, his function was to bring back information of use to his tribe: the answers to such questions as what the enemy tribes were planning; where more game might be found; how to detect a witch; and what treatment to give a sick member of the tribe.
>
> (Inglis 1975, p. 16)

The establishment of formal city-states, empires and their religions brought about a standardization of divination and a restriction of access to the divine. In the historical development of religious consciousness a change occured in social attitudes towards trance states. There was social pressure to dispose of drugs to reach trance states because of their unpredictability, and the possibility that the information obtained in the trance might upset accepted orthodoxy. Thus:

> the time was to come when divination by such means became standardised. The pattern in which the bones fell, the state of the entrails, were consciously "read", as were omens; a bird flying past from one direction meant one forecast; from another direction, a different forecast. In time, divination was reduced to rote – to routine. Dissociation was then no longer needed; and drugs became superfluous. At the same time, the development of patterns of belief – religions – made dissociation an untrustworthy and unnerving experience, because the material pouring out of the unconscious might be at variance with approved doctrine. A safer way was to employ ritual; the regular repetition of words and actions, designed to break down consciousness without inducing a full trance. Ritual required more self-control on the shaman's part, in order that he should be able to reproduce the formula exactly, time after time, dissociation was no help; and drugs were a positive handicap. As a result shamans began to be chosen on other grounds than their ability to induce trances; and it was at this point that, in effect, they became priests.
>
> (Inglis 1975, p. 26)

This had already begun to happen during the Classical era of Greece, which is why opium and other drugs were associated with "deviant" groups such as the Eleusian cults and perhaps other mystery religions of the age. Merlin believes that opium found a place in the Eleusian mystery rites, although it is difficult to be certain since very little was ever written down about them. He thinks that opium may have been used as an antidote along with the hallucinogen, ergot.[3] With the growing complexity of society and the formalization of religions, there were continuing movements to restrict, ban, and otherwise control the use of drugs in a variety of cultures. As drugs moved into the "underworld" they also became more accessible to the individual for personal use. At the same time, medical practice began to divorce itself from religion and so patterns of secular drug use emerged.

Through Galen, Pliny and other physicians of the Classical era, as well as through the lore of everyday healers, a knowledge of opium was passed from the Greeks and Romans to the Arabs and to the medieval Europeans. Whether or not by the seventh century it had been adopted as a "work drug" or an intoxicant is unclear from the sources, but it is possible. There are, however, several considerations that explain why opium was never a very commonly used drug. Unlike wine, and many other intoxicants, opium is very dangerous. On the one hand it is extremely pleasurable. The euphoric state possible with opium is said to be one of the most intensely pleasurable experiences known. An overdose, however, can be fatal. The drug works by slowing down the heart-rate and by "disconnecting" those messages in our nervous systems that are often interpreted as stress. An overdose (and an excess dosage really depends on an individual's tolerance) will shut down the unconscious nervous system to the point where the unlucky user forgets to breathe and his heart to beat. Not many other intoxicants are so unforgiving. Moreover, opium is highly addictive, regular usage of a certain amount over a period of time results in a "tolerance" for the drug. That is, one needs an increasing dosage to obtain the same effects. Ultimately, the euphoria disappears and one needs regular doses simply to remain "normal." Moreover, cessation of use results in rather traumatic withdrawal symptoms causing extreme mental and physical distress. Because of these factors, the use and administration of opium was probably always somewhat restricted.

Whether restricted or not, opium became widely, if not popularly, known through much of western Eurasia and South Asia in the years between Galen and Muhammad. Its use and probably some level of abuse was already established in the Arab world. Its popularity may have been enhanced because of the ban on alcohol in the Muslim world after the eighth century. During this period, cannabis seems to have become the drug of choice in the area and most reports suggest that it was often ingested in tablets or in drinks mixed with other substances, one of which may have been opium. Here the literature is very scanty. Inglis quotes Rosenthal's work on cannabis (Inglis 1975, pp. 32–3) and reports on the debate that took place among religious and secular leaders in the Muslim world over whether or not it should be banned. The movement to suppress cannabis use among Muslims came when it was discovered that "hashish" (a term which then meant all cannabis preparations) was being used as an intoxicant. Thus, along with its use to mask fatigue and ease "labor pains" cannabis, and presumably opium, were already being used in Western and Southern Asia as drugs of pleasure. Perhaps further research in Arab and Persian sources will provide more information on opium use during this period. Western sources on India and the Arab world from a later period report on societies in which the use of these drugs had become relatively common and accepted. Cannabis and opium had also entered the work force and there are reports of their use by soldiers, by messengers and by others who faced demanding but often sporadic work requirements. Thus, in Mughal India:

> In armies the officers and soldiers were addicted to the use of opium which they took in large quantities and enjoyed the pleasing delirium it occasioned. In battles it inspired a false courage and sometimes produced a frenzy which lasted only a short time, leaving those who swallowed this pernicious drug in a state of languor and imbecility until a renewal of the doze [sic] revived the spirits; but its frequent use enfeebled the constitution and shortened the lives of its deluded votaries. Opium was used to a better purpose by the halcarras, who were a set of people employed as messengers and letter carriers. A halcarra took a letter, wrapped it up in some secret fold of his shabby garment, and with a little opium, some rice and a small pot to draw water, he undertook a journey of several hundred miles and received the reward on delivering the letter.
>
> (Singh 1980, p. 79)

In the nineteenth century, it was quite common for mining coolies to use opium in this fashion. If opium and cannabis were available to individuals in such mundane occupations as messengers and soldiers, it seems likely that it was available at most levels of society for whoever wanted it, for whatever reason.

At the same time, opium had turned up in most of the *materia medica* of the age. Chinese sources report the drug being used there as early as the Sung period. Joseph Needham has more precisely placed the introduction of the drug into China much earlier than the Sung. He notes that Nestorian missionaries may have introduced the Chinese to a Byzantine version of Galen's theriaca in 667. Needham mentions the theriaca in the *Pen Tsao Kang Mu* and *Thang Pen Tsao*, two of the more ancient Chinese *materia medica* (Needham 1954, p. 205). Apparently it had reached China via the Eurasian trade route.

> The drug seems to have first come from Arabia or Persia, probably at the beginning by overland route through India. The extension of its use seems to have been more or less gradual. In the Ming dynasty it came into general use in medicine. It was then given as an astringent and sedative in dysentery, diarrhoea, rheumatism, catarrh, coughs, leucorrhoea, dysmenorrhoea and spermatorrhoea, but generally in combination with other drugs.
>
> (Stuart 1979, p. 308)

From Roman times until recently, in one form or another, opium maintained a high place in the medical armory of European and Asian physicians. Nathan Allen, one of the early opponents of the opium trade, in his history of the trade acknowledged opium's status as a sovereign remedy. He quoted one early medical writer who had said "that if he could be allowed only two weapons with which to combat disease, in its multifarious forms, opium would be his first choice" (Allen 1853, p. 30). Even though opium was known in Europe, however, it was not in widespread use. Perhaps since regular cultivation of the drug seems to have died out in the west, it was imported as a luxury from Western Asia. By the Renaissance, practitioners such as the Swiss alchemist and physician, Paraclesus (Theophrastus Bombastus von Hohenheim, 1493–1541), was said to have established a reputation based largely on liberal dispensation of opiates. Even Shakespeare was familiar enough with the drug to put a reference to it in Iago's mouth:

> Not poppy, nor mandragora,
> Nor all the drowsy syrups of the world,
> Shall ever medicine thee to that sweet sleep
> Which thou ow'dst yesterday.
> (Othello, III. iii. 334–7)

Albert Fields and Peter Tararin attributed the lack of widespread use of the drug in Europe to the "cold climate," although it is not clear whether they meant that the poppy would not grow there or because people who live in such weather are unlikely to fall prey to the drug's temptations (Fields 1970, p. 372). They appear to have been wrong on both counts. The expense of importing it seems a more probable cause. When cheaper opium became available in the eighteenth and nineteenth centuries, it certainly was more widely used.

Opium and long-distance trade

Until the late pre-modern period, both China and Europe imported the drug from Western Asia. Two of the current centers, Turkey and Persia, both seem to have been well-established sites of production. By the sixteenth century, the same was true of India. There is no evidence on how the "commercial" production of the crop was then managed, but if it was reaching China in the seventh century, one assumes it must have been a fairly lucrative cash crop. Possibly it was produced by slave labor, or perhaps by peasants as a sideline. Evidence from nineteenth-century India indicates, however, that opium production is fairly demanding and peasants were usually unwilling to produce it unless they had access to the market, and were thus able to keep some of the profit. Otherwise, they were unlikely to grow it unless coerced. However the drug was produced, there was enough of a surplus and enough of a demand in distant places for it to become a regular item of Asian trade. It is almost certain that by the time Melaka was founded in about 1400, opium was traveling on both the overland as well as the maritime trade routes that linked the two ends of the Eurasian continent, and probably had been for centuries.

By the eighteenth century, the long-distance traffic in opium had been transformed into a very different form of commerce than that which had characterized the trade in earlier years. Before the sixteenth century, opium was just one of the many exotic chemicals that made up an element of the traditional long-distance trade. Generally speaking, traditional long-distance trade seems to have focused on four major types of products, or trade goods. Simply put, these were: exotic chemicals, precious metals and minerals, luxury manufactures, and human beings. Prior to the sixteenth century, these four categories summed up virtually all commerce that moved between major urban centers. Opium, along with other drugs, incenses and fragrances, alcoholic drinks, resins, barks, spices, and herbs, made up the first category. These were valuable largely because of their scarcity. In most cases, their value was the result of having traveled hundreds or even thousands of miles to places where they either did not occur naturally or where the local people did not know how to produce them. For a very long time opium was valuable because of the ignorance of its consumers. The opium poppy is fairly tolerant of a variety of climates and with little more than labor and care, the drug can be easily produced. It seems extraordinary, in the case of China, that even though the imported drug commanded enormous prices in the early nineteenth century, it was not until 1820 that domestic production of the drug in China began in earnest. Furthermore, it was not until very late, perhaps not before 1860 that local production began to fill even a small portion of the Chinese demand for the drug. Long-distance trade thrived on opaque markets. *weren't aware*

The other elements of traditional long-distance trade are of importance in the story of opium. When the capitalist transformation began, it affected the economic structures of all the trade items previously mentioned. The trade in precious metals and minerals was often the first affected. There was always a demand for gold and silver and beyond those, a precious metal was largely a relative definition. In ancient times, copper and iron were traded across the Black Sea and the Mediterranean. Value depended on scarcity and quality. With the discovery of America, the first goal of the Spaniards was to find gold. Once Cortez had looted Mexico, Pizzaro had stripped the walls of the Incas and Coronado had failed to locate El Dorado, it was necessary to enslave the Indians to mine it. This slave-based production of gold, and then silver, in the New World was one of the first major steps on the road to the capitalist transformation. In the first instance this new supply of precious metals enabled the Spanish and the Portuguese to purchase much greater quantities of luxury manufactures and exotic chemicals (spices) in Asia.

Luxury manufactures, particularly the products of skilled craftsmen in the urban centers of the world have always been scarce in areas where they were not produced. From the earliest times, textiles, ceramics, and high-quality weapons topped the list of this category. In some cases, even the raw material from which something was made was scarce, such as silk which for centuries was a jealously guarded secret of the Chinese. Cotton was more common, but few could match the quality of the best Indian cottons before the nineteenth century. These products, on the whole, were the general contents of the peddler's pack and made up the cargos of the ships that plied between the ports of the Mediterranean Sea, the Indian Ocean and the western Pacific since ancient times.

The trade of human beings is more diverse than it might at first seem. Certainly, there was, since the beginnings of civilization, a trade in slaves. The Portuguese had already been involved in the slave trade between Europe and different parts of Africa, and once it became clear that native American labor was less tractable and less durable than African, the trans-Atlantic slave trade was born. This commercialization of human labor, together with the production of precious metals, and the trade in East and Southeast Asian luxuries laid the foundation for the global imperial economy. In addition to slaves, the traditional movement of human beings, as mariners, as traders, as missionaries, pilgrims and conquerors on the trade routes of the world was also a kind of exchange. People carried their own personal baggage in addition to their formal trade goods, the most important of which were microbes and information and sometimes both were even dispensed freely. Those who returned home after their travels were often able to make capital out of their unique knowledge. The microbes were not in demand, but they spread anyhow.

On the whole, not much of this trade was relevant to what Robert Heilbroner has called the "economic problem" (Heilbroner 1987). It was not concerned with everyday necessities such as food grains, fuel, housing materials, tools or simple clothing. Societies in general, excepting the new, hybrid societies being created in the New World, lived without it. Nevertheless, the profits from this trade were often immense for those who had the power to protect their earnings from greedy military, political and religious interests. Values and thus profits were usually in inverse proportion to bulk. This was generally a low-bulk, high-value commerce and a rather small share of a ship's cargo could make a sailor rich and could secure a merchant and his family for life, if he did not risk it all on a succeeding voyage. Nonetheless, the trade itself was still extraneous. Neither the products nor the profits were vital to the continuation of society. They may have made it possible for the elite to indulge their taste for the exotic and to demonstrate their wealth and power through conspicuous consumption, but outside of this, the trade was often expendable. Indeed, for states like China, that considered themselves fully self-sufficient in all of the necessities and most of the luxuries that they desired, foreign, long-distance trade was seen as little more than a favor extended to certain barbarians. On the other hand, such trade was vital to ruling elites and their mercantile allies in a number of other ways.

Regarding the "spice trade," Fernand Braudel has challenged those historians who have emphasized the relative insignificance of this trade, especially compared with the production of grain and basic necessities. For instance in 1828, Jean-Baptiste Say pointed out that the shoemakers of France created more wealth than did the mines of the New World. While he concedes the validity of such a comparison, Braudel disputes the conclusion that long-distance trade was thus insignificant as an economic force and stresses the role that it played in enhancing capitalist accumulation.

> The indisputable superiority of *Fernhändel*, long-distance trading, lay in the *concentrations* it made possible, which meant it was an unrivaled machine for the rapid reproduction and increase of capital. In short, one is forced to agree with the German historians and with Maurice Dobb, who see long-distance trade as an essential factor in the creation of merchant capitalism, and in the creation of the merchant bourgeoisie.
>
> (Braudel 1979b, p. 408)

Aside from the new overseas settlements being founded in the sixteenth century, the only states for which trade was the solution to the problem of daily survival were those that lived by trade alone. From fairly early times, groups such as the Phoenicians, who did not produce much of their own food or other basic necessities, found they could procure them from distant sources, and occasionally even carry them from place to place. So long as they controlled a merchant navy, states such as Venice, Genoa or Melaka could thrive on the ebb and flow of long-distance trade alone.

Commodities such as grain were not usually in the top four categories commonly traded, but when there was a famine and the wealthy inhabitants of a city found themselves with short supplies from their own hinterlands, then even grain became worth carrying long distances, but this was usually an extraordinary circumstance and not the sort of thing even a trading state could count on to make a living. Trading states in Southeast Asia, such as Melaka, managed to survive by purchasing rice and other grains from its trading partners. There was a substantial delivery of rice to Melaka throughout its period of commercial dominance. Moreover, the Javanese traders who supplied Melaka, also supplied the Moluccas from which they obtained the spices. The city-states, or port-polities and isolated production zones of island Southeast Asia, were exceptional political economies. As we shall see, it was because many Malay rulers were so dependent on trade that the arrival of Europeans, bent on dominating certain aspects of the trade, made them particularly vulnerable to foreign conquest and influence.

It was the arrival of Europeans at Melaka in 1509 that began to undermine this pattern of traditional commerce. They came, initially, in pursuit of those exotic Southeast Asian chemicals, the spices for which Melaka had become famous. They quickly found, however, that Melaka was the "city that was made for merchandise" and seized it, making it one of their principal bases in Southeast Asia.

In addition to the traditional spices, the Portuguese also discovered opium being cultivated in India in the sixteenth century, and Alfonso d'Albaquerque recommended that the king of Portugal should make it a source of profit. Already at that time, there were two major production areas in South Asia: one in western India, and one in eastern India. In the west, what later became known as "Malwa" opium was then shipped through Cambay. Ralph Fitch, the English merchant who visited India in 1585, noted that the Burmese imported opium from Cambay. He also mentions opium coming from Patna. After escaping from a Portuguese prison in Goa, he traveled from Agra to Bengal "in the company of one hundred and fourscore boats laden with salt, opium, hing, [assafoetida], lead, carpets, and divers other commodities down the river Jumna." This opium was making its way from Patna into the trading networks of the Bay of Bengal and along the same trade routes that later took Fitch to Burma, Siam and Melaka. It is of interest however, that Fitch does not mention it in the Portuguese trade to China, which he claimed was entirely paid for by silver from Japan and India (Fitch 1583, p. 258 and pp. 259–66).

Indian opium was surely being traded to China by the beginning of the sixteenth century, and it was already being used in Melaka and other parts of Southeast Asia. Tome Pires suggests that Malay warriors, whom he styles "amoks" (*amoucos*) may have used it before they went into battle, as did the Indian soldiers mentioned above. Despite the apparent availability of the drug, there is no evidence that it was perceived as a "problem." We must assume that although the people of that era understood that it was both addictive and poisonous, they were not only willing to produce and use it, but they apparently did not see that use as a danger for society at large.

Englebert Kaempfer(o), the German pharmacist, who traveled throughout Asia in the late seventeenth century makes all of this quite clear. He has left us detailed description of opium cultivation and its use in Persia. He classified it as a kind of "kheif," a word generally used in Western Asia for cannabis preparations, and indicates that the Persians also regarded it as identical to the Greek theriaca. In general, all used a name based on the Greek, *afyun*, or some variation of the term from which our word "opium" is derived. He makes no mention of it being smoked in Persia, but indicates that it was ingested.[4] He describes in some detail the way in which the green seed capsules of the poppy were incised and how the sap, which congeals into raw opium, was collected. In addition to describing the different grades and preparations of opium, Kaempfer shows that he and his contemporaries were well acquainted with the fundamental properties that we now associate with opium: that it was an intoxicant; that one could develop a tolerance for it; that it was addictive; and that it could be fatal.

> While a dose of as little as a single grain may prove fatal to a European, those long accustomed to the use of opium may consume as much as a drachm [of the drug] without harm. Yet many injure themselves through abuse and long use, as a result of which the body becomes emaciated, virility slackens, the spirit grows gloomy and the intellect dull. One may see the opium-eaters sitting mute and somnolent in the midst of their companions. I have often been offered a reward of as much as a hundred pieces of gold to cure men of this addiction this side of death. I refrain from adducing here examples of the ravening after opium of which the medical texts are replete.
>
> (Kaempfero 1712, p. 642–5)

Even though the phenomenon of addiction was not perceived as a serious social problem at this time, either by the fellow countrymen of the users, or by European observers, Kaempfer certainly saw it as damaging to those individuals who used it. At this time, it is doubtful that anyone understood that drug use on an extensive scale by a considerable number of people was even within the realm of possibility. Not even in localities where the drug was cultivated do we find reports of widespread addiction. At the beginning of the eighteenth century, it does not appear that the phenomenon we would today call a "drug epidemic" had ever been witnessed.

I would argue that the "drug plague" really was something new under the sun. There do not seem to have been any reports of serious drug epidemics before opium addiction struck China in the eighteenth and nineteenth centuries. For centuries, civilizations had risen and fallen. The causes for their various disasters have been numerous, but among those causes, there is no indication that extensive drug addiction by a large portion of the population has ever been the factor in such a process.

By the latter part of the nineteenth century, things had changed. China and parts of the Malay world seem to have been truly devastated by drug use. Millions of people in China were then using the drug, almost on a daily basis. If we had the exact figures, they would probably show that nearly as much opium was consumed in China in the year of 1880, as was consumed in the entire world during any five years of the 1980s.[5] This includes all opiates consumed for whatever reason: e.g. heroin, morphine, paregoric, codeine, etc., for both medical as well as "enjoyment" purposes. While we must understand that modern chemical technology is able to extract and deliver the active alkaloids far more efficiently than the practice of smoking opium, the sheer bulk of Chinese consumption a century ago was truly enormous. This phenomenon seems to cry out for an explanation.

Drug plagues and capitalism

It seems that a new trend in drug use had emerged by the nineteenth century, but was the Chinese phenomenon the first? Perhaps not. It is clear that during the seventeenth century Europeans were beginning to consume extraordinary amounts of all kinds of drugs or drug products: alcohol, tobacco, tea, coffee and sugar. It is difficult to tell whether alcohol consumption was simply now noticeable because it was being imported and exported, and was thus easier to count, or whether there really was an absolute increase in use. It has been suggested to me that Europeans in the pre-modern era were always drunk, or at least that habitual intoxication was a common and unremarkable phenomenon, and that the concern expressed about the consumption of gin in the eighteenth century was more a matter of a changed consciousness rather than an increase in actual consumption. Jessica Warner seems to agree, but she offers no judgement on whether consumption was actually increasing. In a number of studies, however, she argues that perceptions of addiction and of the occurrence of drug epidemics were important considerations in writings about the "great gin plague" of early eighteenth-century London (Warner 1992; Warner 1993a).

Braudel, however, states categorically: "Drunkenness increased everywhere (in Europe) in the sixteenth century." He notes that in Valladolid in northern Spain, consumption of wine reached 100 liters per person annually, and that in Venice the Signoria took renewed and severe action against public drunkenness in 1598. By the end of the eighteenth century, a Parisian consumed an average of 121.76 liters of wine annually. (Braudel 1979a, pp. 236–41) Braudel stresses the popularization of alcohol which had taken place by the eighteenth century throughout most of western Europe. The production of brandy, gin and rum rapidly increased while consumer prices fell accordingly. Some may take issue with Braudel's hyperbolic comment: "By the early eighteenth century, the whole of London society, from top to bottom was determinedly getting drunk on gin" (Braudel 1979a, p. 246). Nevertheless, it appears that something new was happening. Drug use was increasing and thus the idea of a society ridden by a drug had also come into existence. If we take a broader look at what was happening to the use of other drugs, it appears that there really was something different about the human condition in the modern age and that drugs and capitalism, together, have something to do with that difference.

Even though humanity had been living with a wide range of addictive and intoxicating substances for most of its existence there had been no true perception of a drug epidemic. But, since the discovery of America, Europe in particular, not to mention the Americas, had been swept by massive infusions of new drugs, as well as radically expanded supplies of familiar ones. In particular, the arrival of tobacco, sugar, coffee and tea had drastically transformed European society, not to mention the areas of Africa and the Americas that felt the impact of these changes. It was not simply that new drugs had become available as a result of the Columbian exchange, although this was certainly a factor, but some more profound force had also been unleashed that radically altered the whole economic, social and political constructs of the globe. If we look only at drugs, and drug economies as a class apart from other kinds of commodities, or perhaps more accurately, as the first true commodities, perhaps the capitalist transformation can be seen in a different light.

Some recent studies have drawn attention to the new economies generated by these substances and the new economic structures that accompanied them. Sidney Mintz, Henry Hobhouse and James Walvin have all produced important contributions to this topic (Hobhouse 1985; Mintz 1985; Walvin 1997). Perhaps the most penetrating and enlightening of these studies has been Mintz's book on sugar, *Sweetness and Power 1650–1880* (Mintz 1985). Mintz notes Eric Hobsbawm's comment on the conditions that created the new exchange patterns of the "Commercial Revolution":

> Such a change, Hobsbawm argues, rested on three new conditions: the growth of an expandable consumers' market in Europe itself, tied to changes in production elsewhere; the seizure of colonies abroad for European

"development"; and the creation of colonial enterprises (such as plantations) to produce consumer goods (and to soak up a substantial portion of the products of the homeland).

(Mintz 1985, p. 66)

By the seventeenth century, all three of these factors had begun to work together. On the one hand, there was the growth of a European consumer market not only for sugar, but also for other "drug foods" as Mintz styles them, such as coffee, tea, cacao, as well as real drugs such as alcohol and tobacco. Together with this development came the seizure of colonial territories or the expansion of enterprises in American colonies. The third, and key element was the establishment of plantations and the slave system to produce the new consumer goods in commercial quantities. Mintz relates these to the development of capitalism:

> The profound changes in dietary and consumption patterns in eighteenth- and nineteenth-century Europe were not random or fortuitous, but the direct consequence of the same momentum that created a world economy, shaping the asymmetrical relationships between the metropolitan centers and their colonies and satellites, and the tremendous productive and distributive apparatuses, both technical and human, of modern capitalism.
>
> (Mintz 1985, pp. 158–9)

Mintz is correct in drawing attention to the significance of the consumer market which was created in Europe, it is also important to draw attention to what Europeans were consuming. It is noteworthy that the most important commodities for capitalist growth were, as Braudel has suggested, the exotic chemicals, the drugs. Not only did they come together with modern capitalism, but I would argue that they were the *sine qua non* of capitalism. That is to say, without drugs and drug economies, capitalism could not have come into being. These new consumer markets and the apparatus which served them were not built on wheat, nor wool nor widgets, not even cotton comes close. They were built on commodities that no one had ever really consumed before and which, in general, were totally unnecessary. They were truly nothing more than smoke and water. Their great attraction was their ability to create an addiction for themselves, or at least a habituation.

Capitalism depended upon colonialism and the "free" resources of the New World, but it needed cash in order to finance their exploitation and defense and this came from drugs. Colonialism depended upon the production and export of drug crops. They were the foundation of every successful colonial enterprise, whether settler colonies such as existed in the New World or in colonies of "conquest" such as existed in Asia and Africa.

The history of the Virginia and Maryland colonies are cases in point. Without the tobacco economy that emerged in those territories, it is hard to see how England would have maintained an interest in colonial development in North America. There was little profit for the imperial high flyers of London in the

New England settlements, with its tight-fisted Puritans and its stony soil and atrocious weather. By itself, it would not have been a viable enterprise. The French had taken control of the St. Lawrence and the Great Lakes basin and thus controled the lucrative fur trade. With the slave-based, tobacco economies of the mid-Atlantic settlements and the sugar economies of the Caribbean, however, an adjunct settlement like New England could be useful to Britain. Colonialism was not simply about dumping undesirable elements of the metro-politan population, it had to turn a profit. That profit came from tobacco and sugar, in the seventeenth and eighteenth centuries, and was soon joined by tea and coffee.

The growth of sugar consumption in England went hand in hand with the expansion of the West Indian plantations and the African slave trade. On the other side of the world, the expanding East Indian trade in coffee and tea brought the perfect complement to America's sugar: bitter Asian beverages and sweet American sugar.

> But this is not to say that these changes were intended, or that their ancillary consequences were well understood. The ways in which the English became the biggest sugar consumers in the world; the relationships between the colonial loci of sugar production and the metropolitan locus of its refining and consumption; the connections between sugar and slavery and the slave trade; the relation of sugar to bitter liquid stimulants; the role of the West Indian interest in protecting the plantation economy and winning special state support for sugar; the unexpected suitability of sugar for the crown's desire to impose duties – these and many other aspects of sugar's history must not be thrown together and labeled "causes" or "consequences" as if, once enumerated, they explained anything by themselves. But it is possible to point to certain long-term trends the general consequences of which are readily discerned.
>
> (Mintz 1985, pp. 158–9)

The "profound changes" that Mintz sees here are the expansion of the market and the commensurate lowering of prices that came with the expansion of production. Basic capitalist growth, economies of scale, comparative advantage and division of labour all came together. The producers who first achieved that "comparative advantage" immediately became free traders and worked to break down all the protectionist obstacles which prevent their product from flooding the markets of the world. Free trade of this kind was really a sort of monopoly and thus was the handmaiden of imperialism. Thus, it was no accident that the cry for free trade was the trumpet call of the Opium War, but the victory secured the income of the Indian government's monopoly on opium production.

The increasing wealth of the metropolitan interests which controlled sugar increased their political power in the British government and gave them the capability to further enhance their profits (Mintz 1985, p. 157–62). They eliminated the competition of East Indian sugar from Java by placing a high duty on the Asian import, which stayed in place for an entire century: from the 1680s to the 1780s (Furber 1976, p. 247). The East India Company focused on tea while they left West Indian interests to profit from sugar. In both cases, British economic expansion was led by drug economies. Mintz's comments on the power of imperial "sugar interests" are equally applicable to the tea interests, which in the nineteenth century also became the opium interests.

> The English people came to view sugar as essential; supplying them with it became as much a political as an economic obligation. At the same time, the owners of the immense fortunes created by the labor of millions of slaves stolen from Africa, on millions of acres of the new World stolen from the Indians – wealth in the form of commodities like sugar, molasses, and rum to be sold to Africans, Indians, colonials, and the British working class alike – had become even more solidly attached to the centers of power in English society at large. . . . What sugar meant from this vantage point, was that all such colonial production, trade, and metropolitan consumption came to mean: the growing strength and solidity of the empire and of the classes that dictated its policies.
>
> (Mintz 1985, p. 157)

A class of people had gained power in England through the wealth of the empire. They used that wealth to protect and promote their interests, which included the preservation and expansion of the empire and the creation of structures, both in the metropolitan center and in the colonial periphery to enhance their power. The people that consumed sugar and the people that produced it were necessary to the process of expansion, but also had little control or volition. Capitalism brought a kind of freedom, but not another.

> It was not by processes of symbol making and meaning investment that sugar was made available to the English people, but because of political, economic, and military undertakings the organization of which would have been unimaginable to the ordinary citizen. The immense quantities of coerced labor required to produce sucrose and bitter stimulant beverages also had to be arranged for, or the substances in the quantities desired would not have been forthcoming. Only with these arrangements secured could the wonderful and uniquely human capacity to find and bestow meaning be exercised. In short, the creation of a commodity that would permit taste and the symbolic faculty to be exercised was far beyond the reach of both the enslaved Africans who produced the sugar, on the one hand, and of the proletarianized English people who consumed it, on the other. Slave and proletarian together powered the imperial economic system that kept the one supplied with manacles and the other with sugar and rum; but neither had more than minimal influence over it. The growing freedom of the consumer to choose was one kind of freedom, but not another.
>
> (Mintz 1985, pp. 183–4)

According to Mintz, the desire to buy sugar (and other drugs) made workers work. Sugar provided a sort of symbolic incentive that made them useful to the capitalist classes. On the other hand, sugar, tea and tobacco, also enhanced the wealth and the power of government. Mintz makes an important point, which though relevant to nineteenth-century Europe can be shown to apply to Asia.

> [S]ugar was the most aptly taxable, partly because it was poorly suited to smuggling (unlike tea, for instance). As its yield of wealth to the exchequer grew, so its value as a taxable item was enshrined: there arose a powerful vested interest in its continued and expanded consumption. Like tea or tobacco, it could be counted upon to yield revenues even when scarce supplies drove up its price. And, as Dowell says, because its consumption was so widespread, the pressure was not felt by anyone.' Thus was the new freedom to afford sugar a key to governance itself.
>
> (Mintz 1985, pp. 183–4)

Thus according to Mintz sugar was instrumental in creating the international proletariat, and he makes it clear, that it was not simply sugar, but all of the other exotic drug crops that had found a market in metropolitan Europe.

> Whereas the plantations were long viewed as sources of profit through direct capital transfers for reinvestment at home, or through the absorption of finished goods from home, the hypothesis offered here is that sugar and other drug foods, by provisioning, sating – and, indeed drugging – farm and factory workers, sharply reduced the overall cost of creating and reproducing the metropolitan proletariat.
>
> (Mintz 1985, p. 180)

He is correct in this. Sugar and other drug foods provisioned European and American farm and factory workers. These products helped to turn them into consumers and wedded them to the cash economy. Work brought its immediate reward in capacity to consume these "little luxuries."

Opium too, played in this process. In a sense, English laborers consumed sugar and made "manacles" for the slaves who grew the sugar. Sugar was also consumed with tea, but in the eighteenth century, it was impossible for the European commercial system to enslave Chinese workers so as to make them a part of that system. They were already integrated into a self-contained and self-sustaining Chinese and Asian economy. In fact, English and other European traders could not even get tea directly from the Chinese producers, but had to deal with the Chinese commercial infrastructure. Tea did not exist in the western hemisphere or in Africa, and it was not until the late nineteenth century that the English began to produce it in sufficient quantities in India to change this situation. In 1890, China still exported more tea than all other countries in the world combined, and until 1910, remained the largest single producer (Walvin 1997, p. 126).

In the eighteenth century, tea had to be purchased with silver. The best that could be done, in this case, was to force the slaves in America to produce silver so that it would be available to purchase Chinese tea and other "oriental luxuries" such as pepper and spices. As many students of the tea trade and the East India Company have shown, opium was the answer to the tea remittance. If they could sell enough opium to pay for the cost of the tea purchase it would eliminate the bullion drain from Europe. Beyond that it would reduce the cost of tea to the European proletariat, and even more desirable, increase the profit level of the East India Company and the capitalist structures that lived off the empire. Opium thus functioned, in the first instance as a source of virtually free capital which allowed the English to get their foot into the door of the Asian commercial system.

In order to do this, it was necessary to do to opium what had already been done to commodities such as sugar, tobacco, cotton, and coffee. It was necessary to make it too a "commodity"; to organize its production with a force of cheap and malleable labor, on land that was already controlled for as cheap a price as possible. It would be necessary to create centralized control over collection and processing of the product. It was also necessary to gain access to the market where it could be consumed on a mass basis. This was the course that opium now took.

It was necessary to create an opium epidemic in Asia. Europeans, in particular British traders, did not plan this from the outset and they did not act necessarily from malicious intent, unless the aim of making money and getting wealthy at the expense of another is a crime. Nevertheless, a drug epidemic was begun and promoted, and it was done because it was profitable. It was profitable because it worked. The English trading in China fed that demand because it was there and because it was about the only way in which they believed they could make enough money to pay for tea. They were not ignorant of what sort of substance they were selling. They knew it was a poison. They knew it was addictive. They knew that it did its users no good. From the time of Warren Hastings in the 1770s, the British colonial records and other contemporary materials are full of quotations that indicate a perfect acquaintance with the nature and power of opium. It is in the creation of the opium trade that we can see the invisible hand of capitalism at work.

3   Cleverer than alchemists

The empire and smoke

The previous chapters have looked at the beginnings of human involvement with opium and at the opium trade in pre-modern times. The commodification of the drug trades in tobacco, sugar and tea, were major factors in the earlier stages of capitalist development. These drugs turned the European peasants and urban masses into a consumer-proletariat while they fattened the local bourgeoisie. Opium had a similar impact in Asia. The creation of a market for this drug commodity in Asia, however, did not similarly benefit the Asian bourgeoisie. It did not foster the sort of accumulation which would lead to the same kind of economic transformation in Asia as had occurred in Europe. The same European bourgeoisie which controlled sugar, tea and tobacco, also controlled the flow of opium to Asia, thus much of the profit from opium also ended up in Europe and America, while Asian capitalists enjoyed only limited benefits. The immediate result of capitalism in Asia was the colonial empire. Opium was an important link between the creation of empire and capitalism in Asia.

Between 1750 and 1900, Britain in particular extended its dominions and spheres of influence in Asia from India to China. Most of India came under its control together with Burma, Malaya, Singapore, and part of Borneo. The global reach of Britain's economy became a major force in China and in the other areas of Asia outside its political control. Colonial domination in areas such as French Indochina, the Netherlands East Indies and the Spanish Philippines actually depended on the British strategic position as well as British capital.

The advance of this colonial takeover, while seen as remarkable in itself, has been taken for granted in many respects. European technology, military superiority, the concerted force of nation-states and the productive power of modern industry all seem adequate explanations for this rapid conquest. And yet, so swift and invincible did the nineteenth-century imperial advance seem, that it was often assumed the Europeans represented a superior stage in the evolutionary scale. Social Darwinist explanations seemed to make sense as Eastern Asia literally collapsed into the laps of European conquerors. For centuries, India, the countries of mainland Southeast Asia and China had not only resisted European advances but had continued to pursue their indigenous cultural and political agendas with little reference to the "strangers at the gate." During the nineteenth century however, their political systems eroded, their leaders lost initiative, and their armies either broke and ran or were massacred where they stood. Their economies proved defenceless to penetration and their social structures seemed to dissolve. Was it just guns, money and organization that had made all of this possible?

Prior to the nineteenth century, aside from certain fringe effects, Europeans did not really alter the ground of trade, not to mention political life, in Asia east of Suez. Aside from certain positions of "paramountcy" such as the British had in certain parts of the Indian subcontinent and the Dutch in Java and the Spanish in Luzon, the colonial empires were not very impressive. As Fernand Braudel has noted, the political economies of the established Asian states persisted, more or less intact. In concluding his massive study *Civilization and Capitalism*, he expresses a certain bewilderment at this situation.

> For it can hardly be questioned that until the nineteenth century the rest of the world outweighed Europe both in its population and while the *ancien régime* lasted, in wealth, if it is virtually beyond question that Europe was less rich than the worlds it was exploiting, even after the fall of Napoleon, when Britain's hour of glory was dawning – we still do not really know how this position of supremacy was established and above all maintained.
>
> (Braudel 1984, p. 534)

Opium offers a possible answer to his question. Sidney Mintz's insights regarding the combined impact of drugs, drug foods and capitalism in Europe seem equally applicable to the relationship between capitalism, imperialism and opium in Asia.

For centuries, Arabs, Indians and then Europeans had carried opium from Western and Southern Asia to Eastern Asia. The production of opium for this market was, it seems, already a cottage industry in many parts of the region and a more-or-less standard product had been developed by local peasants and merchants. There is no evidence that Europeans had anything to do with showing the peoples of eastern India, for example, how to process and pack their opium. By the beginning of the eighteenth century, "Bengal" opium[1] was being made into balls and packed into chests for export. Lockyer mentions opium being sold in chests in Aceh and China in 1704, and one assumes it was already a well-established practice. The opium trade, as the British came to it, had a long process of growth and evolution behind it.

The Dutch efforts to expand and establish the opium trade during the seventeenth century were a necessary foundation for the accomplishments of the British. They developed a much more extensive market for the drug than had previously been the case. Particularly in Southeast Asia, the Dutch seem to have been the first to make it a "little" luxury, rather than an exotic medicine. For them, it is clear, opium had already begun to function as a form of capital. By far the most important element in this was the Dutch role in changing the manner in which opium was consumed. The Dutch seem to have been instrumental in bringing the habit of smoking opium to the Chinese, if not to China itself.[2]

Whether it was the Dutch or the Javanese or the Chinese who first mixed opium with tobacco, and thus initiated the practice of smoking the drug, is not clear. Kaempfer's report from 1689 confirms that opium was being smoked in Java, but it is not clear that the Chinese there were using it:

> [There is] also [another] strange use of opium among the *nigritas* [Javanese]; for they mix with it, tobacco diluted with water so that when kindled the head spins more violently. In Java, I saw flimsy sheds [made of] reeds in which this kind of tobacco was set out [for sale] to passers-by. No commodity throughout the Indies is retailed with greater return by the Batavians than opium, which [its] users cannot do without, nor can they come by it except it be brought by ships of the Batavians from Bengal and Coromandel.
>
> (Kaempfero 1712, p. 650)

His use of the term "nigritas" for the smokers he saw in Java, must certainly refer to Javanese. Edkins claims that opium was smoked in Taiwan, and suggests the practice dated from the early eighteenth century. It was reported that "depraved young men without any fixed occupation [who] used to meet together by night to smoke [opium]" (Edkins 1898, pp. 42–3).

John Crawfurd's report which dates from the early nineteenth century, agrees with Kaempfer that the Javanese were smoking opium, but he claims that they learned to do this from the Chinese. Whatever its origin, by 1800, the practice of smoking opium had come to be seen as something peculiarly Chinese. From the European and Indian point of view, it was also considered a particularly depraved and dangerous way of consuming the drug.

> The Indian islanders are well known to be passionately addicted to the habitual *use of opium*, and yet the general use of this drug is but of comparatively recent introduction. They may have been taught the use of it by the Arabs; but the extensive and pernicious consumption which now distinguishes the manners of the Indian islanders, is to be ascribed to the commerce of the Europeans, and to the debauching influence of Chinese manners and example . . . The whole of the tribes of the Indian islands invariably smoke, instead of eating or chewing opium, like the Turks, and other people of Asia. The case is exactly reversed with respect to it and tobacco.
>
> (Crawfurd 1820b, pp. 106–7)

While Crawfurd's assumptions about the antiquity and causes of Javanese use of the drug may be questionable, his observations certainly reflect the changes, both in perception as well as practice, that had taken place by the beginning of the nineteenth century. One important innovation was the appearance of a new method of smoking opium that dispensed with tobacco altogether. This practice, and the "technology" that went with it seem to have been purely Chinese innovations. We see that a rather extraordinary process of hybridization had taken place. Tobacco and the practice of smoking were both elements of the Columbian exchange, and had been brought to the Old World from the Americas by Christopher Columbus and his Spanish successors. Kaempfer's report shows us that by the seventeenth century, opium had found its way into tobacco-smoking mixtures. By the nineteenth century, Marsden indicates that Sumatran Malays were still using opium in a similar fashion.[3]

By this time, however, the Chinese smokers had eliminated the tobacco, but kept, or rather adapted the method of smoking, so that they could consume pure opium in this fashion. This change was of great significance. In addition to the practice of smoking, a new method of purifying and preparing the drug had also appeared, and this too, had come to be associated with the Chinese. Raw opium, as it came from the ball, was dissolved in water, strained, and boiled in a copper vessel until it was thickened. The process was usually repeated and the final product, a syrupy, blackish substance resulted, which was called *chandu*. Smokers then took a small amount of this mixture, held it on the end of a long needle over a spirit lamp for a minute or so, until it started to bubble and was about to burst into flame. Then it was quickly transferred into the bowl of the pipe and the smoke was inhaled. A true "opium pipe" of this sort, was nothing like a tobacco pipe, but was usually a large bamboo, wooden or ivory tube, with a wide metal or ceramic bowl somewhat shallower than a tea-cup, with a small hole in the bottom. This bowl was set over a hole in the end of the tube. Samuel Wells Williams described the process of smoking as follows:

> Lying along the couch, he holds the pipe, aptly called *yen tsiang*, i.e. smoking pistol, by the Chinese, so near to the lamp that the bowl can be brought up to it without stirring himself. A little opium of the size of a pea, being taken on the end of a spoon-headed needle, is put upon the hole of the bowl, and set on fire at the lamp, and inhaled at one whiff, so that none of the smoke shall be lost. Old smokers will retain the breath for a long time, filling the lungs, and exhaling the fumes through the nose. The taste of the half-fluid extract is sweetish and oily, somewhat like rich cream, but the smell of the burning drug is rather sickening. The pipe having burned out, the smoker lies some-what listless for a moment while the fumes are dissipating, and then repeats the process until he has spent all his purchase, or taken his prescribed dose.
>
> (Williams 1907, p. 388)

Wright notes that the authorities in Calcutta were somewhat reluctant to allow the Chinese in Penang to produce chandu:

> The Court's condemnation of chandoo probably reflected the view held in Bengal. Smoking was not customary there and was probably frowned on as a vulgar vice practised in public saloons at the ports by sea-farers, while private opium-eating by the upper classes seemed much less objectionable.
>
> (Wright 1961, pp. 169–70)

This is all by way of saying that the opium trade of the nineteenth century was the work of many hands, and the contours of it had, to some extent, already been established before the Battle of Plassey. Even though the British came to control the production of opium, and both they and the Dutch and other Europeans traded opium, Malays, Javanese and the Chinese themselves dominated the final preparation and distribution of the drug and the Chinese created their own peculiar "culture" for its use. It might be noted, however, that both *chandu* and *madat* appear to be Malay words, which reflects a significant Southeast Asian influence on the emerging drug culture. Opium, once a mere medicine, had been converted into a "recreational" drug. The practice of smoking did more than place it alongside tobacco as a leisure pastime, it also made the use of the drug far less dangerous. It is more difficult to kill oneself by smoking opium than by ingesting it. A person is likely to pass out, fall asleep or otherwise lose consciousness before overdosing. Also, because the effect of the drug is felt almost immediately, within minutes, and more intensely, gratification is more rapid and it is far easier to adjust one's intake. These changes greatly facilitated the popularization of opium in East and Southeast Asia. From the eighteenth century onward, the *smoking* of opium came to be seen as something that was peculiarly Asian.

Anglo-Dutch conflict in Asia

During the second half of the eighteenth century, the British began to move toward domination of the Asian trade and they did it largely by taking control of opium. This brought them into collision with the Dutch for control of the sources of opium, as well as the markets for the drug. Initially, each had a different market in mind. While the VOC had pioneered the opium trade, they had not really focused on developing the China market. Rather, it appears that the original intention of the Dutch was to sell the drug in the Malay world and in Java. Alexander Hamilton's account of the Dutch resident of Melaka, Mr. Lucas, who pioneered the opium trade up the Bengkalis River (just across the Straits from Melaka in Sumatra) is illustrative of Dutch methods and interests:

> The Dutch have another factory right opposite to Malacca, on the side of a large River, called Bankalis . . . The Company sends a great deal of Cloth and Ophium there, and brings gold-dust in Return. That beneficial trade was not known to the Dutch before 1685, that one Mr. Lucas, a Factor in the Company's Service at Malacca, was advised by a Malay to send some Surat Baftees dyed blue, and some Berams, dyed red, which are both coarse Cotton Cloth much worn in that Country; and Ophium is as much in Request there, as Tea is with us. In 10 Years that he kept that Trade wholly to himself, tho' in other Mens Names, he got an Estate of 10 or 12 Tuns of Gold, or about 100,000 Pounds English, and then revealed the Secret to the Company, who took that Trade altogether into their own Hands.
>
> (Hamilton 1727, p. 66)

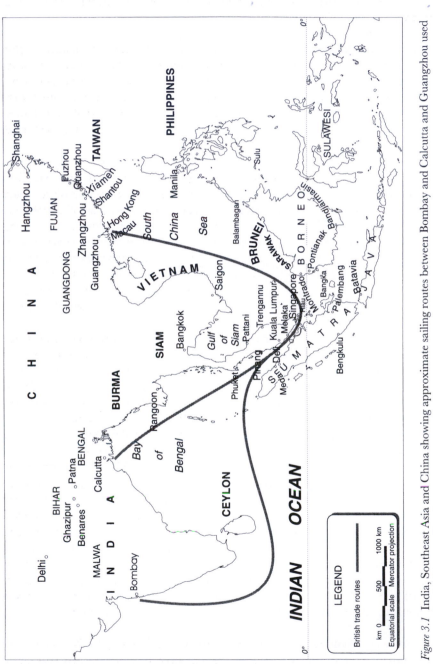

Figure 3.1 India, Southeast Asia and China showing approximate sailing routes between Bombay and Calcutta and Guangzhou used by the Country Traders

Hamilton also reports that the Dutch also traded opium to Palembang (Hamilton 1727, p. 64). The VOC had established itself as the major purchaser of opium in India:

> In their zeal they are said to have fallen on the expedient of training Ceylon elephants and trading them to Bengal merchants for opium and other merchandise. It was in 1659 that they began to procure their supply from Bengal, and when the trade reached its height a century later, they were shipping more than one hundred tons [about 1,400 chests] to Batavia alone.
>
> (Owen 1934, p. 8)

t the beginning of the eighteenth century, the VOC empire in Southeast Asia was by far the strongest and wealthiest of any European presence in Asia. They dominated the trade in all Asian luxuries between Europe and the East. Their navies were the strongest force in the seas between Capetown and Nagasaki and supported a string of fortresses and factories that reinforced the Dutch trading monopolies along the Asian littoral. On the strength of this empire, Amsterdam was the financial capital of Europe and Batavia was the most prosperous trading center in Southeast Asia. It was Holland's Golden Age. Even as the century opened, however, cracks were appearing in their armor, and global economic and political conditions were changing in ways that would threaten the Dutch position.

As Holden Furber notes in his sweeping study of the eighteenth century trade rivalry in Asia, the British were gradually making gains in three areas. First of all, the East India Company, having been rudely expelled from the spice trade and from Southeast Asia in 1623, had built up a credible presence in India, maintaining factories at Calcutta, Madras and Bombay while developing the trade in Indian cottons to Europe. As the Mughal empire began to collapse, in the early eighteenth century, the Company moved into the power vacuum (Furber 1976, ch. 2).

The second advance was the establishment of an EIC factory in Canton which gave the British direct access to China and provided them with a base from which to expand the tea trade, and later the opium trade. After a number of initiatives and tentative contacts, in 1716 the EIC established its council of supercargoes in Canton and placed the tea trade on a firm footing. Between 1700 and 1706, EIC tea imports jumped from 20,000 to 100,000 lbs annually. In 1760 the EIC paid duties in Great Britain on five million lbs of tea and in 1766 they exported six million lbs from China (Mintz 1985, p. 113). The British position left the Dutch at a disadvantage. The strength of the EIC was evident in the shift that had taken place in the trade in calicoes and tea in the early eighteenth century:

> By waiting until 1729 to open *direct* trade in tea at Canton, the Dutch lost their initiative in the China trade to the British, never regained it and soon reverted to their old methods. A mere glance at a few relevant figures shows the difference in the demand for piece goods and tea over thirty years: calico

imports by the English company rose from 500,000 pieces annually during the decade 1701–1710 to 980,000 annually during the years 1731–1740; the sales proceeds on tea rose from £116,000 in 1712 to £348,000 in 1744.

(Furber 1976, p. 131)

The third front of British expansion in Asia was seen in the activities of the group of private English merchants, known as "country traders." They were most important in both undercutting Dutch power and in strengthening the British position in East and Southeast Asia. Ironically, this trade was seen as a weakness by the Dutch since it showed the permeability of the EIC monopoly. The country trade violated those conditions which had been the foundation of Dutch power, and they proved to be its undoing. Furber claimed that the Dutch "reverted to their old methods" after trying to export tea directly from Canton. What did he mean by this? Leonard Blussé's work on eighteenth-century Batavia shows how deeply the VOC leadership had come to rely upon the Chinese by the beginning of the century. The Chinese "junk trade," based largely on the Fujian ports and Shantou, had come to serve all the needs of Batavia. In fact this was seen as a great benefit by Woodes Rogers who visited there around 1700:

> The Dutch have all Chinese commodities brought to them cheaper than they can fetch them; and being conveniently situated for the spice trade, they have all in their own hand . . . Batavia wants no commodities that India affords; it is a pity that our East India Company has no settlement to which the Chinese might resort.
>
> (Quoted in Blussé 1988, p. 128)

At about the same time however, the directors of the VOC, the "Seventeen Gentlemen" in Holland, attempted to control the "abuses" of the junk trade. They realized that company servants and the freeburghers of Batavia and Melaka were buying ceramics and nearly 100,000 lbs of tea annually from these Chinese. Of the tea, they were selling a third to the company (at a profit to themselves), shipping another third home on their own accounts or selling it to other sailors and mariners, while the other third was consumed or sold locally. Aside from this, the tea which was sent to Batavia was an inferior quality to that which was sold to the British in Canton (Blussé 1988, p. 131).

The problem was not one that had an easy solution. By the end of the seventeenth century, Batavia had come to have a trade and life of its own. The Chinese not only carried the Dutch "China trade," but they also had come to occupy a vital place in Batavia's domestic political economy. There was a significant population of resident Chinese merchants in Batavia who not only "managed" the trade, but also provided the sole economic and political link to the thousands of Chinese sugar planters who had settled in the hinterland of Batavia. Chinese officers and middlemen dominated and policed the colony's port and marketplace, collecting harbour duties and taxes levied on ships, markets, customs and the weighing house. They also collected the headtaxes from Chinese and native settlers in the townships around Batavia and farmed the revenues for tobacco, pork and gambling – and, although Blussé is silent on the topic, probably opium as well (Blussé 1988, pp. 124–5).

Batavia had virtually become a Chinese town by 1700, and there were few truly "Dutch" interests in the place that did not in some way depend on Chinese services. It is probable that some Chinese were beginning to merge with the "Indies" population, the Eurasian-Mestizos who made up the Dutch-Indies society as described by Jean Gelman Taylor (Taylor 1983). Blussé, unlike many of his predecessors, does not treat this as an aberration (although the title of his book on Batavia, *Strange Company*, seems to suggest agreement), rather he shows that it was a sensible expedient for solving several of the perennial problems of colonial finance and control.

The "Seventeen Gentlemen" did not aim to spend money in Asia, their intention was to make money, therefore they paid their servants very poorly and sent as few Dutchmen as possible to the Indies. Moreover, they expected the Batavian Council itself to find the costs of maintaining their Asian factories and settlements, all the while providing a steady supply of spices and other Asian produce for the company at rock bottom figures. At the same time, they continued to pay handsome dividends to their shareholders in Holland. Relying on the junk trade prevented the growth of a country trade by their own nationals and servants. The Dutch felt this was a strength of their organization because it was thought to preserve the integrity of the VOC's monopoly. Of course, it did nothing like that (Furber 1976, p. 227).

The excessive demands of metropolitan imperialists however, and the realities of human nature were quite incompatible. The Dutchmen in Batavia cheated the company because it was the only way they could survive. Without the private trade, the "deals" with Chinese merchants, and the marital liaisons with Mestizo families, the average Dutchman in Batavia could not make ends meet. Without such "corruption" Batavia could not have existed, let alone prosper. As it was, it was really quite successful, but the contradictions inherent in the imperial structure could not coexist indefinitely, thus the directors tried to correct the apparent economic irregularities. Aside from unsuccessfully attempting to limit the junk trade, the Seventeen attempted a few other strategies.

They tried to force the Chinese to lower the price of tea they brought to Batavia, but this backfired, and the Chinese emperor banned all Chinese shipping from Batavia in 1716. Luckily the ban was never enforced since the Emperor was on his deathbed at the time and his councillors thought better of it. The threat, however, was enough to convince the Dutch that the policy was unwise. Next, the directors ordered large amounts of tea from Batavia in order to swamp the European market and drive the EIC out of the business, but this failed when the Batavian economy slumped. In any case, Batavia lacked the capital to finance such a move. In 1724, the Seventeen ordered the Governor-General in Batavia to send ships directly to China, but he was reluctant to do this, probably because it would have undercut the private arrangements between Batavian and Chinese merchants. In 1727, the Seventeen finally decided to bypass Batavia altogether and follow the British example by sending ships directly from Holland to Canton.

Between 1728 and 1733, the Seventeen sent six expeditions directly to China for tea and porcelain in an attempt to follow the EIC practice of reserving to itself the direct link between Europe and China. These ventures met with only indifferent success. The Dutch directors discovered they could no more prevent the crews and merchants on these ships from "smuggling" than they could the Batavians. More importantly, the company was denied the profits the British company gained because they had to export silver from Europe to pay for their tea and porcelain purchases (Blussé 1988, pp. 132–3) The British had found a way of overcoming this problem by virtue of their position in India.

The problem of silver

This question of silver was at the very heart of Europe's economic relationship with Asia. C. Northcote Parkinson, prefaces his excellent discussion of the country trade with an eighteenth-century proverb: "He who would bring back the riches of the East must take the riches of the East with him" (Parkinson 1937, p. 317). As Greenberg has pointed out,

> it was the occidental who came out to seek the riches of Cathay, and not the other way. The dominant fact for nearly three hundred years of their commercial intercourse, from the 16th to the 19th century, was that the westerner desired the goods of the East and was able to offer little merchandise in return.
>
> (Greenberg 1951, p. 1)

The Chinese wanted silver for their merchandise, and they usually got it. Even the Chinese junk traders who came to Batavia were reluctant to accept payments in kind. Europeans thus sent enormous quantities of bullion and coin to Asia between the sixteenth and nineteenth centuries. Spanish shipments, via the annual galleons from Acapulco to Manila over three hundred years, totalled around 400 million guilders, and Dutch exports were even greater. For just over 200 years, the period between 1570 and 1780, they sent 590 million guilders to Asia.[4]

> The constant importation of Asian products into the European markets caused a permanent drain of gold and silver from Europe towards Asia. Only a small trickle of precious metals must have re-entered Europe ... The greater part of gold and silver remained in Asia never to return to Europe.
>
> (Schoffer 1977, pp. 230–2)

The idea that the precious metals "never" returned to Europe may be an exaggeration, because the flow was reversed in the nineteenth century. The situation Schoffer describes, however, seems to have been the general pattern of world trade since Roman times. It was a matter of constant concern for the mercantilist-minded Western governments throughout the seventeenth and eighteenth centuries. For a time, the Dutch were able to compensate by shipping Japanese silver to China, but this ended after 1680 when Japan ceased exporting precious metals. To some degree, the Dutch were able to pay for their Chinese purchases with tin, pepper and other Straits produce from Southeast Asia.[5] During the eighteenth century however, these increasingly came to be produced by Chinese immigrants and were often more readily available to free-lancing junk traders than to the VOC, or (worse yet for the Dutch) to English country traders.

Dutch relations with Palembang are a case in point. Although the Malay sultan had signed a treaty with the Dutch guaranteeing delivery of fixed amounts of tin at fixed (usually below market) prices, he invariably broke treaty provisions in which he promised not to deal with other merchants. The Chinese miners of Bangka, where the Palembang tin fields were located, regularly collaborated with the Sultan, his wife and members of his court to sell additional amounts of tin to other Chinese junk traders, to Bugis traders from Riau and to British country traders (Andaya, 1993). As the Southeast Asian economy expanded, there was little the Dutch could do to maintain their monopolies. On the other hand, protecting them was even more expensive than sitting idly by and watching them be violated.[6]

We might ask why the Sultan of Palembang was even willing to put up with Dutch pressures. There were two good reasons. The first was that the Dutch could hurt Palembang either by launching a military action or blockade of Palembang's port. The second was that although the Dutch paid below market rates for tin and pepper at Palembang, they paid in silver (Vos 1993, p. 25–6). Except in the case of Java and parts of the Moluccas, where the Dutch were able to demand forced deliveries of spices, coffee, sugar and other commodities, their trading position in Southeast Asia still depended upon their ability to pay in cash. A century later, the first American envoy to Asia, Samuel Shaw, observed that the inability to find silver was a great disadvantage for the Dutch:

> The Dutch, for the past three or four years, have laboured under great disadvantages, owing to their not sending from Europe a sufficiency of specie; their company having depended too far upon remittances to be made from India to Europe through the medium of their treasury. This has obliged their supercargoes to draw bills on the company, which being given to the Chinese merchants, are by them disposed of, at a discount of 20 or twenty-five percent. The business is called *transfer*, and has introduced a kind of stock-jobbing which cannot fail of being highly injurious to the interests of the company.

> (Shaw 1847, p. 299)

The massive inflow of silver into China during the seventeenth century seems to have been at least partially responsible for the extraordinary prosperity of China during the mid-Qing years. In particular, the century after 1680 saw a remarkable period of growth in China. Population nearly doubled and the Chinese demand for all imported commodities increased markedly. This increasing demand had two major repercussions in Southeast Asia. The first was the growth in the junk trade. Blussé describes the years between 1680 and 1740 as the heyday of the junk trade. The arrivals of junks at Batavia nearly doubled from 9.7 junks per year to 19.5 junks (Blussé 1988, pp. 122–3). The second result was the appearance of Chinese coolies, or laborers, in Southeast Asia to produce products marketable in China. The chronic Southeast Asian labor shortage led Chinese merchants and Southeast Asian rulers to adopt the expedient of importing Chinese labor to mine tin and gold and to plant sugar, pepper and gambier. (Trocki 1990, chs 1 and 2) Blussé has discussed the migration of Chinese sugar planters to Batavia, between 1680 and 1720 (Blussé 1981). In the early eighteenth century, the Sultans of Sambas and Pontianak in western Borneo welcomed Chinese gold miners to develop mines in the Kapuas River watershed. Not long after, Chinese tin miners began works in Bangka on behalf of the Sultan of Palembang. By the 1760s, Chinese miners and planters were boosting production of Southeast Asian commodities throughout the Malay world and in Siam.

It was unfortunate that some Dutch officials tended to see the activities of these Chinese as a threat rather than an opportunity. In fact, many of them understood the great resource which the Chinese traders and laborers represented. Barbara Andaya reports that the Dutch resident of Perak advised the Malay ruler to bring in Chinese to mine tin (Andaya 1979). In 1785, the Dutch governor of Melaka urged the Batavian council to throw open Melaka to the junk trade, but his plea came too late (Harrison 1953). In 1740, the Dutch at Batavia panicked and massacred most of the Chinese inhabitants of the town and killed many of the laborers who had once grown sugar. While the Chinese ultimately returned, the Dutch had lost any control they once might have had on Chinese activities in the Archipelago. The years between 1740 and 1780 mark an upsurge in the appearance of Chinese laborers' settlements in Southeast Asia, particularly in areas outside of Dutch control. It became even more difficult for the Dutch to restrict production of products such as tin and pepper. Indeed, it was probably a mistake to try to do so, since the import of these items reduced the Chinese demand for silver. Nevertheless, China continued to import silver until the early nineteenth century. The Dutch not only lost their most intimate contact with these burgeoning Chinese producers, but they did so at a time when, as a result of advances in India, British trade was once again expanding vigorously into Southeast Asia.

The Battle of Plassey, and all that . . .

The sequence of events that followed the Battle of Plassey in 1757 and ended with the grant of the *diwani* of Bengal (the ruler's right to collect taxes) to the EIC are seen as the foundation of the British Empire in India. By 1767, Robert Clive and his associates had placed the company in the position of governing one of the richest and most productive regions of the subcontinent. At the time, "Bengal"

Figure 3.2 Shah 'Alam (Mughal Emperor, 1759–1806) conveying the Grant of Diwani to Lord Clive, August, 1765. The Emperor is seated on his throne under a canopy. He is handing the grant to Lord Clive, on his left
Source: Oil painting by Benjamin West, *c.* 1818. By permission of the British Library, OIOC Prints, F29

included much of what is today West Bengal, Bangala Desh, Bihar, Varanasi (Benares) and Oudh. The immediate result of Clive's victory was that the various "councils" of company servants based in the towns of Bengal arrogated to themselves the rights to collect taxes on behalf of the company and virtually confiscated every other branch of commerce that seemed in the least bit profitable. Those Indian merchants that continued in business did so only by grace of the enormous bribes they paid to the company servants in these councils. Since this area included one of the major opium-producing regions of India, it was not long before the members of the Patna Council in Bihar and the Ghazipur Council in Benares had appropriated to themselves control of the most lucrative opportunities within their grasp.

Patna had long been a center of opium production, although N. Sinha argues that its cultivation was not encouraged under the Mughals. Ralph Fitch's remarks suggest, however, that it was an important product of the Bihar-Benares region in the Mughal era. With the decline of Mughal power in the early eighteenth century, a group of Indian merchants in Patna appears to have gained a monopoly on the purchase of the drug from the ryots. They quickly amassed fortunes by selling it to Europeans: particularly to the Dutch at Chinsura; but also to the French at Chandernagore and the English at Calcutta. Of these, the Dutch were the most important customers:

> From the beginning the Dutch took the lead in the opium export trade from Hughli, and though in the first half of the eighteenth century the British succeeded in establishing a predominance of them in the trade in cotton piece goods and in silk goods and raw silk, the Dutch succeeded in retaining their lead in this item. They exported opium to Ceylon, the Malacca straits and the Malay Archipelago . . . Before Plassey the French and the English together did not export even half the quantity of opium which the Dutch exported.
>
> (Sinha 1956, p. 56)

These Indian merchants enjoyed a monopoly of the opium trade in return for an annual payment or "peshcush" to the Mughal court. Although this legal monopoly probably died out between 1739 and 1757 during the "period of confusion," the merchants effectively kept their monopoly until the British arrived and appropriated it for themselves. And until 1773 when Warren Hastings took over the monopoly on behalf of the company, the Patna and Ghazipur councils controlled the opium trade of Bihar and Varanasi. In addition to enriching themselves, they immediately set about to ruin the Dutch, the French and their other rivals (Sinha 1956, p. 189). This was a blow to the Indian merchants and to the Indian economy in general. The Dutch had usually paid for their purchases of opium and saltpeter with silver.[7] The English, on the other hand, simply appropriated Indian goods and bullion using them to cover the costs of the China trade. Verelst, who was the EIC governor between 1767 and 1769, boasted that he had been able to cover the entire trade expenditure of the company for the year 1771 (a sum of £768,500) with the "revenue of the country," without importing a single ounce of silver from Britain (Woodruff 1953, p. 111).

This was the age of the nabobs, when down-at-the-heel members of the English gentry and aristocracy purchased places in the company and came out to India to make their fortunes by "shaking the pagoda tree." Karl Marx commented on the revelations of graft and corruption that were exposed during the impeachment trial of Warren Hastings. There were three charges against Hastings for giving contracts to his favorites which were described as "glaringly extravagant and wantonly profuse." One of these was the opium contract to Stephen Sullivan for four years in 1781. Other contracts were granted to Charles Crofts for bullocks and to Sir Charles Blunt for horses, etc.

> His favourites received contracts under conditions whereby they, cleverer than alchemists, made gold out of nothing. Great fortunes sprang up like mushrooms in a day; primitive accumulation went on without the advance of a shilling . . . Sullivan sold his contract for £40,000 to Binn, Binn sold it the same day for £60,000 and the ultimate purchaser also made enormous gain.
>
> (Marx, *Capital*, I, p. 777, quoted in Sinha 1956, p. 213)

Hastings, nevertheless, was responsible for taking the monopoly out of the hands of private individuals and giving at least some of the benefits to the Indian state. He instituted a contract system, the object of Marx's comment, in which a single individual would contract with the government to deliver a certain number of chests of opium. The contractor would then carry on his own affairs with subcontractors, local chiefs and village headmen to pay advances to the peasants to grow opium. This system lasted for the next twenty years.

By the late 1770s, critics of Warren Hastings and of the EIC had raised a storm of protest against the abuses of the opium system in India. Edmund Burke authored the Ninth Report in 1782 which reviewed the "evils" of the opium system. Owen summarized the findings noting that the real concern of the critics was Hastings' monopoly:

> There was evidence, for example, that cultivators had been the victims of oppression, and there had been rumors of trouble between the agents of the contractor and the subordinate revenue collectors, so that "the Plowman, flying from the Tax Gatherer is obliged to take refuge under the wings of the Monopolist." The subject could not be dismissed without a eulogy of free trade by the committee, whose ignorance of the opium industry was exceeded only by its penchant for applying doctrinaire economics indiscriminately. No ethical questions were raised in regard to the opium trade itself. On the contrary, the blows of the investigators were showered upon the restraint of commerce practised by the company.
>
> (Owen 1934, p. 34)

Hastings, on the other hand, anticipating his critics, had defended the opium monopoly in his argument before the Bengal Council in 1773.

> Ordinary commerce, "which always languishes under confinement," might prosper best without governmental restraint, but to increase the production of an article not necessary for life would be no advantage. And opium "is not a necessary of life, but a pernicious article of luxury, which ought not to be permitted but for purposes of foreign commerce only." The drug market was a highly limited one, and a profitable trade therefore depended upon a restricted output.
>
> (Owen 1934, p. 23)

Free trade, it was feared, would result in competition, violence, oppression, adulteration and worst of all, overproduction. Despite the monopolization of opium production in India, the EIC decided very early on to leave the shipment and sale of the drug in Asia to free traders.

Opium, the EIC and the country trade

Well before the eighteenth century the English had already begun to realize that the "country trade" could be a substitute for silver. Whether royal agents, companies, company servants, or private traders, Europeans found that the local trade of Asia offered an opportunity to turn over their capital. The trade of the Persian Gulf, the Red Sea, both coasts of India and that from India to Southeast Asia and China were all fair game. In addition to generating profits, it helped offset the other costs of doing business in Asia. Among the primary commodities involved in the country trade "to the Eastward," that is, to Southeast Asia and China, were Indian cloth and opium. And, until quite late in the eighteenth century, Indian cotton and cotton cloth were the favored products. Virtually every part of Southeast Asia was a potential market for Indian cloth, provided one knew which type of cloth was habitually purchased by whom. Opium, too was always a reliable commodity, particularly after the efforts of the Dutch to promote the trade, but it does not seem to have been of overwhelming importance until the late eighteenth century. The English, following their takeover of Bengal, pushed opium to the forefront as the primary exchange commodity in Asia.

The "country traders" were the independent English, and more often Scottish, merchants who had established private firms in India. Parkinson maintains that there was actually very little about these firms that was English other than their names, and the presence of one or two well-mannered white faces in the front office.

> As far as one can judge, the British business men brought to their affairs neither capital, energy nor ability. They were certainly not in a position to teach the natives anything about business methods. They could introduce nothing novel in the way of banking, but they were white men and therefore able to inspire confidence in other white men . . . With this advantage they were able at least partially to elbow the natives out of . . . ship owning and insurance.
>
> (Parkinson 1937, p. 320)

While this may have been the case in the early part of the eighteenth century, by the beginning of the nineteenth century, these trading houses, or agency traders as they came to be called, were an important element of European commerce in Asia. By the time of the Opium War in 1839, they had become the keystone of European economic involvement in Asia.

In the early eighteenth century, however, the country traders were little more than the vehicle through which, according to Parkinson, the servants of the East India Company, both military and civil, managed their personal fortunes. Although they remained in India with permission of the EIC, they were often seen to operate just beyond the bounds of what was formally acceptable. They went into partnerships with Indian, Muslim and Parsi merchants and formed companies with the Portuguese. They did business with the Dutch; they smuggled, and when they set off on their voyages through the South China Sea, it was best not to ask where they went or what they did. Rather than losing status, however, they gave legitimacy to the native merchants with whom they were affiliated. They came to perform an important function for the EIC. They were able to deal in goods that were inconvenient for the company or else illegal. Their most important function, so far as the trade with China was concerned, was the opium trade.

The EIC's main commercial interest was in carrying valuable Asian cargoes to Europe. During the eighteenth and early nineteenth centuries, their main interest was the tea trade between Canton and Britain. In return they carried European merchandise, primarily English woollens and some iron and steel, to Asia. On the face of it, the EIC ran a trade imbalance, and contributed to the silver drain from Europe to Asia, just as the VOC. Owen remarks that during the period 1600 to 1750, "vast quantities of bullion were sent to the Far East" by the EIC to purchase tea and silk. In the period 1792–1809 the company shipped £16,602,338 worth of goods to China[8] and imported goods worth, £27,157,006 from China. Thus, there was a balance of over £10 million against the company. During these same years the company shipped about £2,500,000 of specie to Asia, which still left them £8 million short. This trade was never self-supporting and regularly ran at a loss of at least 5 percent a year. Pritchard remarks that European cargos were often sold for less than their purchase price: "This was part of a settled policy of dumping them into the market in order to provide funds for the homeward investments, and in order to drive out Dutch and other European competition" (Pritchard 1936, p. 157). The balance was made up from the country trade of India, and as time passed, mostly by opium.

These private trading companies owned ships that sailed between the major British factories in India and other parts of Asia. For the opium trade, the most important were the runs between Bombay and Canton and between Calcutta and Canton. In the early years of the eighteenth century, the ships carried fairly mixed cargoes of Indian goods, including cotton textiles, raw cotton, raw silk, saltpetre and opium. They also, as it turns out, did a fairly extensive trade in armaments. Lockyer reports that two to three country ships visited Dutch Melaka with calicos, silk and opium in 1704. Even though opium was then illegal, the private trade with local Chinese and Dutch merchants flourished. The Dutch traders were considered very reliable even though they usually paid 2 or 3 percent less than other traders. At that time, the price of opium at Melaka was 312.00 rixdollars per chest (Lockyer 1711, p. 66). Another important destination for the country traders at this time was Aceh, which imported opium as well as saltpetre, rice, ghee, cotton and silk from Bengal, as well as tobacco, onions, calico, muslins, brown and blue longcloths, sallampores, chintz and gunpowder (Lockyer 1711, p. 34). The cargoes of these vessels were quite valuable, each vessel often carrying several hundred chests of opium, each valued at anywhere from $300 to $1000 depending on the season and the place.

Their aim was to turn over a significant portion of the cargo on their way through Southeast Asia, exchanging textiles, opium, guns and ammunition for pepper, tin, spices, silver and other Straits produce which were in demand in China. By the first decade of the nineteenth century, opium had become the most important item in these cargoes and most of it went straight to China. Pritchard notes that opium accounted for 50 percent of their imports to China while cotton made up 14 percent. The next three items in order of importance were tin (7 percent), pepper (4 percent), and camphor (3½ percent). All of the latter came from Southeast Asia (Pritchard 1936, pp. 174–5).

Initially the ships were large, teak vessels constructed in Bombay, Surat or Calcutta, of between 700 and 1200 tons. As time passed, they grew smaller, sleeker and more specialized. Parkinson claims they were the finest ships in the world in their time, built by the best Parsi craftsmen of the best materials in the world. The only true European contribution to them, aside from their overall appearance, were the fittings. Since they had to pick their way through Southeast Asia, and often had to fight off pirates or unfriendly trading partners, they were well-armed, carrying anywhere from 10 to 30 guns.

> A fleet grew up, of English ships, built by Parsees out of local, or at least Indian, materials; officered by English seamen; manned by lascars; and owned either by English or Parsee firms.
>
> (Parkinson 1937, p. 331)

They usually only had four or five Europeans on board, and a native crew of about 70 to 130 lascars. Everything, according to Parkinson, "depended on the courage, energy, honesty and intelligence of the captain" (Parkinson 1937, p. 334–5).

> In such a world the trader was at once bold and guarded, jealous of his rivals and tenacious of his secrets. He was eternally watching for symptoms of treachery, both in his crew and among his customers. He was always ready to shoot, so as to be on the safe side. Sometimes he made a fortune and sometimes he was killed.
>
> (Parkinson 1937, p. 348)

A return voyage from Bombay would take at least two years in the late eighteenth century because these ships, although capable of sailing upwind, were generally sailed with the monsoons. Thus, they would leave Bombay around February and catch the last of the northeast monsoon down the Malabar Coast to Dondra Head. By May, they could pick up the southwest monsoon to take them across the Bay of Bengal to Aceh, down through the Straits of Melaka and on to Canton arriving sometime in August or September. After winding up the trading season in Canton, the Bombay ship could catch the first of the northeast monsoon, in November or December, to get back across the China Sea, and the Bay of Bengal. Then, the southwest monsoon in May would take it back up the Malabar coast to Bombay, a voyage of nearly two years if everything went according to plan (Parkinson 1937, pp. 342–3). While these ships probably always carried some opium, it was not the mainstay of their trade until the 1780s. By the 1830s, the opium trade had become so important that the old country ships were no longer sufficient and they were superseded by the opium clippers and their voyages are quite another story.

The opium ships from Calcutta really pioneered the trade to China. These were, as Parkinson notes, voyages of high risk and high profit, and were often viewed as "mere buccaneering." Their trade in Southeast Asia was mostly in contravention of Dutch treaties and monopolies. Nevertheless, they usually stopped at both Melaka and Batavia on their way to China with full knowledge of the VOC. In addition, they traded at numerous places throughout Southeast Asia, including: Aceh, Kedah, Riau, Brunei, Trengganu, Patani, Pontianak, Banjarmasin, Sulawesi, Maluku, and Sulu. At the time, most of this region was still unsurveyed and unknown to most European mariners. Their trade in opium was not only illegal so far as the Dutch were concerned, but was also contraband in China, Burma, Siam and Vietnam. While many of the Malay rajahs were customers for opium, others had already decided, either from economic or moral considerations, to ban it. Nevertheless, there was always a market for it. In China, the bans were not rigorously enforced and it was usually possible to bribe local officials. In the early years of the trade, however, that was done by Chinese dealers. The British found they could carry on the trade in the Portuguese colony of Macau, in fact, a number of the firms that managed the trade were Portuguese.

The traders served a dual function for the EIC in the years after 1780, when Warren Hastings took over the monopoly of drug production in northeastern India. First of all, they bought the drug from the company, which sold it at auctions in Calcutta. The company was thus able to dissociate itself from the drug and disclaim all responsibility for the manner and places in which it was marketed. The revenue from these sales soon came to provide an important source of support for the Indian state and ultimately constituted nearly 20 percent of the annual revenue of the Indian government. Secondly, traders made these funds available where the company needed them most, in Canton.

By the 1780s, these traders increasingly ended up with a surplus of cash at the Canton end of their journey. For instance, British trade from India to China in 1792 showed a balance in favor of India. Country ships delivered a total of £943,000 worth of goods, both legal and illegal. The illegal trade included 2500 chests of opium valued at £250,000 (the price was then $400 per chest, or about £100). The bulk of the legal trade was made up of cottons which totalled about £571,464 by both country and company ships. The country traders only exported about £322,877 worth of goods in that year, thus leaving a balance in favor of India of £620,971. Lord McCartney, who led the failed mission to establish diplomatic relations with the Chinese state in that year, believed that the balance was likely to tip even further:

> for the cotton of Bombay and the opium of Bengal are now become in great measure necessaries in China, the latter having grown into general demand

through all the southern provinces, and the former being preferable to silk for common use, as a cheaper and pleasanter wear.

(Cranmer-Byng 1963, p. 260–1)

Since they did not want to carry the silver back to India with them, and since the company in Canton was always in need of hard cash to cover the tea investment, the company became a banker. Traders paid their silver into the EIC treasury in Canton and took bills of exchange. The company used the silver to buy tea and the traders received a piece of negotiable paper. By the early nineteenth century, it was possible to buy these bills, redeemable not only in Calcutta or Bombay, but also in London. And, when the Americans and the small "dummy" east India companies (such as the Ostend Company and the Imperial Company, and to some extent the Danish Company) began to do business in Canton, it was possible to buy bills negotiable almost anywhere in the West.

The coalescence of these functions of banking, shipping and insurance around the opium trade was one of the most remarkable features of the era. Not only did they service the opium traffic, but they became the foundation of a commercial infrastructure that ultimately supported a wide range of trade. In fact, the entire commercial infrastructure of European trade in Asia was built around opium. However, while opium was being used to build capitalism and empire, it was also eroding the traditional political and economic order in Asia.

The impact of opium in Southeast Asia

As Crawfurd suggests, most of the opium sold in Southeast Asia was used by members of the elite, or the rajahs. Writing in the 1830s, George Windsor Earl claimed that opium had debauched the entire elite of the Malay state of Sambas in western Borneo. The Sultan as well as most of the other rajahs and *pangerans* were opium smokers. "Here, as at every Malay town that I had hitherto visited, the nobles were both mentally and physically inferior to the lower classes, a circumstance chiefly owing to the dissolute mode of life pursued by the former" (Earl 1837, p. 224). Although Earl indicates that the lower class Malays did not smoke opium, it may have been different in the case of Bengkalis mentioned by Hamilton. Reports from the nineteenth century indicate that miners and pepper planters tended to be opium users. Although the Bengkalis miners, who were most likely Minangkabaus, were commoners, as miners they certainly would have had an income that gave them purchasing power. This pattern of opium consumption among individuals engaged in commodity production, proved to be common in this era. Chinese coolies, who would have found opium smoking prohibitively expensive in China, very rapidly adopted the habit once they came to Southeast Asia and found employment as miners or planters. On the other hand, those engaged in subsistence activity, particularly rice farmers, rarely saw more than a few coppers' cash a year, and thus were unable to afford the habit. In any case, there was a similar propensity here as in Europe for individuals on a cash income to become drug consumers.

Tobacco, sugar, and tea were the first objects within capitalism that conveyed with their use the complex idea that one could become different by consuming differently. This idea has little to do with nutrition or primates or sweet tooths, and less than it appears to have with symbols. But it is closely connected to England's fundamental transformation from a hierarchical, status-based, medieval society to a social-democratic, capitalist, and industrial society. The substances transformed by British capitalism from upper-class luxuries to working-class necessities are of a certain type. Like alcohol or tobacco, they provide respite from reality, and deaden hunger pangs. Like coffee, or chocolate or tea, they provide stimulus to greater effort without providing nutrition. Like sugar they provide calories, while increasing the attractiveness of these other substances when combined with them. There was no conspiracy at work to wreck the nutrition of the British working class, to turn them into addicts, or to ruin their teeth. But the ever-rising consumption of sugar was an artefact of intraclass struggles for profit – struggles that eventuated in a world-market solution for drug foods, as industrial capitalism cut its protectionist losses and expanded a mass market to satisfy proletarian consumers once regarded as sinful or indolent.

(Mintz 1985, p. 186)

We see very much the same processes at work in Asia that were noted in Europe. On the one hand, opium was rearranging class lines in Southeast Asia and ultimately in China, by the proletarianization of significant populations, while at the same time, creating political-economic structures that were inimical to the traditional "gift economy" of Southeast Asia, and the agrarian economy of China. Charles Lockyer, who visited Asia in the early eighteenth century reported on the popularity of opium among the Malays and Acehnese:

The Mallayans are such Admirers of Ophium that they would mortgage all they hold most valuable to procure it. They that use it to excess are seldom long-lived, which they themselves are very sensible of, yet they are no longer satisfied than their Cares are diverted by the pleasing Effects of it. I have been told by an *Englishman*, who accustomed himself to it at *Bencoolen*, it is a difficult Matter to leave it, after once experiencing the exquisite Harmony, wherewith it affects every part of the Body. On a larger Quantity than ordinary, he found such a tickling in his Blood, such a languishing delight in everything he did, that it justly might be termed a Pleasure too great for human Nature to support.

(Lockyer 1711 pp. 60–1)

Opium prepared the ground for capitalism by creating mass markets and proletarian consumers while undermining the morale and morality of political elites throughout Asia. The picture that Earl paints of Sambas was, as he indicates, typical. The opium-soaked Malay rajah was a stock figure of nineteenth-century Southeast Asia. There was at least one such individual in every one of Conrad's

Southeast Asian stories. On the other hand, as I have suggested in *Prince of Pirates*, the Malay rulers who survived and prospered were the ones who profited from its sale to their subjects, or perhaps even more preferable, profited from its sale to Chinese settlers in their domains. For the nineteenth-century rulers of Johor, Perak, Selangor and other places, this was the key to success (Trocki 1979).

There were those Southeast Asian rulers who took a different view of opium, even as early as the eighteenth century. Vlekke reports some Javanese chiefs, such as the ruler of Bantam, were successful in petitioning the Dutch to end sales, and in stopping its usage in their domains. "You know how much money is spent in these parts on opium," a Dutch official wrote in 1756, "now sales begin to diminish, mostly because the princes object to it and the common people follow their chiefs" (quoted in Vlekke 1946, pp. 122). Opium shipments to Ambon were stopped at the request of the local chiefs. Nevertheless, the Dutch were importing £100,000 of opium to Java in the mid-eighteenth century. There were, moreover, other areas where the Dutch not only continued to sell the drug, but they actually used the drug as cash, paying their regents with opium. It is questionable, however, that even where the drug was prohibited, the ban was maintained for any length of time. In 1708, the Sultan of Palembang banned the import of all but three chests of the drug per year into his domains, (Hamilton 1727, p. 64) but imports appear to have been resumed under Sultan Mahmud Badaruddin after 1724.

However, after 1760, Dutch attempts to reduce opium sales were probably an indication of their own decline as well as of the serious challenges they were now facing from the British country traders. With the sources of the opium supply now firmly under the control of British agents, the Dutch found it increasingly difficult to procure their supplies. The British had taken over the very regions from which the Dutch had habitually drawn their supply. Even though the EIC eventually agreed to provide the Dutch company with an annual provision of 400 chests, it was offered at a much higher price than before and the quantity was far less than what they had formerly obtained. Previously, the Dutch, while never able to buy directly from the producers, were able to purchase opium from local sources at a discount. The Dutch were now forced to purchase opium from the EIC at the average rate fixed by the periodic auctions in Calcutta. Thus, the EIC took a clear profit of at least 100 percent, and probably more, on the opium the Dutch received.

The second problem for the Dutch was the country traders. On the one hand, it was possible for the Dutch to supplement their supplies by making purchases from the country traders, who were quite happy, in fact eager, to stop in Melaka and Batavia to trade some of their opium for pepper, tin and other Straits produce. On the other hand, while they were legally in Dutch waters, they could just as easily engage in some smuggling. Local Chinese merchants, Dutch freeburgers and even VOC company servants were quite willing to oblige them. In fact, not only in Java and Sumatra, but throughout the archipelago, country traders found ready markets for their opium. The period between 1760 and 1785 saw the crystalization of a group of new trading patterns as well as new economic forces in Southeast Asia, and the opium trade was a major element in their emergence.

Together with the country traders, the Chinese junk traders, now less tied to the Batavia trade, ranged at will throughout Southeast Asia. Between 1770 and 1800, the Chinese-Mestizo rulers of Siam, Phaya Taksin and the new Chakri dynasty, established firm links with the junk traders, who now came to dominate the entire trade of the country. (Cushman 1993a; Viraphol 1977). Much of the trade of the Vietnamese states, before, during and after the Tayson uprising, were dominated by Chinese, many of them the same traders who had established themselves in Bangkok. Indeed, the entire Gulf of Thailand and the Gulf of Tongkin now enjoyed a major upsurge in commerce as a result of these Chinese traders. The same was true in the island world where the growing "coolie" settlements of pepper, gambier and sugar planters and gold and tin miners, increased the need for stable and regular commercial links with China. This traffic seems to have owed little to the expanding country trade, but the two virtually simultaneous movements reinforced one another. It was during these years that the Anglo-Chinese "partnership" that came to typify the economies of nineteenth-century Singapore and Hong Kong was created. The country traders, with their cargoes of opium, weapons, Indian cloth and silver were ideal trading partners for the locally established Chinese merchants who serviced the settlements of Chinese laborers. During these years, opium became the preferred "work drug" of the coolies who now began to move in increasing numbers into the Southeast Asian rainforests.

A third set of actors were the indigenous peoples of the archipelago who now began to seek political and economic advantage from the new opportunities presented to them. Malays, Buginese and Tausugs all responded in their own way to the availability of the guns and drugs now offered by the British, and to the expanded trade with China offered by the junk traders (Warren, 1981). In *Prince of Pirates*, (Trocki 1979), I have drawn attention to the interplay of economic and political relations between the Chinese and British traders and the resurgent Malay–Bugis polity of Riau-Johor in the second half of the eighteenth century.

By the 1780s, the Dutch had come to see the port at Tanjong Pinang in Riau, as a major threat to their political and economic position in the Malay world. This fear led them to dispatch a punitive naval expedition from Holland to destroy Riau. Riau had leaped to prosperity on the basis of the expanded junk trade from Southern China, the settlement of Chinese pepper and gambier planters, and the growth of trade in the archipelago. The locally settled Chinese merchants also carried on a thriving trade with "smugglers" who carried Bangka's tin to Riau – often on behalf of Sultan Badaruddin and his successors. Likewise, the Chinese "kongsi" settlements in the interior of western Borneo, which had opened gold mines at Montrado and other sites on the Kapuas River were other markets which received British opium via Riau.

James Warren's studies of the "pirate" state of the Tausugs in Sulu during the late eighteenth and early nineteenth centuries also call attention to the connection between the country traders and these expansionist sea-rovers (Warren 1981;

Warren 1990). The combination of drugs and guns from the British was a volatile infusion into the political life of the islands. We see here, on a much smaller scale, a pattern similar to larger ones in Africa and the Atlantic. There, Yankee traders with rum and rifles, provided encouragement for the "Barracoon" states of West Africa to provide them with slaves, who were then traded for sugar and tobacco, and thus became the means for reproducing the supply of sugar and tobacco. Drugs and slavery went together. The Sulu raiders, the Illanun pirates who terrorized the Philippines and the coasts of Borneo in these years, likewise procured slaves as a labor force to service the Chinese demand for sea-slugs, mother of pearl, jungle produce and other trade goods.

By the end of the eighteenth century, nearly a third of Bengal's opium production was going to Southeast Asia. Some part of that may have been going on to China via the junk trade, but it is impossible to say exactly how much, since there are only anecdotal sources on this aspect of the trade. Certainly a portion of it was going to Chinese settled in Southeast Asia, whether to coolies or merchants. Other parts of the region were also seeing an expansion of their economies. Everywhere Chinese settlers provided consumer markets for opium and products for export. The Southeast Asian trade configuration was opium for tin, pepper and gold; opium for pearls, mother of pearl and sea-slugs; opium for silver.

If some Malay states benefited, others suffered. If their chiefs and aristocrats did not become opium addicts, then there were other uncertainties. They could lose the economic advantage to other more adventuresome states. The Sultanate of Sulu grew at the cost of Mindanao and Brunei. In the western part of the archipelago, the Malay polities of Riau and Palembang flourished while those of Jambi and Siak declined. Above it all, the British gained immense advantages in the Southeast Asian trade while the Dutch languished. It was clear that opium was not merely a threat to the "morality" of individuals in Asia; a drug trade on this scale was a threat to the entire political economy of the region.

Other rulers in Southeast Asia, where they were able to exert their authority, banned the drug. By the beginning of the nineteenth century the mainland Southeast Asian states had all banned opium imports and use. One of the arguments advanced against the trade as early as 1808 by the Grand Jury of Penang, was that it had been banned in Burma, Siam and Vietnam, as well as in China. Each of the three mainland states had, by this time, been through a period of upheaval, revolution, and invasion and had emerged under strong, self-confident and somewhat traditional rulers. Each saw the elimination of opium as commensurate with the expulsion of foreigners, especially Europeans. For a while, these states seem to have managed to resist the pressures of British commercial and military force, but in the end, either through outright invasion, diplomatic pressure, or the corruption of their own subjects and officers, all were forced to accept the European presence and with them, opium.

For Asian rulers at the end of the eighteenth century, there were two choices. They could accept the westerners, and allow them "free trade," which meant trade in opium and all of the consequent economic and social disadvantages that came with it. If they were lucky they could survive and if they were able to secure for themselves a piece of the trade, they could even prosper. This was the course taken by the kings of Siam and the rulers of Johor in the nineteenth century. Alternatively, they could resist, they could close their doors to the trade and attempt to keep foreigners out of their countries. In the end, all those who tried this course failed. The rulers of Burma, Vietnam and China, all fell to foreign pressure. Opium was not the major cause of their downfalls, although we may make a good argument for the case of China, but the attempts to exclude foreign trade, and the trade in opium, led them to restrict all foreign entry, and that policy left them unprepared to meet the greater threats of western imperialism.

4 In compassion to mankind

Opium the "keystone" of empire in Asia

The years between 1780 and 1842 were formative years for the opium trade. They were also the formative years of the British Empire. The opium agriculture in India changed from an informally cultivated cash crop to a centralized, systematized state-run industry. Before the Battle of Plassey, opium had probably served to provide a small buffer of cash for the peasant or was carried on at the demand of the landlord. Already by 1780, cultivation in Bihar and Benares was regulated and controlled. It was produced under a government monopoly, and it remained as such into the early twentieth century. Opium made the same transition earlier accomplished by sugar and tobacco, from an exotic chemical to a fully "capitalist" drug commodity. At the downstream end, opium trading became, not only the major concern of the empire's businessmen, but also the most closely managed and well-financed enterprise in the European-run parts of Asia. It had, moreover, begun to lay the foundation for a truly mass market of consumers.

Seen from an ecological point of view, opium functioned as the "keystone" factor (Mills 1993) of the British, and all European, Empire in Asia. The concept of a "keystone species" as it is used in ecological studies, seems to apply most appropriately to opium. That is, it was the one element in a larger system upon which the entire complex of relationships came to depend. If we look at the trading world of Asia as a system of interdependent relationships, the role of opium emerges as a pivotal agent of change. For most of the nineteenth century, the drug was the major export from India to China, pushing aside Indian textiles as the most valuable of India's products. At the same time, the drug revenue was the second most important source of income for the Indian government. For 50 to 60 years, it was China's major import from the outside. It was the major concern of Europeans and other Asian merchants gathered in Macao and Canton during the first half of the nineteenth century. Profits from opium not only offset the cost of the East India Company's tea investment, but by the beginning of the nineteenth century, they began to reverse the centuries-old flow of silver into the Middle Kingdom. It was the realization by Chinese authorities that for the first time they were exporting silver bullion, that galvanized their opposition to the trade and led to the Opium War. In addition, the new flow of cash out of China went into the hands of British and American merchants who used the money to bankroll their own transition to modern industrial and corporate capitalism.

The problem of Europe's sudden spurt forward in the nineteenth century is one that has recently attracted considerable attention. David Landes has suggested that the roots of this advance into "modernism," including capitalism, industrialism and global empire, can be traced to deep-seated cultural traits which appeared in western Europe. He has been answered, in some respects by Asian specialists, or others who see themselves as global historians, such as R. Binn Wong and Andre Gunder Frank, both of whom have maintained that Europe had nothing by way of cultural or economic or technological advantage over China, or some other Asian powers, prior to about 1750, or perhaps even 1800 (Frank, 1998; Landes, 1998; Wong, 1997). While the complex arguments raised regarding the relative merits of east versus west are too large to dismantle here, none of these writers has looked closely at the role that drugs have played in this process. It seems that despite the advantages Europeans gained in discovering the New World and in developing a global trading system, that nothing much changed until global productive forces were significantly rearranged, and that did not take place until Europeans began to develop the global drug trade that gave them the clear edge. Even then, with their dominance over sugar, alcohol, tobacco, coffee and tea, it was still not enough to crack Asian resistance. Asia had to be brought down by something else, and that was opium.

Beginning in about 1760 or 1770, opium began to affect every aspect of the European presence in Asia and to actually transform the environment. Alone, it was not the most extraordinary or seemingly significant element of the empire. It did not occupy all or even most of the time and effort of most colonial officials. Perhaps what is extraordinary about it is the way in which it faded into the background and became unnoticeable precisely because it was ubiquitous. It seems to have been the object of few, if any of the many wars that Britain fought in India or in Southeast Asia. In comparison to the whole economy of India or of China, it was only a small item. But, like the yeast in bread dough, like the kangaroo mouse in the desert, and the fungi around the roots of forest plants, it was that upon which the entire structure depended. Though difficult to prove beyond question, it seems likely that without opium, there would have been no empire. Opium, both in the case of capitalist development as well as in the case of colonial finance, served to tighten up those key areas of "slack" in European systems and facilitated the global connections that in effect, were the empire.

While it is impossible to rerun history and try to determine the fate of European efforts in Asia without opium, we can still look at the role of opium in the various structures of empire and form some idea of its significance. So far as China is concerned, it would have been far more difficult for Europeans to penetrate as far as they did without opium. If as Parkinson suggested, Westerners had little to teach Indians and Parsees about business, it goes without saying that they had even less to teach the Chinese. Access to opium was, for much of the nineteenth century, the sole commercial advantage which European merchants had over the Chinese, both in Southeast Asia and in China itself.

Perhaps the British, Americans and other Europeans would have gone on buying tea, silk and ceramics while trying to pay for them out of the country trade or with their own bullion, but it does not seem likely. Tea was shipped halfway around the world because the EIC and other large interest groups in Britain found it profitable. If there was no profit in it, something else would have been found. Britons probably could have been convinced to renew their appreciation for coffee. After all, the taste for tea had been drummed up by the EIC when it was forced to stop importing Indian cloth at the urging of domestic manufacturers (Furber 1976). The real problem with tea, according to Henry Hobhouse, was the fact that it was so easily smuggled. This was partly how difficulties began with the Americans and, throughout the eighteenth and early nineteenth century, virtually every town on the west and south coast of England was a haven for tea smugglers.

The other alternative, and perhaps the more likely one, was that the cultivation of tea in India might have been developed earlier. The fact was, however, that the tea trade caused a trade deficit with China and it was only met by the opium trade. Command of Southeast Asian products was another element of growing European influence in China. Here again, it would have been far more difficult for the British to extend their control over Southeast Asia and its commodity exports without opium. All the levers of power that Europeans exercised in Asia began to turn on the fulcrum of opium.

These, of course, are economic considerations. The building of the empire was also driven by strategic concerns, such as the global competition with Holland, with France and later with Russia. There were cultural differences with China and conflicts over newly contrived points of international law. Many of these conflicts, however, actually had their roots in trading situations and the securing or breaking of monopolies and the security of the trade routes. In Asia, there was a general tendency for the flag to follow trade. Factories and settlements were established to facilitate trade, and the trade turned more and more on opium. As time passed, these territorial installations grew larger, developing a strategic rationale of their own and demanded defence, access and administration. Even though they developed their own dynamic, opium was still at the heart of things.

As the nineteenth century opened, Britain was locked in a global struggle with France. Among the major military events in the Asian theater was the occupation of Java between 1811 and 1816, during which Thomas Stamford Raffles administered the island as Lieutenant-Governor. Within two or three years, Raffles, and his superiors, the directors of the East India Company (for in war there was hardly a distinction between the national forces of Britain and the EIC), found the administration of a large and populated territory a considerable drain on their finances. This and strategic questions relating to the European balance of power led to the return of the island to the Dutch in 1816, much to Raffles' dismay. The would-be empire-builder had to rethink the possibilities. His ultimate conclusion was that British interests in Southeast Asia could best be served by a mere trading port at the mouth of the Melaka Straits. Here all the merchants of the islands could enjoy the benefits of free trade; and most importantly British traders on their way to China (with opium) could find security for the Southeast Asian leg of their journey. The opium trade provided a great part of the rationale for the establishment of Singapore (Trocki 1990, ch. 3).

At the beginning of the nineteenth century, the free ports, such as the Straits Settlements, were Britain's answer to the expenses of colonial administration. It was already too late to stop the cycle of territorial expansion, administrative expense, and ultimate financial catastrophe, which had begun in India and would culminate in the collapse of the EIC before mid-century. It may not have lasted as long as it did, were it not for the supplementary income from opium. In Southeast Asia, opium paid for free trade, and as we shall see here, it really financed all of the colonial empires in Southeast Asia.

Another aspect of the years after 1815, was the global silver situation. Lin Man-huong has argued convincingly that the period between 1820 and 1850 was one that saw a shortage of silver throughout the world. This was caused mainly by the collapse of the Spanish Empire in Latin America and the faltering production of the mines of Mexico and South America. It was several decades before American production reached pre-Napoleonic War levels. In the meantime, Britain alone found itself in control of a commodity that could be passed off as easily as cash: opium (Lin 1989, p. 267 and 1991, pp. 4–6). Thus, at a time when silver was scarce the British possessed a double advantage. Not only could they use opium as a medium of exchange for tea, they could also trade it for all other commodities as well, including silver. The years after 1820 saw opium production and exports skyrocket, and they continued to increase until 1880.

Cultivation and production in British India

In India, the economic impact of British rule was far-reaching and decisive. K.N. Chauduri's claims that between 1770 and 1840, there was a "conscious attempt on the part of Britain to exploit her overseas dependencies for economic purposes" (Chauduri 1971, p. 2). This was accomplished partly through foreign trade and partly by restructuring the roles of the peasantry, the merchants and the craftspeople. Government transmuted the traditional land revenue into cash payments and thus peasants found themselves required to produce commercial crops for export rather than food crops. Traditional craft producers in India were denied access to their former markets as metropolitan manufacturing interests first blocked the import of Indian textiles and then pressured the EIC to aid in the dumping of British textiles to Asian markets. In Bengal, company servants aggressively pushed Indian merchants, bankers and brokers to the wall as they appropriated tax-free privileges. Merchant dynasties, such as the Seths, and the other *dadni* merchants, who had once acted as middlemen between the local economy and foreign traders now found themselves cut off from their former sources of wealth. It was only in western India, where British political control did not yet exist, that native merchants were able to take advantage of the economic opportunities of the capitalist transformation.

Capitalism cannot develop in a society so long as peasants do nothing more than simply squat on land, growing enough food to feed themselves, and the ruling class does no more than occasionally squeeze a surplus out of them. Peasants have a persistent tendency to put personal survival ahead of grander designs such as economic development. Peasants also understand that any true surplus that they might produce will usually be confiscated by other agents, thus there is little incentive to accumulate assets that will only attract the greed of those in power. These attitudes are a great hindrance to capitalist accumulation. Peasants do not voluntarily abandon a subsistence mode of life without some form of coercion, at least that has been the historical rule. In the past few centuries, the great motor for transforming peasant agriculturalists into producers for, and consumers from, the market, has been brute force and arbitrary confiscation. Peasants have been kidnapped into slavery or driven by starvation, tax-collectors, landlords and money-lenders into some form of production that would enhance the process of accumulation. In most cases, the power of the state has been brought to bear against the peasant in order to effect the transition. If it has not actually required them to undertake this or that form of production, then it has punished them for refusing to do so. We see all of these factors at work in the organization of the opium cultivation in India. The longer one looks at imperialism and capitalism, the more they resemble the phenomenon which William H. McNeill has characterized as "macroparasitism" (McNeill 1980).[1]

In the years between 1773 and 1793, the East India Company, in its quest for a rationalized monopoly over the opium trade tried a number of alternatives. Some failed, some did not and, as time passed, a "workable" opium system was devised that served both imperial and capitalist interests. Initially, the EIC had experimented with a "contract" system. This was instituted in 1773 when Warren Hastings, then Governor-General, declared the company's monopoly over production of the drug and took it out of private hands. The company contracted with a private individual to deliver so many chests of opium at an agreed upon price. It was Hastings' opium contract to his friend, Stephen Sullivan, that provoked Marx's comment about alchemists. After Hastings, the contracts were let at auctions. There were, however, a number of difficulties from the company's point of view, and neither the contractors nor the peasants found the system satisfactory. Narayan Singh's dissertation on the opium and saltpetre industries highlights these problems (Singh 1980). The Company demanded the opium at a low price, while it required the contractor to pay the cultivator a relatively high price.[2] There was little room for the contractor's profit, if he played by the rules. If he attempted to squeeze his agents and subcontractors, then they simply passed the cost down to the ryots, who responded by adulterating the drug they delivered. The company was displeased when it was found that the opium contained sugar, earth, poppy rubbish and, worst of all, flour mixed in with the opium.[3]

As a part of his "permanent settlement," Lord Cornwallis took the opium monopoly under the direct management of a government agency in 1797. Cultivation was restricted to specific areas within the states of Bihar and Benares. The opium agents of the government then undertook, through a network of go-betweens called *gomastahs*, *matoes* and *sudder matoes*, to make advances to peasants

Figure 4.1 Warren Hastings, first Governor-General of India, 1773–1785
Source: Painting by George Romney, *c.* 1800. By permission of the British Library, OIOC Print, F1, FCO

who had contracted to cultivate opium. Much of this part of the system had already been in place, perhaps as early as the 1760s, but now it was formalized and regulated much more closely. Ultimately, the advances were given in four installments: the first when the fields were measured and the size of the crop estimated; the second after the crop was sown; the third just before harvest; and the fourth upon delivery of the raw opium (Singh 1980, pp. 50–60). Another aspect of Cornwallis' policy was to restrict the output of British Indian opium to less than 5,000 chests annually, instituting strict measures of quality control and guaranteeing the company a substantial and reliable profit. The figures in Table 4.1 show that the average prices at the Calcutta auctions steadily increased between 1797 and 1821.

Figure 4.2 Marquis Charles Cornwallis, Governor-General of India, 1786–1793 and
again July–Oct. 1805. His career apparently did not suffer following his
surrender of the American Colonies at Yorktown in 1781
Source: Painting by Arthur William Devis, 1792–3. By permission of the British Library, OIOC Print,
F6 FCO

Most opium was to come from Bihar, through the agency in Patna, and only
about a quarter was expected from Benares through the agency that was
ultimately set up in Ghazipur. The system, as Cornwallis left it, remained
essentially in place for the next century. The only modifications were subsequent
increases in production and more frequent auctions. But, for the next twenty-five
years or so, the system ran with considerable profit to the company, according to
Cornwallis' blueprint (Owen 1934, pp. 36–7).

Table 4.1 Calcutta auction: opium prices (1787–1822)

Year	Ave. price per chest		
1788	Rs	466	(Patna only)
1789		577	"
1790		595	"
1791		560	"
1792		535	"
1793		628	"
1794		533	"
1795		480	"
1796		236	"
1797		286	"
1798		414	(Ave)
1799		775	
1800		687	
1801		790	
1802		1383	
1803		1124	
1804		1437	
1805–1809 n/a		–	
1810		1589	
1811		1639	
1814		1813	
1815		2149	
1816		1975	
1817		2178	
1818		1785	
1819		2065	
1820		2489	
1821		4259	
1822		3089	

Sources: NAI, SRC, LCD, 30 Jan. 1822, 8 April, 1821, and
11 July 1827, also from Crawfurd, 1820, p. 518

A body of regulations was enacted to govern the system and to protect the government's revenue as well as to ensure the welfare of the cultivators. As may be expected, these measures performed the former function more effectively than the latter. Opium cultivation was forbidden to everyone within British-ruled India except those who had received advances from the government. Ideally, peasants were not to be forced to cultivate opium against their will. The government, however, had little control over those Indians who carried out these policies on the local level, and there are many accounts of coercion being used; even to the point of food crops being uprooted to make way for opium. During the contract period, coercion seemed to be the rule. In 1777, complaints were filed about such tactics:

a considerable tract of land in the neighbourhood of Ghya was covered with green corn, and which would have been fit to cut in about a month or six weeks: this corn was suddenly cut down in order that the land might be prepared for the immediate cultivation of the poppy.

(Quoted in Singh 1980, p. 81)

Even in years of famine, farmers were forced to give up grain cultivation in favor of opium. The government was aware of these conditions and frequently placed clauses in contracts forbidding coercion, but the abuses persisted throughout the nineteenth century (Goldsmith 1939, p. 50). Moreover, the government itself required that opium land should remain opium land, thus, if the cultivator did not wish to grow opium, he would often be forced off his land. He usually did not own it in any case, thus as a tenant had little say in the selection of crops. Opium cultivators were not free agents.

Although there is some debate on the topic, peasants appear to have been unwilling to cultivate opium. This reluctance was because opium could not be cultivated at a profit by most Indian ryots. The rate of payment from the government was minimal at best. Exact figures for the amounts paid to peasants prior to 1820 are unavailable, but the cost to the government per maund fluctuated between Rs85 and Rs112 between 1814 and 1822. This means that the cost per seer (about 1.9 lb or 0.9 kg), was usually above Rs2, and never more than Rs3 (NAI, SRC LCD, 8 April 1821 and 11 July 1827). Statistics for gross opium revenue and charges for the period 1809–1827 show that before 1820, the government regularly netted ten times more than it paid out for opium, and that included all expenses, not simply payments to the ryots (Singh 1980, p. 163). For the period from 1820 to 1859, peasants in Bihar and Benares received Rs3.5 per seer of raw opium.[4] By contrast, at about the same period, a ryot in western India, cultivating Malwa opium, was receiving around Rs8 for a seer of "pukka" or prepared opium.[5] Because the company was so niggardly with its payments to the peasants, most could not afford to grow poppies. Only one particular caste, the Koeris, managed to carry on the cultivation with some degree of efficiency. They were able to do this because they could employ their wives and children to help out with the tasks of opium production.

the entire family of the Koeri assisted him in poppy cultivation, in the preparation of land and in the extraction of the drug. The Koeri had not to pay for hired labourers. In fact, without this unpaid labour of the entire family, poppy could not have been grown at all. Poppy cultivation, on the basis of capitalistic farming, could not have been possible at all without a basic change in the organization of production.

(Singh 1980 pp. 74–75)

Although other castes, particularly in Bihar, found themselves required to cultivate opium, many of them were forbidden by their own caste rules from using their wives as field labor. These included: the Awadhia, Kurmi, Dhanuk, Ahir, Rajput and Brahmins. British administrators reported that the Koeris were the most "laborious and industrious order of ryots" and even as late as the 1890s were still thought to be the best opium cultivators. As if these requirements were not onerous enough, the ryots were also expected to deliver their opium to the government factory or some other central "weighment" site at their own expense. This could mean a trip of up to several days or even weeks' journey (India 1871, p. 27). The administrators of the Opium Agency were quite unsympathetic to the complaints of the cultivators.

> It goes without saying that complaints of the impossibility of cultivating poppy at a profit, at the price paid for its products, have always been rife. This is the grievance upon which the poppy cultivator has always most insisted; but we do not in this place propose to consider it.
>
> (India 1883, p. 38)

There was, looking at the numbers, little incentive for a peasant to plant opium. The price was quite low, the work was hard and like any form of agriculture, dependent upon the vagaries of nature. The only advantage was that the government made cash available to the peasants so they could pay their taxes. The Indian government , on the other hand, rarely made less than 100 percent net profit on opium, and that was in a bad year (Crawfurd 1820a, pp. 518–19).[6] Overall, however, it is difficult to say whether the opium growers of Bihar and Benares were any worse off than the Bengali peasants who were engaged in the "private" but commercialized jute and indigo agricultural systems. In all three cases, peasants were usually under some form of compulsion, if not from the government, then from their landlords and creditors, to produce crops that could be sold (Bose 1993, ch 2).

John Malcolm estimated the peasants in Malwa, during this same period, actually gained very little from opium cultivation. Even though the ryots there received about Rs8 per seer, the best they could do was to clear Rs12 per *bigha* (about 2/3 acre) in a good year, while in a "tolerable season" they might net only Rs1. In a bad year, they could lose as much as Rs9 (Malcolm 1823, pp. 359–60) (See Appendix 4). Singh concludes that:

> It was generally agreed that poppy cultivation was more costly and laborious but less remunerative than the cultivation of other crops. Colebrooke observed: "that it is less profitable is apparent from the circumstances of the peasants not ambitioning this culture except in few situations which are peculiarly favourable to it." . . . Colebrooke found that the ryots willing to grow poppy were those whom the landholders' exactions made poor and helpless.
>
> (Singh 1980, p. 85)

The reports of the opium agents give a good overview of the system of opium production in Bihar and Benares during the 1870s and 1880s. A number of these have been preserved in the Indian National Archives. Poppy was a *rabi*, or cool season, crop. It was planted in November or December and harvested between

February and April, depending on local conditions. Since this is the dry season in India, the crop needed some form of irrigation. As a rule, poppy had to be watered nine times during the season, or roughly once a week until the flowers set. It was not good to water the crop after it had flowered, or to have rain then because it would make the sap too watery and dilute the alkaloids. Also, rain could damage the flowers and prevent the fertilization and formation of a seed capsule. The need for water led the government, through the opium agents, to provide special loans to the ryots to dig wells. This solicitude was never shown for other crops. Poppy fields also needed special preparation. They had to be fertilized with manure (another reason why caste regulations might deter some Hindus from this cultivation) and the crop required regular weeding. It was among the most demanding of crops. David Fiengold has calculated that the production of a *vis* of raw opium (about 1.6 kg., or approximately equivalent to an EIC "ball" of opium) in the Golden Triangle today requires 387 man-hours.[7] It is doubtful that opium-production technology has changed at all in the past 200 years. From this measure we can calculate that the average peasant who, according to Opium Agency Reports, cultivated about 10–15 bighas with each bigha producing about five seers or roughly five kg., would have produced a total of 50 kg. (or about 30 *vis*) of raw opium in a season.[8] This amount would require somewhere between 11,000 and 15,000 man-hours, or more correctly, man-woman-and-child-hours. Certainly the entire family, or a large population of low-paid labourers, would have to be involved in this production, perhaps as many as ten to twelve people working 100-hour weeks for the twelve weeks of the poppy season.

When the seed capsules were ripe, the peasant would go through a section of his field in the afternoon and score the capsules with a small knife which had three or four blades tied closely together so that it would make a series of parallel incisions for the sap to bleed out. The following morning, he would return with a scraper and collect the droplets of congealed opium sap. Then he would incise the capsules in another part of the field in the afternoon. Each capsule could be tapped three or four times to obtain the maximum amount of sap during the short time the capsule was still green. Depending on weather and soil conditions, the peasant could hope for a production of four to five seers, or about four to five kg per bigha (India 1871, p. 1). That would give the ryot a gross income of about Rs17.5 per bigha, or perhaps as much as Rs200 for 14 or so bighas. It is doubtful that there would be much left over in an average year.

In 1871 in Bihar, about 450,000 bighas were under poppy cultivation for at least part of the year, then producing about 25,000 chests, and in Benares there were another 260,000. In that year, however, the government had resolved to increase production to 50,000 chests and thus aimed to bring a total of about 800,000 or 900,000 bighas under cultivation. At that time in Bihar, opium was cultivated in eleven districts and in. Varanasi there were seven districts where opium was grown.[9] (See Figure 4.3.)

After the harvest, the peasants did little to prepare the opium other than clean it as much as necessary to please the agents, and pack it to be carried to the

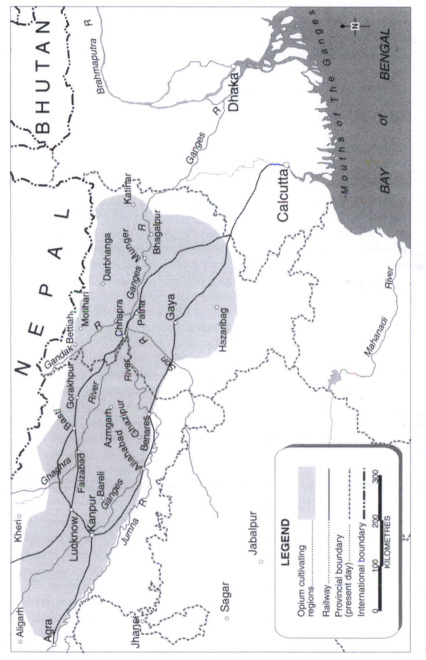

Figure 4.3 The opium-producing areas of Benares (Varanasi) and Bihar States in Eastern India

weighment. Opium had to be delivered in clay pots known as *challans*, also provided at the peasants' expense. Peasants were also able to sell the government some of their poppy leaves and petals as "trash," which were used in wrapping the final product. In Bihar and Benares, weighing began in March and continued through April and into May. This meant a journey to some central location in the district where thousands of cultivators would gather at an appointed time to turn their harvest over to the government agent and to collect the fourth installment of their payment, or otherwise reconcile their account. If they did not produce the contracted amount they had to pay back the deficit. There were heavy penalties for adulteration and generous rewards to informers. By the 1860s, the Opium Department was already employing chemical tests to determine whether certain adulterants had been mixed with the opium.[10]

The "Sudder Factories" as they were called, in Patna and Ghazipur were extensive establishments, employing thousands of men and boys in the business of preparing the opium for shipment: cleaning, drying, turning, "cake-making," packing, etc. In January and February, the factories would be just sending off the last of the previous year's crop to Calcutta. In February and March they would clean up the factory and prepare materials, such as leaves and trash for the incoming crop which would start to arrive around the beginning of April. By May, the factory would be in full swing with the specialized craftsmen, the cake-makers, busily turning out cakes or "balls" of opium at a rate of about sixty per day. In Patna, there were 1000 men employed as cakers, who worked from 10 a.m. to 4 p.m. every day in the huge sheds erected for the factory. They labored throughout the hot season in temperatures of up to 40°C (103°F). A bell was rung every twenty minutes and each cake-maker's output was checked. The average output for the Patna factory was between 16,000 and 20,000 cakes daily. Caking continued through June and some of the staff would continue to make "excise" opium, which was sold locally to Indian consumers, and medical opium. The opium prepared for export to China and Southeast Asia was known as "provision" opium and accounted for about 90 percent of the factory's output. During August and September, the cakes, which were placed on shelves in the factory, would dry out and required turning. Each cake had to be given a one-quarter turn once every six days. This was called "sattai," and the factory employed 65 boys per 10,000 balls.

By September, the Opium Agents would begin to gather the mango-wood chests[11] in which the opium balls were to be packed. First the chests were smeared with dammar, to seal them; and strips of wood for the partitions were prepared. This continued through October. Finally, they collected the trash and began to pack the chests. Forty cakes, or balls were packed into each chest. There were two layers, twenty on the bottom, twenty on top. They were separated into pigeonholes by the wooden strips. The chests were covered with burlap and powdered with clay dust to seal them. They would then be directly shipped downriver to Calcutta. As early as 1870, opium was being shipped from Patna to Calcutta by rail. The work of packing and dispatching the opium crop would continue into February (India 1883, pp. 150–80).

Figure 4.4 Weighing of opium in the 1880s
Source: By permission of the British Library, Photo 703(14).

In Calcutta, the new season's crop would be ready for the first auction of the year in January. The auctions would be held in the exchange rooms at Tank Square just a few blocks north of Government House (Fay 1975, p. 14). Until the 1820s, the company only held two auctions per year. By the middle of the nineteenth century, the size of the provision had increased to over 50,000 chests. With the advent of clipper ships and then steamers it became possible to maintain a constant flow of opium and other goods to China, and auctions came to be held on a monthly basis. The government then divided the crop into twelve more or less equal portions and auctioned off one of them each month. They also used the auctions to manipulate the market so as to obtain the highest possible price for their opium. An auction could be cancelled to keep up a price or to prevent the market from being glutted. On the other hand, the merchants and speculators who traded in the "Calcutta Bazaar" as it was known, knew well the current price of the drug in China as well as the prices in various Southeast Asian centers. They also knew the weather conditions under which the crop had been produced and usually had some idea of the quality of a particular crop. If they did not know these things in January, then they knew them as soon as the first ships had returned from Canton with sales reports from the year's crop. The correspondence in the Jardine Matheson collection shows an active correspondence between the Canton traders and their agents and affiliates in Calcutta and

Figure 4.5 Examination of opium in the 1880s
Source: By permission of the British Library, Photo 703(15)

Bombay. There was a continual interchange of market information, particularly for opium. Jardine Matheson regularly provided their constituents with information on the Asian opium market through their regular "Opium Circulars." (See Appendix 2.)

Once the opium was sold, it was out of the company's hands. Unofficially however, and in fact, sometimes even officially, there was a deep and abiding interest in the health of the illegal market in Canton, or the China coast, or in Southeast Asia. All affected the ultimate price of the commodity, if not this year, then the next. The company and the Indian government had to take a long view. They thus maintained a high level of quality control over their produce. No one can read the enormous number of reports and studies from the Opium Department without noticing the concern for a pure and consistently high quality of opium as well as for efficiency, economy and security. Indian officials worked hard to maintain the reputation of their product. Patna and Benares opium were, as I have suggested earlier, virtual trademarks. By the first decade of the nineteenth century, Chinese smugglers who otherwise suspected every coin, blandly accepted without question or inspection, entire consignments of hundreds of chests so long as they bore the familiar markings of the company's opium.

Figure 4.6 Drying balls of opium at the Sudder Factory in Patna, *c.* 1851. In this room the balls of opium were stacked prior to their being packed in boxes from transmission to Calcutta and eventually to China. At that time 450 boys were engaged in stacking, turning, airing and examining the balls or in rubbing them with dried and crushed poppy petal dust to clear them of mildew, moths or insects. This room contained 300,000 cakes valued at about £900,000

Source: From Sherwill, 1851. By permission of the British Library, OIOC, IOL X 401

Table 4.2 Opium market report from *Calcutta Overland Price Current*, Tuesday Jan. 22, 1856

Reports first sale of 1854–55 opium season on 10th Jan 1856

	Chests	*High (Rs)*	*Low (Rs)*	*Ave. (Rs)*	*Proceeds*
Patna	2440	920	910	914+	2230675
Benares	1020	60	905	953,12,9	972875

Source: Quoted in U.S. Consular Reports, M450, Reel 2, Calcutta Consular Rept., Huffnagle to Secretary of State

Meeting the competition

By the 1820s, opium had come to be the second largest source of government revenue in British India, regularly constituting about 15 percent of the total. Even though the land revenue was always the largest, opium had certain advantages that the others did not. Land and salt taxes were collected in small amounts, and squeezed, as it were, rupee by rupee from peasants and landlords all over the countryside. It was then passed through several layers of sticky fingered intermediaries. The opium revenue, at least that from opium exports, was paid in large

...ents, either directly to the government at the auctions in Calcutta, or ... or negotiable paper (Bills of Exchange) wherever it was most needed. ... ... eighteenth century and early nineteenth century, it was most often paid into the EIC treasury in Canton, to finance the company's China trade. When not paid in cash, it was often paid in the company's own bills. Outside of treasure extracted from India itself, opium was really the only form of revenue that was negotiable outside of India.

In addition to being a major source of revenue, it was also a major export, constituting the largest single item of export for the first two-thirds of the nineteenth century. By the late 1870s it had dropped to second behind raw cotton (in some years) and was also second to all cotton products combined (i.e. raw, twist, yarn and cloth) in other years. By the middle of the century, opium was regularly about a third of all exports, and thus, by itself was a major prop of the colonial Indian economy. It had become too valuable a resource to abandon, and for the next 80 years, the Indian government resisted every effort and every situation that would have led them to stop growing opium. We could say that they were as hooked on the drug as its consumers.

Following the institution of the Agency system, the company sought to maintain a desired level of profit as well as the monopoly, but it was really too lucrative an opportunity for outsiders to leave it to the government. Soon others wanted some of the opium profits. By the 1820s, after nearly 50 years of producing and shipping between 4,000 and 5,000 chests of opium, it was clear that the market had changed. For one thing, in 1820–1 the price of a chest of opium had risen to about Rs4259 in Calcutta. Crawfurd pointed out that the rise in price was evidence "that the quantity produced and brought to market was unequal to the demand, and that, acting as a bounty of the opium of other countries, it has been the cause of a great importation of Turkey and Malwa opium" (Crawfurd 1820a, p. 518).

Realizing that the Chinese market had become far more elastic than they had previously imagined, the government decided to increase production in order to meet competition from foreign and Malwa opium. And, rather than attempt to restrict the supply and maintain the price, they adopted the opposite strategy: of producing as much as possible and hoping to drive the competition out of business by running down the price. Despite the usual blandishments about native welfare, increasing blocks of land were brought under opium cultivation, particularly in Bihar state, and more peasants were dragooned into the business of poppy cultivation.

> we are of opinion that the principle ought to be invariably adhered to, not to introduce the culture of the Poppy into any District where it has not hitherto obtained, but that the Provision should be increased, either by improved management in those parts of the Country where Agencies are already established, or by the introduction of Government Agency into districts where the Plant is known to be cultivated for purposes of clandestine trade.
>
> (NAI, SRC, Letters from the Court of Directors to the Governor-General in Council, 24 Oct. 1817, par. 77)

It was a comforting argument, but in fact a lot of new land now came under the poppy. This expansion of cultivation was justified by the Court of Directors, quoting the exact words that Warren Hastings had used to defend himself for declaring a monopoly.

> After all, we must observe that it is our wish not to encourage the consumption of Opium, but rather to lessen the use, or more properly speaking, the abuse, of the drug, and, for this end, as well as for the purpose of the Revenue, to make the price to the Public, both in our own and in foreign dominions as high as possible having due regard to the effects of illicit opium trade in our own dominions, and competition in foreign places from Opium produced in other Countries. Were it possible to prevent the use of the drug altogether except strictly for the purpose of medicine, we would gladly do it in compassion to Mankind, but this being absolutely impracticable, we can only endeavour to regulate and palliate an evil which cannot be eradicated.
>
> (NAI, SRC, Letters from the Court of Directors to the
> Governor-General in Council, 24 Oct. 1817, par. 85)

There were three sources of competition. The first on the scene were the Americans, who were selling Turkish opium in markets where once British Indian opium had been the sole product. The second source of competition was considered far more threatening to EIC interests, that was the trade which had sprung up, apparently after a period of abeyance, in western India, in the Malwa area. The Portuguese and Ralph Fitch had mentioned the existence of "Cambay" opium being traded to Southeast Asia in the sixteenth century. The source of this opium was the region that later came to be known as "Malwa" in the nineteenth century. Today it is largely included in the state of Madya Pradesh, and part of Rajahstan. At first, the company sought various means to eliminate both supplies, but these were never feasible projects. Ultimately it came to terms with both, a strategy that fundamentally changed the nature of the opium trade. Outside of these, the third source of competition, and one generally ignored at the time, was the appearance of significant poppy cultivation in China itself, particularly in the provinces of Yunnan and Sichuan.

As soon as they had thrown off British rule, Yankee traders from the harbors that had once smuggled tea in violation of the company's monopoly, were turning up in the western Pacific and the South China Sea. There were already American ships in the Pearl River in 1784 when Samuel Shaw, the first official United States trade representative arrived in Canton in the *Empress of China*. By 1786, four US ships called at Canton, and by the end of the century twenty to thirty US vessels were calling at Canton every year, as well as carrying on an active trade in pepper with Aceh and the west coast of Sumatra.

At first, Americans financed their tea, silk and chinaware purchases with silver, mostly from Mexico. They also shipped ginseng and sandalwood, and found a ready source of trade goods in the furs of the Pacific northwest, but these resources were either quickly exhausted or else the market was rapidly glutted. There was a great rush into the fur trade between 1793–1797 by both American and British traders, when 3,500,000 seal skins were sent to Canton. By 1820, the fur trade was ruined with both fur seal and sea otter populations of the northwest coast being near extinction (Blue 1982, pp. cxxxii, cxxxiv–cxxxv). Americans quickly grasped the importance of the trade between Southeast Asia and China and soon began to compete with the country traders in Batavia, Melaka and all the other harbors of Southeast Asia. Samuel Shaw had seen the attractions of this traffic and with it the utility of the opium trade.

> The free merchants derive no small advantage from the company's annual remittance to China towards purchasing tea for Europe. The company's opium is disposed of at public sale, and the merchant who buys it, upon giving security to pay the amount at the current exchange, into their treasury at Canton, has the benefit of a credit. Silver can sometimes be obtained on similar terms. This, together with a part of the opium, is applied to the purchase of tin and pepper from the Malays and at Batavia, on which a handsome profit is made at Canton, as well as on the remainder of the opium, for which they there find a good market.
>
> (Shaw 1847, p. 265)

Initially prohibited from purchasing opium in Calcutta, Americans found a new source of opium in Turkey (Stelle 1938, pp. 1–2). In 1803, William Stewart, the first US Consul at Smyrna filed a lengthy report on the trade of that port. He noted that direct commercial relations between Turkey and the US would be advantageous to both. Turkey needed many goods that US shippers could supply cheaply and without going through Italian middlemen.

> Our trade with the East & West Indies and South America will always afford us the means of supplying Turkey with the principal articles of its consumption. The productions of these countries are sent from Europe to Smyrna which is the general deposit of all foreign productions consumed in Turkey, as also of the commodities of that country and Egypt.
>
> (William Stewart, US Consul Smyrna to SoS, 25 April 1803)

He also reported that Turkey was an important source of drugs and of opium. The first documented American purchases of opium at Smyrna took place in 1804 and for the next three decades or so, Americans did a thriving business in the eastern Mediterranean. By the 1820s Americans were shipping hundreds of chests of Turkish opium to Southeast Asia and China.[12] In 1824, twenty US vessels stopped at Smyrna and exported over 1600 chests of opium (David Afflee, US Consul Smyrna to SoS, 31 Dec 1824). Turkish opium sold for $300 to $400 less per chest than Bengal opium, but was not produced in the same quantities as the Indian product nor was it as popular.[13] It was never really a serious competitor for Indian opium and Americans began to carry Bengal opium as soon as it was available to them. As late as 1830 however, imports of Turkish opium to Canton could still reach 1400 chests (see Table 5.1, p. 95). Shortly after this the Turkish imports declined sharply. Even though often considered competitors to the British traders, there was actually a great deal of cooperation, if not a real symbiosis, between between American and British traders.

The Malwa cultivation was a far more serious problem. Since the turn of the century, the Indian government had been trying unsuccessfully to eliminate this branch of the trade. Amar Farooqui's recent study of the British attempts to "annihilate" the Malwa cultivation is instructive for a number of reasons. On the one hand, he shows the deep, almost panicked concern of the Calcutta authorities, as well as the Directors in London, at this threat to the Indian revenue. Secondly, he traces the series of measures which British authorities attempted in order to control or end the trade, which included treaties and pressures on the surrounding Indian states to forbid the passage of the opium through their territories. These issues have already been examined by Owen and Wright, but Farooqui also looks at the Indian traders involved in this activity and offers an analysis of the growth of Indian capitalism in western India.

Unlike Bengal, where British traders and company servants essentially pre-empted the businesses of native merchants who had previously controlled the opium trade, the company did not govern the regions where Malwa opium was produced. Although the earlier production of "Cambay" opium seems to have dropped to a fairly low level in the early eighteenth century, by the later part of the century, attracted by the profits being reaped by the company in Bengal, native merchants had reactivated the western Indian cultivation of the drug. Once they had established themselves in the market and constructed their own network of brokers, moneylenders and markets, the Malwa merchants were able to withstand sustained British efforts to eliminate their commerce.

Table 4.3 Malwa poppy cultivation districts, ca. 1820

District	Area sown	District	Area sown
A. Madhya Prahesh			
Mandsaur	26,301 bighas	**B. Rajasthan**	
Ratlam	8,082 "	Jhalawar	3,133 bighas
Ujjain	16,417 "	Chittaurgarh	3,770 "
Dewas	3,078 "		
Dhar	3,747 "	**C. Unidentified**	
Shajapur	4,961 "	9 parganas	4,774 "
Rajgarh	2,972 "		
Vidisha	6,200 "		
Sehore	3,535 "		
Bhopal	160 "		
Jhabua	91 "		

Total Malwa cultivation area in 1820: 50,800 bighas
Total EIC cultivation area in 1818: 45,492 bighas

Source: Farooqui 1995, p. 467

Malwa opium may have been exported as early as the 1770s, but it was not until 1803 that the Bengal government took notice of the trade. At that time, the Governor-General urged the Bombay government to take immediate steps necessary for the "complete annihilation" of the Malwa trade. This was easier said than done, and for the next twenty years, the British Indian government tried to cut off access to the sea for shipments of opium from Malwa production centers which were all located far inland. First it was forbidden to ship it through Bombay, whereupon the trade shifted to the Portuguese ports of Goa, Damão and Diu. The British government then made treaties with the Portuguese and were confident that the trade would stop, but it did not. Between 1805 and 1810, Britain occupied the Portuguese ports in India because of the Napoleonic Wars, and the Malwa trade declined, but it sprang up again after the ports were returned. In addition to the Portuguese ports, Malwa opium was also shipped from Ahmadabad, Cambay, Surat, Jamusar, Baroda, Bharuch, Bhavnagar and Jafarabad. Treaties were made with the Indian rulers of nearby states to prevent the passage of the drug through their territories, but again these were ineffective. If the rulers did not themselves violate the treaties, then their officials or local merchants did. It was simply too lucrative to forbid. When they blocked access to the Gujerat coast, the trade moved to Sind. The company was never successful in choking it off. In 1803, when the British first began throwing obstacles in the way of the trade, the estimated output from Malwa was about 300 to 600 chests of one pikul each, but there are no certain figures. By 1817, production had increased to about 900 chests (Farooqui 1995, p. 450–3). The following year, the price of a chest of Malwa opium in Canton was $680, while that of a chest of Patna opium was at $840.

In 1819, the British government decided to adopt a new strategy to control the Malwa production. If it was impossible to choke off production by blocking access to the sea, then it might be possible to simply go into the marketplace and purchase Malwa opium on the company's account. They could thereby control the supply, and thus be able to set the price so that it could not undersell the company's opium. The company would auction the opium, either at Calcutta or Bombay, and it could be shipped by the same merchants who dealt in Bengal opium. This plan too was unsuccessful, at least insofar as the company's objectives were concerned. Not only was it impossible to gain control of the supply, but it only encouraged the Malwa merchants to increase production. The more the company bought, the more they produced. The merchants thus sold a great deal of opium to the company while continuing to ship, through a variety of outlets, additional opium to China. In 1821–2, 1,718 chests of Malwa opium were sold in China. The following year the total had increased to 4,000 chests and the next year to 4,172 chests. With the company delivering a similar amount, this meant that the supply of opium reaching China had nearly doubled in the course of three years. Moreover, the increased and now legitimate traffic in the drug in Bombay, had seen the growth of a locally based community of opium merchants.

As might be expected, the increase in supply had caused the price per chest to fall precipitously. In 1821–2, the Chinese paid $8,314,600 for 4,628 chests of opium, both Malwa and Bengal combined. This meant an average price of about $1,796 per chest. In 1823–4, they paid $8,515,100 for 7,072 chests, an average of $1,204 per chest. The rough value of a chest of opium had lost nearly one-third of its value within two years (Greenberg 1951, p. 129). The price drop was not simply a result of the increase in supply. In their eagerness to throw as much opium as possible into the market, either the cultivators, or the merchants in Malwa sold a quantity of substandard opium to the company. Both the fall in the opium price as well as the poor quality of the Malwa opium being sold under the company's mark led to strenuous complaints from the Canton opium dealers. Charles Magniac, wrote to India:

> The unfortunate state of the opium market . . . [is] a natural consequence of the extraordinary proceedings of your Government, incomprehensible to us on every ground of wisdom of policy, in offering a premium on the production of Malwa by purchasing 4,000 chests, and thus overlaying and stifling the drug produced in Bengal from whence the Company were deriving a profit which in respect of the first cost is almost unequalled in the annals of commerce, a profit which in one season . . . actually rose to such a pitch as nearly to pay for the whole Chinese investment for cargoes for 20 ships of 1,400 tons – a profit which no person in their senses would have dreamed of until it exhibited in itself symptoms of decay. To such a profit . . . the government have given a death blow.
>
> (Greenberg 1951, pp. 127–8)

Magniac predicted that opium prices would drop to $350 to $500 per chest, a level at which they had stood in about 1800. He and other opium traders demanded compensation from the company for losses they had suffered because of the company's policy. Magniac's fears, as it turned out, were correct, but the fall in price did not destroy either the trade or their profits. While it was difficult for dealers at the time, the increase in supply and the fall in prices meant that consumption was increasing. The market for opium was actually quite elastic. Although many smokers were certainly addicted to the drug, financial constraints did make a difference in consumption patterns. High prices meant that less opium was purchased, and low prices saw consumption increasing with new users being introduced to the drug and moderate users increasing their consumption. John Crawfurd related his experience with opium sales in Java while he was administering Yogyakarta during the British occupation.

> The effects of this principle were illustrated in a most striking manner in all the sales of Java, of which I had personally a remarkable example in those under my own authority, within the territories of the sultan. When the retail price was about 5000 Spanish dollars per chest, as it was on the British first taking possession of the island [in 1811] the whole consumption was only 30 chests per year. When the price fell to about 4000 dollars, the sales rose to 50 chests, and when the price finally sunk to 3500, the consumption

advanced to near 100 chests. When the price was moderate many had recourse to the drug who never used it before. When it was extravagantly high, many who had before used it moderately, desisted altogether, and those whose habits were more confirmed, had recourse as substitutes to native narcotic drugs, less agreeable and more pernicious.

(Crawfurd 1820a, p. 520)

As the table of Canton prices shows, (Table 4.4) the trend of opium prices in China, and elsewhere, was inexorably downward until a new "optimum" price was reached, this time at about $400 per chest. What is also notable in both comments is the extraordinarily high prices and high profits that the company was reaping from opium at this time.

Like other free-trade liberals, Crawfurd was a critic of the company's monopoly. He argued that the company had invited competition by maintaining its opium monopoly. The monopoly, not the drug business was immoral and unnatural. Competition would bring the drug to market at something like its "natural" price. And, if unshackled, it might expand, and thus provide the company with a greater source of revenue in terms of ground rent and other taxes. He felt that the Malwa cutlivation, which operated without a government monopoly, prospered because it functioned as a free trade system. In the sense that it was not controlled by the government, trade was indeed free, or so he thought:

> It would be absurd, then, we repeat, to suppose that a liberal government should, by the exercise of a petty monopoly, producing but a few hundred thousand pounds of revenue, sacrifice a great national advantage, the amount of which might be realized by an export duty of some thirty per cent, levied on strangers directly, without detriment to its own subjects. For the last thirty years the opium revenue derived from the monopoly has been stationary, or rather, indeed, declining – a monstrous state of things, when it is considered that within the same period, the quantity of the article exported has multiplied tenfold, and the value at least fivefold; but such is the sure result of all monopolies.
>
> (Crawfurd 1837, pp. 251–2)

Crawfurd's understanding of the Malwa trade was perhaps correct, but the company did not take his advice. Rather, the monopoly was maintained through the nineteenth century, but the Malwa cultivation was allowed a measure of latitude by the Indian government.

Government decided to allow the Malwa production to continue. Their price for allowing relative freedom for the Malwa opium industry was the imposition of a "pass duty" on each chest shipped through Bombay. With the advance of the company's conquests in western India, particularly with the defeat of the Mahratas and the Pindari by 1820, the British Indian government was in a position to impose treaties on most of the states between the Malwa areas and the sea. The traffic was channeled through Bombay, which was actually the shortest

Table 4.4 Prices of opium per chest, in Spanish $ as given in Canton, Macau or Hong
Kong

Mon/Yr	Patna	Benares	Malwa	Mon/Yr	Patna	Benares	Malwa
7/1800	557	525	–	9/1830	800	795	565
9/1800	580	–	–	3/1831	1025	1045	645
11/1801	570	–		9/1831	980	975	770
–/1802				3/1832	945	970	550
–/1803	1200	1200		9/1832	790	769	475
7/1804	1320	1300	–	3/1833	720	700	640
4/1805	1430	1430	–	10/1833	640	–	680
9/1805	1395	1375	–	3/1834	560	–	610
3/1806	1140	1140	–	9/1834	540	520	605
9/1806	815	795	–	7/1835	675	630	575
4/1807	1000	–	–	12/1835	750	710	610
9/1807	1200	–	–	4/1836	820	740	425
–/1809	–	–	–	11/1836	785	705	785
–/1809	–	–	–	3/1837	760	700	600
3/1810	1090	–	–	12/1837	630	580	480
–/1811	–	–	–	3/1838	465	410	420
–/1812	–	–	–	10/1838	585	540	565
–/1813	–	–	–	–/1839		no prices	
–/1814	–	–	–	–/1840		no prices	
–/1815	–	–	–	–/1841		no prices	
–/1816	–	–	–	9/1842	580	570	450
–/1817	1300	–	–	3/1843	725	640	570
–/1818	840	–	680	9/1843	835	800	730
4/1819	1170	–	–	3/1844	600	570	650
10/1819	1250	–	–	8/1844	750	720	680
6/1820	1380	–	–	3/1845	640	580	–
12/1820	1550	–	1450	4/1846	690	670	700
6/1821	1700	–	1100	9/1846	635	615	620
–/1821	–	no sales		4/1847	645	630	600
1/1822	1850	–	1100	9/1847	620	600	530
5/1822	2500	–	1800	3/1848	430	420	520
4/1823	2100	–	1350	9/1848	510	490	730
12/1823	1000	–	920	5/1849	530	574	700
4/1824	1030	–	830	9/1849	470	490	650
8/1824	950	850	580	4/1850	510	515	595
3/1825	1450	–	–	11/1850	450	455	605
4/1825	780	–	580	5/1851	470	450	550
10/1825	970	–	770	11/1851	495	475	530
4/1826	1050	1060	880	4/1852	540	540	560
12/1826	900	1175	875	11/1852	510	530	490
3/1827	850	1300	910	4/1853	435	445	425
10/1827	1200	1240	1400	9/1853	340	355	335
4/1828	970	960	1210	4/1854	370	385	440
9/1828	1010	980	1025	9/1854	310	320	410
4/1829	905	870	970	4/1855	320	335	420
9/1829	850	820	880	9/1855	400	410	510
3/1830	800	–	745	3/1856	425	428	505

continued . . .

Table 4.4 continued

Mon/Yr	Patna	Benares	Malwa	Mon/Yr	Patna	Benares	Malwa
9/1856	405	420	510	4/1869	695	705	745
3/1857	440	435	490	–/1869	–	–	–
9/1857	750	730	870	3/1870	532	507	640
3/1858	715	725	665	9/1870	580	540	570
9/1858	712	710	635	3/1871	600	555	630
4/1859	755	765	600	–/1871	–	–	–
10/1859	725	725	585	4/1872	660	650	650
4/1860	782	770	600	9/1872	640	627	595
10/1860	827	815	720	4/1873	610	547	590
6/1861	855	850	725	9/1873	576	555	620
10/1861	860	870	720	4/1874	580	550	575
3/1862	742	725	755	9/1874	575	550	605
10/1862	655	632	705	4/1875	595	570	570
6/1863	675	640	727	9/1875	595	575	585
12/1863	570	560	550	4/1876	620	585	555
4/1864	575	495	750	9/1876	565	527	560
9/1864	505	470	675	4/1877	582	550	555
3/1865	415	397	635	12/1877	673	–	–
12/1865	580	585	865	4/1878	613	–	–
4/1866	500	475	720	9/1878	615	–	–
9/1866	700	680	870	3/1879	570	–	800
4/1867	750	682	850	9/1879	532	–	740
10/1867	715	710	785	10/1880	610	–	720
4/1868	730	715	730	0/1881	–	–	–
10/1868	715	705	730	9/1882	575	545	620

Sources: Taken from various correspondence in the JM Archives (Mostly Opium Circulars in C/10 series, also, A7/145 opium sales books and A7/144 opium purchases.
Note: Prices are given semi-annually where available

and easiest route from the interior markets to the sea. In 1831, the company began to impose a pass duty of Rs175 per chest for every chest of Malwa opium going through Bombay.

This was a reasonable price, for it represented no more than the difference between the cost of shipping the drug through Bombay, and that of other more distant ports. However, because a number of traders continued to evade the duty, it was lowered to Rs125 in 1835, and it remained at this level for the next eight years. In 1843, the British annexed the state of Sind and now held the entire seacoast with the exception of the Portuguese territories (with which there were treaties) and the duty was promptly raised to Rs200 per chest. Two years later, it was bumped up to Rs300 and in 1847 it was pushed up to Rs400 (Watt 1893, pp. 94, 282–5).[14] Malwa opium production was now a source of profit to the Indian government and began to produce a regular and substantial supplementary income for the government at very little cost to itself. By the 1880s, it was yielding a revenue in the neighborhood of Rs25 million annually (£2.5 M).

Sowing the seeds of capitalism

According to Farooqui, a number of writers, including Owen (Owen 1934, p. 83) and B.B. Chauduri, have misconstrued this idea of freedom in the Malwa system. While the merchants may have operated without the restriction of a government monopoly, the cultivators certainly did not freely undertake the culture of the poppy any more than their compatriots in Bihar and Benares. Malcolm's figures given in Appendix 3, suggest that the ryots of Malwa were no more likely to profit from growing opium than their counterparts in Bihar and Benares, and with good reason: the profit was taken by those who controlled the trade.

Malwa opium was a different product than that produced by the company. As in the east, the Malwa peasants planted their opium in October and November and harvested it in February and March. However, when the peasants gathered the opium sap from the seed capsules, they immediately put it into vessels containing linseed oil. This was thought to give the opium a "certain consistency" and at the same time the oil acted as a preservative and prevented evaporation. Whereas Bengal opium could only keep for about two or three years before it began to deteriorate, Malwa could easily keep for four years. In fact, sometimes it was aged for a year to give it a "superior mellowness" (Farooqui 1995, p. 461).

Unlike the east, there were no great factories for the processing of Malwa opium. Here it was a cottage industry of sorts. The opium was gathered from the peasants by the individuals, called *mahajans*, who had advanced them the money for their crops. They further processed it by combining it into small cakes weighing from one quarter to one-half of a seer (200 to 500 grams) which were then allowed to dry without direct exposure to the sun. This process lasted through the monsoon season, and was often interrupted during the rains between June and September. These small dealers then sold or delivered the drug to the larger wholesalers in the major market towns. It is doubtful that these small operators were completely free agents either, rather the trade was dominated by wealthy merchants in the large regional centers who were often both revenue farmers and money-lenders. They functioned like the East India Company in supplying the capital which they lent to *gomastahs, banias, sahukars* and other *mahajans* who took responsibility for making advances to peasants and gathering up the harvested opium. Although Malcolm calculated that the peasants received Rs8 per seer, Farooqui indicates that prices could fluctuate considerably: between Rs4 and Rs10 per seer. At the wholesale level, where opium was sold by the five-seer unit (the *panseri*), prices were 50 to 100 percent higher than what the peasant received (Farooqui 1995, pp. 463–5).

B.B.Chauduri and Owen (Owen 1934, p. 83) assumed that cultivation of Malwa opium was free and therefore probably more remunerative for the peasant, but Farooqui argues:

> Evidence from Malwa, however, indicates that the absence of a monopoly did not necessarily imply complete freedom *at the level of the peasant* . . . The enormous political authority wielded by big revenue farmers in major

opium-growing tracts . . . made the producer succumb to pressures both in terms of choice of crop as well as extra-economic considerations which bore on procurement prices.

(Farooqui 1995, p. 459)

Very often, peasants found themselves required to undertake poppy cultivation in order to meet revenue obligations or debts which had already been contracted. Taxes on opium land, for instance were about four to five times higher than on land used for food grains. The large opium dealers were often revenue farmers or individuals who had significant political connections and were in a position to use a combination of both financial as well as political muscle to advance their interests. For example, Appa Gangadhar, an opium dealer of Mandsaur, was also a revenue farmer. He actually collected double the tax from the peasants on opium land (Rs24 instead of the official rate of Rs12) and simply pocketed the surplus.

If the Malwa opium trade did little for the peasant, it was highly profitable for the Marwari merchants and others who dominated the trade. These groups tenaciously held their ground against several EIC onslaughts and ultimately prevailed. The Indian government found itself with no choice but to accept their control of the cultivation and to allow them a share of the profits. Farooqui claims that the opium trade thus served as a major vehicle for the development of the Indian capitalist class.

> The adeptness shown by indigenous opium enterprise in western and central India in creating a viable alternative commercial base for itself deterred the East India Company from arbitrarily deciding on an opium policy for Malwa. A set of favourable circumstances provided opportunities which Indian businessmen were quick to seize upon: the possibility of producing in this region an item of trade – opium – the demand for which was constantly expanding; and the relatively late establishment of British rule in this region as compared to, say, Bihar, Bengal, etc. Ultimately it was the ingenuity of the Indian traders that helped them get the better of colonial intervention. Gradually after having conducted, and not succeeded with, various experiments during the 1820s, official thinking on the matter veered round to the view that private indigenous enterprise in the commodity would have to be tolerated. Indigenous Malwa opium enterprise thus became a critical factor in redefining the balance of forces in western and central India during the colonial period.

(Farooqui 1995, p. 473)

This experience laid the foundation for a much more dynamic economy in western India than in the east accounting for, to some extent, the current development of Bombay over Calcutta (Farooqui 1995, p. 448).

Thus opium now called into existence the forces of capitalism on both sides of India. In Malwa, groups of independent merchants, revenue farmers, moneylenders and other financial leaders in the major provincial towns of the region rose to prominence through the opium trade. They were able to succeed because they had already controlled networks of indebtedness that reached into hundreds of villages. This gave them leverage over the rulers of the states in which they operated, thus they controlled the political forces in their areas. They further developed links to the outside, through the various ports between Karachi and Goa, and finally in Bombay itself. In these outlets they forged alliances with Parsi, Jewish and Western merchant firms that were involved in the imperial economy. The very same country firms that had worked under the wings of the company, were also ready to do business with the opium "smugglers" when they had a product to compete with Bengal opium.[15] A few of these firms, such as the Sassoons, had their own *gomastahs*, who were actively involved in the business of making advances to peasants, but most simply purchased their opium from the regional markets in Malwa through agents who were dispatched each year.

If the company monopoly stifled native Indian capitalism in Calcutta, it certainly encouraged the European and Asian firms based in that city which likewise dealt in the imperial economy. The Calcutta firms, many of which had links to some of the Bombay firms also had connections to agency houses in Canton and other parts of Southeast Asia. These came to dominate the international trade in opium during the middle years of the nineteenth century, which was a period of explosive growth for the opium industry. Not only was the situation with the Chinese government continually unsettled, since opium was illegal throughout this period, but with production constantly increasing in India, the price was subject to radical fluctuations. This meant that the mortality of opium dealing firms was quite high. In the beginning of this period, there were some 50 or 60 firms dealing with opium in India. By 1860, there were only a few left and these had a dominating position in all other areas of trade as well. It was survival of the fittest.

The new Malwa policy was even more unsettling in China. John Crawfurd remarked on changes in the status of the trade in the early nineteenth century.

> Until the last few years, the whole consumption of the Archipelago was supplied by Bengal. There has been a great revolution in this branch of the trade, in common with almost every other, in consequence of the trade of the Americans, and the enlargement of the British trade, and a considerable quantity of the consumption of the islands comes now from Turkey and Malwa.
>
> (Crawfurd 1820a, pp. 518–19)

The revolution in the trade was larger than Crawfurd might have supposed. Even he could not have imagined the explosion that now took place in the opium trade. In the years between 1831 and 1839 both the Indian government and the Malwa producers began taking measures to enlarge their share of the trade. As all of the records show, prior to 1820, the total amount of opium leaving India never amounted to much more than 4,000 or 5,000 chests. During the 1820s, the

Malwa production, largely because of the company's policy of purchasing opium, had moved up to a slightly smaller amount than the company, so that in 1831, the total amount of opium reaching China was probably not more than 7,000 chests. On the eve of the Opium War, in 1839, something like 20,000 chests of opium would be confiscated by Commissioner Lin Cexu in his drive to eradicate the trade.

Opium did far more than simply play a role in "fixing" the trade imbalance that had existed between Britain and China. It did more than help the EIC service a part of its massive debt. It also did more than make a small number of Englishmen, Indians, Chinese and a few others very rich. Opium, as the new drug commodity of Asia, changed the overall environment. Perhaps it is misleading to look at political economies as existing in a sort of ecosystem which was in some way balanced, if we assume that balance meant lack of change. Obviously, history is about change and many factors must be considered when determining causes and effects, and not many situations are monocausal, and not many events or developments are restricted in their short- and long-term effects. Nonetheless, some factors have greater influence than others. And, just as in ecosystems, which are gradually changing and going through various sorts of cycles, occasionally, a new and extraordinary factor is introduced. In ecological terms, these are "keystone modifiers." They are species like beavers that radically alter a habitat by their creation of dams, new lakes and other such features (Mills 1993). The opium trade, as a complex economic system, touched on many of the critical areas that determined the integrity of the pre-existing political economies of Asia as well as the course of European expansion in the nineteenth century. It acted as a keystone factor in rearranging the relations of production for large numbers of people in India. By the 1880s, the requirement to cultivate opium impinged on the lives of at least a half-million peasant households in both the Malwa area as well as the Bihar/Benares areas. It occupied nearly half-million hectares. It must be seen as a system of forced cultivation, although the instruments of coercion were sometimes not directly applied. Despite the frequent defenses that if they did not promote and control the opium trade, then others would, the Indian government so actively protected its monopoly and so richly profited from the trade, that we must suspect either their sincerity or their awareness. Opium was the major foreign exchange-earner.

The British did not create the empire in order to trade opium, nor did the opium trade become the rationale for every major imperial policy. On the other hand, opium touched many parts of the system, and when crucial issues were decided, they were never decided against the trade or against the opium revenue until very late in the game. The interests of the trade guided the expansion of the empire by closing certain avenues and opening others. With the trade went the growth of the capitalist system, outside of India more obviously than inside of the subcontinent. The advances of the empire in Southeast Asia and China were likewise driven by the opium trade – particularly in Malaya, Indonesia and Siam. In India itself, the relationship was less apparent in that wars and territorial advances often took place because of the needs of frontier defense.

In China, however, the first great test of this protection came in 1839 with the outbreak of the Opium War on the China coast.

Opium had become like the other great commercial drug trades. In India, opium was, like tobacco and sugar in America, produced by forced labor. It was now a market-driven system that was almost completely monopolized by a tiny privileged group. It also created, around itself, a system of trade, financing, banking, insurance, transportation and distribution. Opium now did for Asia what tobacco, sugar, alcohol and tea had done for Europe. It created a mass market and a new drug culture.

5 The most gentlemanlike speculation

Drugs and cultural decline in China

While most scholars acknowledge that the Qing state had passed its apogee in the early nineteenth century and was exhibiting many of the signs of dynastic decay, not many have linked that systemic decline directly to the consumption of drugs. Normally, the phenomenon of drug use has been seen as a cause of social decay rather than an effect. Because opium came from outside, it was easier for Chinese statesmen to view it as an "external" problem.

> Opium . . . was viewed as an agent of barbarian aggression, a 'moral poison' which debased people's minds. Like 'heretical religion' it dissolved the proper social relationships (*lun-yi*) which distinguished man from the beasts, and Chinese from barbarians. If people continued to sink ever deeper into the selfish languor of the addict, argued the censor Yüan Yü-li in 1836, 'Fathers would no longer be able to admonish their wives; masters would no longer be able to restrain their servants; and teachers would no longer be able to train their pupils . . . It would mean the end of the life of the people and the destruction of the soul of the nation'.
>
> (Wakeman 1978, p. 179)

Admittedly, drug use may have hastened decline, but there is no reason why it cannot have been both an effect as well as a cause in the case of nineteenth-century China. The collapse of the Qing would have happened without opium. The decline had its origins in other causes than the opium trade, or even the activities of foreigners in Canton. On the other hand, we can assume that if the state were stronger, it might have been able to prevent the growth of the drug plague that struck the country during the nineteenth century.

Compared to contemporary European and Asian cultures, it is clear that China was unable to muster the political will to protect itself against the opium merchants, whereas others were. Perhaps suppression was easier for the western countries because at that time the world's major drug dealers were Anglo-Americans. In both Britain and the United States, opium use had become quite widespread by the middle of the nineteenth century, yet by the 1890s both countries had been relatively successful at reducing "recreational" opiate consumption and had placed legal restrictions on the opium trade and on drug use in general (Berridge and Edwards 1987; Courtwright 1982; Parssinen and Kerner 1983; Terry and Pellins 1970). Likewise, Japan, which had been almost completely closed until 1854, opened its doors at a time and under conditions that allowed it to get the United States to agree to ban the trade. The formal commitment, by one western state, along with other internal factors seems to have made a difference. Even though the Tokugawa regime collapsed and the Japanese state was reformed during an unsettled period which lasted until the 1870s, it was not subject to the same extent of foreign intervention as were other Asian states. At all times, and no matter what the level of political disturbance, the Japanese state was always able to keep out opium. Thus, one of the great contrasts between Japan and China in the nineteenth century was the ability of Japan to protect itself against the opium plague. Later, in its drive to graduate to a status equal to that of the European imperialist powers, Japan itself became a drug-dealing country, seeking to profit from the export of morphine in the wake of the opium suppression movement.

On the other hand, virtually all of the countries of Southeast Asia that came under European domination or influence during the nineteenth century were required to accept the opium trade and at least to allow its legalization for consumption by Chinese immigrants so that a revenue could be collected. While we may quibble about whether opium was "forced" upon China, there can be little doubt that legalized drug use was forced upon most of Southeast Asia. Likewise, a case can be made that cultivation of the drug was forced upon many unwilling Indian ryots. In India, where opium had been moderately used prior to British expansion, the records of the excise revenue show that consumption began to increase at a significant rate in the latter part of the century.

The decision by a state to sell opium to its subjects always took place in situations of political decline or at least relative weakness. In Southeast Asia, the integrity of most states was completely abrogated by European colonial rule during the nineteenth century. In every case, the sale of opium was authorized without reference to the peoples of these territories. None of the states of island Southeast Asia were ever in a position to protect themselves against the opium trade or opium use for any length of time. Palembang had tried to do so for a short period at the beginning of the eighteenth century. So too, did some of the Javanese principalities, but these prohibitions were not effective for very long. Palembang was selling opium to at least some of its subjects (i.e. Chinese miners on Bangka) by the mid-eighteenth century and by the nineteenth century, virtually all of the Dutch possessions had some sort of opium revenue concession. In fact, many rulers appear to have embraced opium as a ready source of revenue. This was certainly the case in Johor, Perak, Selangor and Pahang, not to mention nineteenth-century Siam. The importance of opium revenue farms will be examined in more detail in the following chapter. Only natives of the Philippines seem to have been relatively free of the drug plague, but this was probably more a function of their poverty than the ethical principles of their rulers.

At the beginning of the nineteenth century, all of the large mainland states (Siam, Vietnam and Burma) were, like China, attempting to exclude both opium and European traders. None were successful. Each in turn, was either completely taken over and required to allow opium sales, or was required to accept a treaty that legalized the opium trade. It must be said, however, that in each of the three, there is good evidence that a fairly active smuggling trade existed prior to European intervention. Either European traders or Chinese junk traders had been able to introduce opium to these states prior to colonization or the signing of unequal treaties. In all of these cases indigenous political and military agents were unable to prevent the import of opium. On the other hand, the opium trade itself was rarely the immediate cause of colonial takeovers. Opium simply came along with free trade and colonialism. Conversely, where states did have the power to control their own borders, the opium trade could be prevented.

Inability to stop smuggling was one thing, and possessing the means to consume was something else. Despite their relative permeability, no Southeast Asian state possessed a very large population to begin with, and the size of the opium market in each state was quite limited (Steinberg *et al.* 1971, p. 233).[1] Even at the end of the nineteenth century, all the countries of Southeast Asia combined, never imported more than 20 percent of the output of Indian opium. That figure may be a little high since even some of this opium was transhipped to China. Also, it should be noted that the largest single category of opium consumers in Southeast Asia were resident Chinese.

In comparison with Southeast Asia, China was a wealthy country, and although the wealth may have been concentrated in the hands of only a small percentage of the population, its very size meant that there was an extraordinarily large number of potential consumers. Moreover, it seems that there was a greater propensity to consume opium among nineteenth century Chinese than among any other contemporary populations. However, it is very difficult to demonstrate this objectively, other than simply to show that Chinese were using more opium than any other people at the time. The explanations for this circumstance are yet to be fully established. Clearly the inability of China to police its borders effectively was one factor. Another was the affluence of certain sectors of the Chinese population and their relatively high level of disposable income, but these circumstances in themselves do not adequately explain the Chinese drug plague.

Eighteenth and early nineteenth century China was a civilization that was close to its peak in terms of cultural accomplishment and wealth. It had a sizeable "leisure class." Considering the type of society portrayed in works of Qing literature such as *The Story of the Stone* by Cao Xueqin (Cao 1973) and *The Scholars*, by Wu Jingzi, (Wu 1957) it is clear that there were a lot of people with not much more to do than entertain themselves, or to be entertained by others. Beyond anecdotes however, very little is known about who used drugs and even less about why they used drugs. We have only the vaguest notions of how many people consumed opium, how much they consumed or how many true "addicts" existed among the population of consumers. Nor is it entirely clear where they lived. Owen and the standard accounts of opium use in China suggest that the habit began in Taiwan and then moved to the maritime provinces of the south, especially Fujian and Canton, and then moved inland and into northern China. In 1820, the Chinese foreign affairs expert, Pao Shih-ch'en claimed that the city of Suzhou had 100,000 addicts. In 1836, foreigners estimated that there were 12.5 million smokers in China, and in 1838 Lin Zexu insisted that 1 percent of the population used the drug. But these are largely guesswork figures. Sir Robert Hart, the head of the Imperial Maritime Customs, estimated in 1881 that two million Chinese (about 0.65 percent of the population) used the drug (Hart 1881). Even Hart's contemporaries felt this was far too low. More recently, Jonathan Spence estimated that 10 percent of the population was probably a more accurate estimate for the late 1880s and that perhaps 3 to 5 percent were "heavy smokers" (Spence 1975). This would have put the 1890 figure at about 40 million smokers.

> But the figures these literati cited were not as important as the appearance of opium smoking. In urban centres or along the routes of trade and in densely-populated river deltas, its existence could not be ignored. Since addiction was costly, it went with leisure time and extra income. Therefore it was usually found among wealthy members of the gentry, officials of the central government (some said one-fifth were addicts), yamen clerks (Lin Tse-hsu estimated a four-fifths addiction rate) and soldiers. While the court was terrified at the thought that the entire government was rotten with addiction, it was also alarmed by the economic consequences of the increasing export of bulk silver.
>
> (Wakeman 1978, p. 178)

It seems likely that at least before 1830, opium was a relatively scarce and expensive item, not many but the very wealthy would have been able to purchase it. If large numbers of the gentry were using the drug, it is probable that at least some gentry women also smoked opium. Studies of opiate use in nineteenth-century England and the United States indicate that large amounts of opium were consumed as a pain-killer. We should also assume, that many upper-class Chinese used or began using opium as a pain-killer. Certainly women with bound feet would have found frequent occasion for using it. Unfortunately, I know of no studies which have explored this issue.

In *The Scholars*, Wu Jingzi, with satirical humor tells the heart-breaking stories of some of the thousands of hopeful members of the literati, desperately studying and sitting for the provincial examinations with the aim of becoming an official. Wu depicts the system as it was in the early eighteenth century, presumably before the rot had really set in, but even then chances of success were pretty slim. By the mid-nineteenth century, the Qing examination system, while it still managed to select a few scholars of high quality, was also open to considerable corruption with degrees being sold to the highest bidders. With such large numbers of candidates and so few offices available, the high level of competition naturally meant a correspondingly high level of failure in the exams. This resulted in widespread unemployment (so far as their preferred careers were concerned) and a high level of frustration among the best-educated and most affluent people of the country. Ichisada Miyazaki, in his classic study of the Chinese examination system estimates that only one in three thousand licentiates, or higher degree holders (those qualified to sit for the provincial examinations) actually were able to secure civil service positions.

> To become an official was the most lucrative as well as the most honorable career in imperial China. Therefore the sons of the propertied intelligentsia converged upon the narrow gates of the examination system, doing their best to pass through them. Those who succeeded all the way to the *chin-shih* degree were delighted, naturally, but inevitably the system also produced a large number of men who experienced the bitterness of repeated failure and spent gloomy lives in hopeless despondency, lamenting their misfortune.
>
> (Miyazaki 1976, p. 121)

This relative lack of opportunity among the most ambitious sector of the traditional elite had always been a major problem as dynasties began to decay. Many of China's rebels had sprung from the ranks of failed examination candidates, and they continued to do so. In 1850, Hong Xiuquan, a four-time failure, would lead the vast Taiping uprising. For those not yet ready to risk their lives challenging the system, however, there was the pipe to ease their pain. While none of these factors are sufficient explanation for why large numbers of the Chinese elite began to use opium, they may at least be taken as evidence of the general intellectual and spiritual malaise that had stricken Chinese culture. In such a situation, the availability of a drug like opium could only exacerbate the decline.

In the years between the beginning of the eighteenth century and the third decade of the nineteenth century, a culture of opium use had been created in China. Even though forbidden, the practice became entrenched, and since this culture was associated with the elite, it became an object of emulation for the lower classes. Like the consumption of other drugs, in other cultures, there was a tendency for the practice to move down the social scale as the item became cheaper and more readily available. It is probable that the demand came to exist before the supply to satisfy it was available. Sidney Mintz (Mintz 1985) shows that this happened with sugar, and Jessica Warner shows a similar phenomenon in the case of gin in eighteenth-century Britain. (Warner 1992; Warner 1993a; Warner 1993b; Warner 1995)

There was too, in China, a fairly well-developed internal economic infrastructure most of which had been in place for centuries. In the half century between 1780 and 1830, a network of trading links had been developed to bring the drug from the southern coast to the interior and to distribute it throughout the country. William Rowe's studies of Hankou show that the city was a major opium trading center. Hankou was already the major trading link between the Lingnan macro-region of Southern China and the rest of the country, so its role in the opium trade was not extraordinary. Opium was never mentioned among Hankou's leading items of trade, but by the 1830s, there were several large warehouses devoted to the local wholesale market in the drug. There were also a number of highly capitalized dealerships operated by Cantonese traders (Rowe 1984, p. 229). Given the existence of an active network to transport and finance the distribution of the drug, it can be assumed that the foundation of a sizeable consumer market was already in place. Very probably, there was a large population of individuals who had perhaps just had a small, tantalizing taste of the drug and who would have taken more, but who could not afford it. Thus, when extraordinarily plentiful supplies suddenly became available in the 1830s, the rapid expansion of the market appears to have been a relatively easy process.

In the 1830s James Holman reported opium smoking to be widespread in the Canton area:

> The use of opium has become so universal among the people of China, that the laws which render it penal, and the proclamations which send forth their daily fulminations against its continuance, have not the slightest effect in checking the prevalence of so general a habit. Smoking houses abound in Canton; and the inhabitants of every class who can furnish themselves with the means to obtain the pipe, are seldom without this article of general luxury. It is a propensity that has seized upon all ranks and classes, and is generally on the increase.
>
> (Quoted in Allen 1853, p. 14)

There was another side to the coin. If the increase in China's user population were not enough of a problem, the opium trade also provided opportunities for many less savory elements of the Chinese social spectrum. Since the trade was illegal, criminals, pirates, petty merchants, secret societies, the riff-raff and marginal people of Chinese society now fell heir to much of the new wealth being generated by the opium trade. As the political and social crisis deepened, many of these individuals now found it possible to develop power bases of their own or to seek protection under other illicit umbrellas. There was also shelter under the wing of the new foreign military and political power that was introduced into China with the system of unequal treaties.

The Opium War and the opium trade

The expansion of the opium trade that occurred with the settlement of the Malwa question led directly to the Opium War between China and Britain. John Crawfurd writing on the eve of the war noted the changed situation in the trade as these events began to unfold.

> Opium is an article calculated to become of vast importance to the agriculture and commerce of India. The growth of the poppy is, at present, confined to a few districts of the lower provinces of Bengal, pretty much in the

same way as the growth of tobacco is confined to a few districts of France, for the purposes of the government monopoly in that country. In the great province of Malwa, however, in the centre of India, it is now freely cultivated, paying an export duty; and to this we, in fact, owe the vast increase which has taken place in the trade in it, within the last twenty years. In India there is a considerable local consumption of this article, especially in some of the northwestern provinces; but the great marts for its consumption are the Malayan islands, the countries lying between India and China, and above all, China itself. We believe we shall not overrate the whole export produce of opium from India, at 24,000 chests a year; nor the export value of every chest, at £120 sterling; making a total value of £2,880,000. The wholesale price of the article to the consumers will certainly amount to a sum of not less than three-and-a-half millions sterling. This is probably a larger sum than is paid by foreign nations for all the wines exported from France, Spain, and Italy.

(Crawfurd 1837, pp. 250–1)

It was worth even more than Crawfurd suggested, Wakeman points out that in 1836, China imported opium valued at $18 million (or about £4 million) which made it the "world's most valuable single commodity trade" of the nineteenth century" (Wakeman 1978).

Although the trade was growing rapidly, the course of expansion was not necessarily a smooth one. The increasing amounts of opium which began arriving in China in the years before the beginning of the Opium War could not be assured immediately of a ready market. Even though the Chinese appetite for the drug had also begun to increase, supplies could easily jump ahead of demand, and the market would be dislocated. Despite the increases in quantity of opium imported, the amount of money which the Chinese actually spent on the drug increased at a far slower rate. According to the figures for opium shipments to China and the total value of the yearly provision, we get some idea of what was happening to the opium market in the four decades before the Opium War (Table 5.1).[2]

The numbers show a couple of things, first is that at the beginning of the nineteenth century, the Chinese were spending between 2 and 3 million Spanish dollars annually for about 4,000 chests of opium or about 160 metric tons. While the availability of price and quantity data is somewhat erratic for these years, the overall trend is fairly clear. Ten years later, (although exact figures are not available) they were spending about twice that, or between 4 and 5 million dollars, but the amount of opium had remained constant. By 1820, they were spending about 8 million for roughly the same amount of opium. The regular supplies of opium reaching China in these years had created a considerable demand for the drug. In 1821, when the Indian government decided to start buying Malwa and auctioning it to traders in Bombay and Calcutta, the system lurched out of control as Malwa producers sought to take advantage of the situation and began to boost their output. There were a series of booms and busts in the trade and a constant tendency to speculate, which in the short run, made the trade seem very risky. Indeed, the traders were very wealthy, or at least they could command vast sums

Table 5.1 Opium shipments to Canton and expenditures 1800–1839

| | Number of Chests | | | | |
Year	Patna and Benares	Malwa	Turkey	Total	Value ($)
1800–1	3,224	1,346	–	4,570	2,376,080
1801–2	1,744	2,203	–	3,447	–
1802–3	2,033	1,259	–	3,292	–
1803–4	2,116	724	–	2,840	–
1804–5	2,322	837	–	3,159	–
1805–6	2,131	1,705	102	3,938	–
1806–7	2,607	1,159	180	4,306	–
1807–8	3,084	1,124	150	4,358	–
1808–9	3,233	985	–	4,208	–
1809–10	3,074	1,487	32	4,593	–
1810–1	3,592	1,376	–	4,968	–
1811–2	2,788	2,103	200	5,091	–
1812–3	3,328	1,638	100	5,066	–
1813–4	3,213	1,556	–	4,769	–
1814–5	2,999	674	–	3,673	–
1815–6	2,723	1,507	80	4,321	–
1816–7	3,376	1,242	488	5,106	–
1817–8	2,911	781	448	4,140	–
1818–9	2,575	977	807	4,359	–
1819–20	1,741	2,265	180	4,186	–
1820–1	2,591	1,653	–	4,244	–
1821–2	3,298	2,278	383	5,459	8,314,600
1822–3	3,181	3,855	–	7,773	7,988,930
1823–4	3,360	5,535	140	9,035	8,515,100
1824–5	5,960	6,663	411	12,434	7,619,625
1825–6	3,810	5,563	–	9,373	7,608,205
1826–7	6,570	5,605	56	12,231	9,610,085
1827–8	6,650	5,504	–	12,434	10,382,141
1828–9	4,903	7,709	1,256	13,868	12,533,115
1829–30	7,443	8,099	715	16,257	12,057,157
1830–1	5,672	12,856	1,428	18,956	12,900,031
1831–2	6,815	9,333	402	16,550	13,796,960*
1832–3	7,598	14,007	380	21,985	13,728,339*
1833–4	7,808	11,715	963	20,486	–
1834–5	10,207	11,678	?	21,885	–
1835–6	14,851	15,351	?	30,202	–
1836–7	12,606	21,427	243	34,776	–
1837–8	19,600	14,773	?	34,373	–
1838–9	18,212	21,988	?	40,200	–

Sources: Greenberg 1951, pp. 220–1 and other JMA records

of money; on the other hand they could easily lose great sums in speculation on the trade. George Alexander Prinsep was quite concerned about these waves of speculation because he feared that they would force out the "reputable" traders. He favored the company's policy of monopoly and recommended a controlled supply. Writing in 1823 he commented:

Now the consumption of China appears to be almost stationary, extending to about 6,000 chests; so that, had the company limited their sales thereto, the assumed average price of 3,000 rupees in Bengal might probably have been supported. The additional 1,500 chests have had the effect of raining the market and destroying at least four-fifths of their opium revenue. The mischief has been augmented by the vain attempts of the speculators of 1822 to keep up the prices in China by holding back, and the consequent influx into that market of more than the excess of the total supply, the imports of last season being stated at 9,000 chests to meet a consumption of 6,000. If the Company devise means hereafter to reduce the total quantity of Malwa opium from about 5,300 to 3,000 chests, prices may again come round, although there must still for some time be a dead stock of former years unsold.

(Prinsep 1971, p. 148)

Obviously, he was wrong about the level of consumption remaining stationary. It was in fact rising, something which the speculators probably knew better than he did. Despite their worries, there is no hint in the sources that the company, or anyone (except perhaps the "speculators") should get out of the opium business. The unsold stocks did not remain "dead" for very long.

With the rise in production the price per chest did indeed fall, but consumption also began to increase. In each year after 1821, successively larger amounts of opium were thrown into the Chinese market and the aggregate sum of money which the Chinese spent on the drug continued to rise, albeit at a slower rate. The other factor, which is much more difficult to measure, is that the demand which had come to exist by 1820, had spurred the development of native Chinese opium cultivation. Recent studies indicate that Chinese domestic production had begun in earnest around 1820 (Benedict 1994; Benedict 1996, ch 2; Lin 1993a). This opium, considered to be of lower quality, fetched a much lower price and was thus attractive to the less affluent consumer. It is difficult to be certain about the extent of this cultivation, but Lin Man-huong estimates that by 1836 China was producing about 5,000 pikuls or a bit less than 5,000 chests, mainly in the provinces of Yunnan and Sichuan. The decision then, by the East India Company in 1831, to allow Malwa production to rise freely and to deliberately increase the production of Patna and Benares opium as well, had a further destabilizing impact on the market. The British do not seem to have been able to stop themselves, so much of their capital was now tied up in opium and so much of India's trade depended on opium, that it seems they would have been foolish to give it up. Crawfurd's figures from about 1836 give an idea of the extent to which opium now overwhelmed the trade of India (Table 5.2). For India, opium had come to make up nearly one-third of her total exports. And for China, by 1839, opium was indeed a drug on the market.

The Chinese government continued to oppose the trade on an official level. Its policy, however, was filled with ambiguities. Because of the high level of corruption, the trade had grown and flourished since the 1780s, and the government had

Table 5.2 All British India's exports, ca. 1836

Product	Quantity	Value (£)
Opium	24,000 Chests or 1,640 T	£2,880,000
Indigo	10,000,000 lb	2,500,000
Cotton wool	100,000,000 lb	1,500,000
Cotton Mfgrs	n/a	250,000
Raw silk	1,600,000 lb	950,000
Silk Mfgrs	n/a	200,000
Corn and grain	468,750 qrs	375,000
Sugar	16,000 T	256,000
Saltpetre	14,000 T	160,000
		Total £9,071,000

Source: Crawfurd 1837, p. 253

not been able to muster the will to stop it despite repeated campaigns. As soon as the heat was off, the traders went back to business as usual. So far as many Chinese bureaucrats were concerned, the laws against opium were little more than an excuse for squeezing the traders. The sudden expansion of the trade in the 1830s, however, together with the realization that millions of taels of silver were now flowing out of the country and that thousands more Chinese were falling victim to drug addiction all led to a stiffening of resolve.

In 1839, the Daoguang Emperor sent Commissioner Lin Zexu with instructions to stop the trade. Thus began the final chain of events that led to the first Opium War. This, however, was simply the final, almost inevitable step in a much longer process that had been underway for over a half-century. The opium trade had developed as a "necessary aberration" alongside the EIC's monopoly of the China tea trade and the so-called Canton system, by which the Chinese government conducted foreign maritime trade. The system was complicated by the fact that the Canton system was also what passed for China's system of international relations. Legitimate trade as well as all other foreign relations with the "southern barbarians" were conducted by the Cohong, a guild of the principal merchants of Canton who were authorized by the Chinese government. It was from them that the EIC purchased tea and the other products of China which it shipped to Europe. The Cohong dealt with all foreigners in Canton.

Initially, there were no country traders nor was the trade in opium considered to be of great importance. Because the opium trade had been banned by imperial decree since 1729, the EIC did not officially involve itself in the opium trade in China. It seems, however, that it was often carried on company ships as part of the private cargo of the captains, crew members or other company servants who were permitted shares of the cargo. Although the company had made one or two attempts to extend its control of the trade "downstream," these all ended in loss and failure, thus by the 1790s the company decided to leave the opium trade to others. Nevertheless, in Canton, the country traders operated under the aegis of the company, which was responsible to the Cohong for their conduct. Thus, the trade in opium was always conducted with a certain degree of subterfuge, while on the other hand, officers of the company, the Cohong and all of the Canton officials knew of the trade and many, as individuals, were involved in it.

The role of the British government was even more ambiguous, at least on the surface. If the Chinese opposed the opium trade officially, but unofficially allowed it to flourish, the British government occasionally condemned it (at least in these early years) but did nothing to impede it and by their actions, generally promoted it. This was nowhere more apparent than in the Opium War itself. In many key historical events it is often possible to see a point, at least in retrospect, where things might have been changed, or, where the outcome turned on the personality of a single individual. In the case of the Opium War this does not seem to be the case. While it is clear the war might not have erupted so sharply had someone other than Commissioner Lin been sent to Canton, it seems inevitable that sooner or later the Chinese would have felt themselves required to take forceful action against the trade. Conversely, it is hard to find a moment when the British might have turned things around and given up the trade.[3] Despite W. E. Gladstone's famous condemnation of the British position as "morally indefensible," the British government was not deterred in 1839 from sending a fleet to China to defend its opium traders. Moreover, Owen maintains that Gladstone's statement was little more than "political manoeuvering" (Owen 1934, p. 177). Certainly when he himself became Prime Minister, little was done to impede the trade. Assuming that the tacit support of the government actually reflected a reluctance to stop the trade, it seems almost inevitable that there would be an Opium War and even more inevitable that China would be defeated.

The problem of silver also seemed to make the prospect of war inevitable. Lin Man-huong has concluded that there was a net outflow of something like $150,000,000 (Spanish/Mexican) from China between 1814 and 1850. This sum comprised 13 percent of China's total silver supply and 11 percent of the country's money supply. Clearly the opium trade had a great deal to do with the onset of the financial difficulties in southern China that led up to the Opium War and then to the Taiping Rebellion (Lin 1989, p. 267; Lin 1991, pp. 4–6).

China's loss was the gain of others. Britain and the United States were the major beneficiaries of this peculiar cash flow. A great deal of this sum, although largely credited to India, actually found its way back to London, New York, and Boston by means of bills of exchange. Only enough to refinance the next year's crop and to help the Indian government cover the deficits for its many wars seems to have remained in India. Thus, at a time when the entire world was suffering from a generalized silver shortage the British, and to a lesser extent the US, were able to use opium as capital. For China, the same was true, opium began to circulate as currency, but did little to benefit the local economy. Awareness of the monetary crisis was one of the factors that led the Daoguang Emperor to appoint Lin Zexu to carry out the opium suppression policy.

China had waited too long, however. If firm action had been taken earlier, it might have been possible to force the British/Indian government to abandon the trade. Perhaps even the 1820s would not have been too late, although it is a moot point. The traders were vulnerable to crackdowns and, if their products could not be sold, then they could not turn over their capital. That was their great concern. They needed to get their capital back again every year so that it could be reinvested in the next year's crop and so the company, and later the Indian government, would have the cash flow to pay off its own debts. In these cases, the Indian government was the lender of last resort. And, by the mid-1820s, the trade had become so valuable and so necessary to the Indian government that they really could not do without it, despite John Crawfurd's opinion.

If the trade failed completely, or if speculation was so extreme that the traders could not retrieve their capital, then the Indian government would, and did, bail them out. In late 1836, speculation in the Calcutta bazaar drove prices up to over Rs1,200 per chest. In Singapore, the price of Patna opium reached $700 per chest (or about Rs1400). In November of 1836, the Canton price was quoted at $785. This rise was partly driven by rumors that the Chinese government was about to legalize the opium trade. It seems also to have been connected to speculative booms in Britain and the US. When the rumors proved false, the price dropped dramatically. John Prinsep, who was Secretary to the Government of India, wrote a minute in 1837, which told the story of this boomlet. The Calcutta and Canton speculators stood to lose in the neighborhood of Rs2.5 million (Trocki 1990, pp. 61–2).[4] Of course, they were only paper losses, since the money was actually owed to the Indian government. That sum was based on the total that had been bid on opium at the Calcutta auctions in January and February 1837. Rather than hold the speculators to their offers, the government decided to ignore the bids made at the January and February auctions and recalculate the value of the opium based on the prices for which it actually sold. The government justified writing off this huge amount so as to ensure that the opium brokers in Calcutta would still have "capital to work the trade" in the future.

While the government might be expected to forgive these traders their debts on one occasion, it seems doubtful that they could have been expected to continue to do so on a more or less permanent basis. They were faced with a similar situation in 1839, when Commissioner Lin confiscated 20,000 chests of opium in the hands of Canton traders. In this case Elliot promised the traders that they would be reimbursed if they turned the opium over to him, so he could give it to Lin. In that case, the traders were reimbursed out of the indemnity the Chinese were forced to pay after the war,[5] so again, in this case, it cost the government none of its own money.

Given the technological and organizational advantages now enjoyed by the European states, China's defeat was virtually a foregone conclusion. The British victory, however, did not legalize the opium trade. The Treaty of Nanking in 1842, opened the five Treaty Ports, ceded Hong Kong to Britain and placed China under one of the first "unequal treaties" in east Asia. It established a new system of foreign relations between China and the west which ultimately came to include consular jurisdiction over British subjects and extraterritoriality. Because this and the subsequent treaties which Europeans made with China, all contained a "most-favored-nation" clause, every new concession which was wrested from

China, was shared by all. Among other things, the treaty also restricted China's ability to tax trade, but opium was not even mentioned. Outside of the initial conflict between Commissioner Lin and Elliott, the opium trade apparently ceased to be an influential force in Anglo–Chinese relations. The British certainly did not claim they were fighting for the opium traders, although many opium traders certainly fought for the British. The government defended itself against critics maintaining that the opium trade was irrelevant to the war.

The role of opium, while not apparent, remained important, and, opium traders did much to influence the outbreak of the war and the peace treaty. The manner in which the British government was able to obfuscate its reasons for making war upon China however, gave the enterprise an air of deniability. This has made it possible for an entire generation of historians to claim that it was not really an opium war (Tan 1978). For a time in the 1950s and 1960s, it was fashionable among some British empire historians to call it the "Anglo-Chinese War" and to suggest that if they had been trading beans, then it might have been called the "Bean War." It would be tedious here to recapitulate what has already been eloquently argued by so many others in the years since Fairbank first began to write about China. Fay, Wakeman, Tan Chung and Chang Hsin-pao, Arthur Waley and others, have all made the case for an Opium War quite convincingly, and there has been no credible response from those who would argue the contrary (Chang 1964; Fay 1975; Tan 1978; Wakeman 1966; Wakeman 1978; Waley 1958).

Opium, however, was no longer the most pressing problem that faced the Qing dynasty. Not only did foreigners now descend on China in greater numbers and with even more demands, but the humiliation and social and economic dislocations of the war had a devastating impact on south China. Wakeman's groundbreaking study of the period shows that the war was a direct cause of the Taiping Rebellion (Wakeman 1966). There was a rise in secret society activity in Guangdong province; a relocation of the pirates, from the coasts to the rivers where they now preyed on the wealthy villages of the delta; and a rise in banditry from former militiamen who kept their weapons. There was also a rise in clan feuding and wars between speech groups, especially the Hakka and Pundi.

> In Canton city itself, urban crime increased in step with unemployment. For, when the Treaty of Nanking opened Shanghai to foreign trade, much of Canton's commerce was diverted north. This shift also affected the hinterland because tens of thousands of boatmen and coolies who had once packed tea and silk down Kiangsi or across the Fukienese mountains found themselves out of work.
>
> (Wakeman 1975, pp. 141–2)

The Opium War did not solve the opium question. Although matters were not as they were before, opium was neither forbidden by the British nor legalized by the Chinese. This was, so far as the most influential opium traders were concerned, the best of all possible worlds. Since the end of the company's monopoly in 1834, the country traders and the community of brokers in Canton had become the leading force in relations between China and the west. It is time to look at their role as events unfolded both before and after the Opium War.

The opium agents

By the time of the Opium War, the country traders had been transformed. The major ones had settled down and set up private agency houses. Initially, the status, indeed the very existence of these trading firms in Canton was anomalous according to the formalities that had governed trade between the various European companies and the Cohong. In the half-century that had passed between 1779 when John Henry Cox turned up in Canton to collect a debt for some of his father's clocks and the Opium War, the firm he founded and others like it had made a place for themselves in the China trade (Williamson 1975, p. 11). Most of these were connected to trading firms in Calcutta or Bombay, which in turn were connected to firms in London. There were also links with similar communities of Anglo-Scottish and American traders in other parts of Southeast Asia, particularly the Straits Settlements, Batavia, Manila, and as time passed, Australia.

By 1840, however, the traders in Canton, together with their "friends" in Calcutta and Bombay, were the primary traders in opium. Most of these firms survived by taking consignments from others on commission. Only occasionally did individuals in these firms "adventure" to trade on their own accounts. While they were also the primary dealers in Indian cottons and Straits produce, the bulk (or rather the greatest value) of their business was in opium and had been since the beginning of the century. The most famous and long-lived of these agency houses was Jardine Matheson and Co. which was, in fact, the mid-nineteenth-century successor of Cox's firm (Greenberg 1951, pp. 222–3).[6]

> In the first years of their partnership [e.g. from 1822 to the 1830s], Jardine and Matheson traded almost entirely in opium. It was, in Jardine's opinion, 'the safest and most gentlemanlike speculation I am aware of' . . . Jardine's avoided speculation by working on commission except when they could buy very cheaply. Prices could vary as much as $550 to $1375 per chest. Their average profit was $20 per chest. By the 1830s they handled over 6000 chests per year for an annual profit of over $100,000. After the end of the EIC's monopoly, they went into the tea trade and later into insurance and banking.
> (Crisswell 1981, p. 33)

Their handling of opium had come, as we have seen, from an incidental sideline of the India–China country trade. On the China coast, their trade had gone through a number of rearrangements. There were three discrete phases in the management of the trade. Between 1755–1820 was what might be called the "Old Canton system," which largely concerned the trade between the EIC and the Cohong. Country traders appeared during these years and became involved in products outside the company monopoly. Like the company servants, they were not allowed to remain at Canton during part of the year and thus maintained a base at the Portuguese settlement of Macau. The opium trade was then run at Macau and the actual landing and storage of the opium itself was done at the island of Whampoa some thirty miles up the Canton River from its entrance at the Bogue, or the Bocca Tigris, where the Chinese forts were. The days of the Macau trade ended in 1820, during one of the periodic crackdowns on the opium trade by the Chinese government and a coincidental attempt by the Portuguese government to monopolize the opium trade for itself.

In order to avoid the complications of Macau and to find a new storage and landing site for the opium which was not so close to Canton as Whampoa, the agencies began to station receiving vessels at the "Outer Anchorages," as this phase of the trade was known. These were more or less safe anchorages near Lintin Island and in a number of other spots near Hong Kong harbor, and what were until 1997, the New Territories. These vessels, most of them simply hulks, were actually floating warehouses, many of which were owned and managed by the large American firms, such as Russell & Co., but the British firms of Dent & Co. and Jardine Matheson also maintained their own receiving vessels at these anchorages. The European and other opium traders (many of the firms were Parsi, Armenian, Jewish, Spanish, etc.) actually conducted business in Canton or Macau. Chinese opium wholesalers would come to the Canton offices, arrange for a purchase of so many chests of Patna, Benares, Malwa, or Turkish opium and make their payments to the agents there either in silver or in bills of exchange. Upon receiving proofs of payment, they would send their smuggling boats, the so-called "fast crabs" or "scrambling dragons," to pick up the assigned number of chests at the receiving ships at the Outer Anchorages near Lintin. The whole transaction was done with complete trust and without any of the parties actually seeing through the entire transaction. It was, for all but the men on the actual smuggling boats, a system clad in complete "deniability."

> The fact remains that the parties who bought the drug at Calcutta did not themselves sell the drug at Canton, while the actual sellers there were not the owners. As for the original producer, the Government of India, it turned its back the moment the Tank Square auctions were over. One might suppose that to diffuse and dilute responsibility had been the whole intent of the arrangement.
>
> (Fay 1975, p. 45)

While it may be difficult to demonstrate intent in this case, it certainly was the effect.

The third phase, the "Coast Trade" began in 1832. After attempts by the Chinese government to shut down the trade in the early 1830s, Jardine and Dent began to seek other locations for the trade that were outside the Canton delta area. They began sending fast and well-armed opium ships up the coast and having the captains negotiate with the local merchants and mandarins for direct opium sales. We get an intimate picture of some of these early voyages from the journals of James Innes, one of the more daring opium traders. Two of his logs are included in the Jardine Matheson Archives. On his first voyage in December, 1832 aboard the *Jamesina*, one of Jardine's ships, he wrote how liberating and profitable it was for him to be able to sell opium without a broker, as was done in Canton. At "Chinchew Bay," he describes a scene in which eager purchasers flocked to the vessel. For several days, the ship was virtually overrun with Chinese, while he, the shroff, and another European sat up far into the night selling opium to "all comers, high and low." While waiting, some smoked opium and fell asleep on the couch in his cabin and others occasionally napped on the floor while the abacus rattled, and Chinese and Europeans communicated by sign language. In four days, he sold opium worth 187,877 Taels or about $200,000 (JMA, A7/231, Log of James Innes, "Jamesina" 1832).

To some degree aspects of the outer anchorage and coast trade systems prevailed until 1860 and the legalization of the trade. With the Treaty of Nanking in 1842, the trade entered a fourth phase, the Hong Kong period. From this point on, the new port became the major opium depot, thus obviating the need for the receiving ships to be located far from the head offices. Now the agency houses were able to store the opium in nearby receiving ships or their own warehouses, because it was on British soil. Alexander Matheson remarked in one of his first letters from Hong Kong:

> We are gradually settling down here – and I doubt not we shall find ourselves more comfortable in the course of a month or two than we have ever been in China. It is an immense Convenience having our shipping almost within hail of the office and enables us to carry on the Coast trade with far more facility.
>
> (JMA, C6/3 PLB, Alexander Matheson, to David Jardine,
> Calcutta, 27 March 1844, p. 345)

The coast trade expanded and while the treaty ports were now open to "legitimate" trade, the opium trade continued as a contraband activity beyond the bounds of these ports and at other places not included among the treaty ports (Greenberg 1951, 46–9).

With each of these changes in the trading system, the actual amounts of opium flowing into China increased, so that by the mid-1840s, opium shipments rapidly surpassed 50,000 chests annually. Perhaps the jumps were not so spectacular as had taken place during the 1830s, but they now became a consistent feature of the trade.

Opium and the sailing revolution

The prohibitions of the Chinese government were not the only difficulty with which the opium traders had to cope in these early days of the trade. The decision by the Indian government to increase opium production put unprecedented strains on the transportation system. The old "country wallahs," as the original country trading ships were known, could only make one trip a year at best from Calcutta, and one every two years from Bombay. This was not enough, Fay notes:

> By the late 1820s, however, too many chests of opium were trying to reach the China coast to be accommodated in so leisurely a fashion. Opium merchants wanted something faster. They wanted to be able to buy breaks of Patna or Benares at the Company's January sale and put them on the China coast in February. They wanted to be able to load again in May and have the ship back at Calcutta in time to load a third time in July. They wanted, in short, several round trips a year. That meant defying the pattern of the monsoon.
>
> (Fay 1975, pp. 50–1)

Although they could tack, the country ships, and most of the other merchant vessels of the era were incapable of making the run from the Straits of Singapore to the China coast into the teeth of the northeast monsoon. The answer to this obstacle was the clipper ship, a new style of vessel with a relatively small cargo space, a slim, streamlined hull and as much canvas as it could possibly carry without capsizing. These were ships completely made for the opium trade. They needed to be heavily armed and thus had to carry large European crews of well-trained men who could not only sail, but be ready to fight off pirates and coastal officials to protect and deliver their high-value, low bulk cargoes, and be depended on to come back with the profits. Until the second half of the twentieth century they were the fastest things afloat.

The first clipper to sail to Canton against the wind was Jardine's *Red Rover*, which was built and sailed by Captain William Clifton in 1830. The ship was modeled after the American *Prince de Neufchatel*, a blockade runner in the War of 1812, the only difference was that the *Rover* was rigged as a bark and the *Prince* as a brigantine (Scott 1969, pp. 31–3).[7] Charles Burton Buckley tells the story of one of the vessel's early passages through Singapore in January, 1832. The ship had attracted a lot of attention when it first arrived, and there were many who believed that she was incapable of beating up to China into the teeth of the northeast monsoon. There was heavy wagering against her chances.

> One morning, about a month after her departure from Singapore, the mercantile community was thrown into a state of considerable excitement by the appearance of a crippled vessel, flying a St. Andrew's white cross on a blue field – 'Jardine's private flag.' Her main-top-gallant mast was gone; the fore top-mast, evidently a jury one, had a royal set for the top-sail. The mizen mast looked all askew, and, in fact, the 'bonnie barkie' was a wreck. Of course, the 'I told you so' were triumphant. 'Impossible, we knew it.' Their opponents were as dejected as the others were jubilant. Meanwhile, Captain Clifton came on shore to breakfast with his agent. The worthy skipper's face was a picture of melancholy. He was limp with fatigue. He threw his hat on a

Figure 5.1 The clipper ships *Ariel* and *Taepeng* in a "tea race" near the British Isles. In Asia the *Ariel*, which belonged to Jardine Matheson and Co., frequently carried opium on its way to China
Source: By permission of the National Maritime Museum Neg. No. A7187

table, tumbled into a chair, and seemed as if about to burst into tears. His host and others tried to cheer the mortified mariner, who refused to be comforted; but, like many others on similar occasions, he rather overdid his part. A suspicion was raised in the mind of one of those present, who, quietly rising from his seat, went into the verandah and examined the cast-away hat, withdrawing from it a Macao newspaper only a week old. The 'gaff was blown,' as the vulgar expression is; the secret was out, and, the wily captain burst into a hearty laugh. He had beat up against the monsoon in eighteen days without losing a spar; all the ravaged look of his vessel was a comedy, and the 'I told you so' party, frightfully 'sold', suddenly collapsed.

(Buckley 1903, pp. 324–5)

These ships changed the China trade completely. They could make three voyages per year from either side of India and they did not have to stop along the way to buy or sell miscellaneous cargo as did the country ships. Their loads of opium and specie were so valuable that they could afford to be dedicated to them alone. For the recently founded British colonies in the Straits, this was not an entirely welcome development. The clippers had made them virtually redundant because it was no longer necessary to have a safe stopover halfway between Calcutta and Canton. Moreover, Straits cargoes were not as necessary as they once were to balance the trade deficit. As a result, those European traders who had settled in Penang and Singapore in the hope of controlling a share of the opium trade to China were disappointed and they now had to find a way of making a living out of their immediate hinterlands if they were to survive. In the meantime, the advantage in the opium trade passed to traders such as Jardine Matheson and Dent & Co. who were positioned in Canton and ready to forge ahead when any opening might occur in the China market. Jardine Matheson, Dent and the American firm, Russell & Co. quickly emerged as the dominant houses in the China opium trade. Each firm soon had its own fleet of clippers almost constantly at sea between India and China. Opium now came to the China coast in a steady stream, each ship carrying 500 to 1000 chests.

The opium was stockpiled at Hong Kong and from there shipped by smaller clippers up the coast to smaller receiving vessels stationed at various ports along the coast. Since the opium trade was still illegal in the 1840s and 1850s, the trade avoided the five Treaty Ports and established itself elsewhere. In 1847, Jardine had receiving vessels stationed at Amoy, Namoa, Chmmo Bay and Whampoa. Four or five small vessels were constantly plying between these ports and Hong Kong with fresh supplies, while at the same time the firm had five larger clippers carrying opium from India to Hong Kong. Jardine's also had a 700 ton receiving ship anchored in Hong Kong harbor. Besides Dent and Russell, other firms then in the trade included Burns, Macivar & Co., Gilman & Co., Pyver & Co., a Parsee firm, Rustomjee & Co. and the Bombay-based firm of David Sassoon & Sons. The opium fleet, in 1847, consisted of about 50 vessels in all, including both the larger 200–300 ton clippers running between India and China and the 60–150-ton vessels in the coast trade (Allen 1853, pp. 15–16). The *Lanrick* was typical of these clippers.

> The vessels conveying the drug from India to China are probably the finest boats in the world. The *Lanrick*, of 283 tons register, built at Liverpool, cost £13,000, belonging to Jardine & Co. is superior in sailing on a wind to any man-of-war. I made a voyage in her down the China seas to Java, in 1845, in the teeth of the monsoon, when she was under the command of one of the most skilful and daring seamen that ever sailed. Frequently we were running eight and nine knots close hauled, and carrying royals, when a frigate would have reefed top-sails and coursers. In one of her voyages the *Lanrick* carried 1250 chests of Bengal opium, valued at £200,000. The *Lanrick*, like other vessels of her class, was fully armed with long nine-pounders, musketry, etc . . . Their commanders are generally educated men, of gentlemanly manners, very hospitable, of generous dispositions, well-skilled in seamanship, and of a courage and boldness unsurpassed.
>
> (Allen 1853, p. 18)

We can calculate that if Jardines made its usual $20 per chest commission on that shipment, the vessel would have paid back nearly half of its original cost. Of course, such a vessel normally made three voyages a year. Thus, the capital costs of the opium business were rapidly paid off, and this was important. Given the difficulties of the trade, a few of these ships were lost every year. Basil Lubbock mentions pirates, typhoons, and other maritime hazards (such as the Paracels' reefs) as some of the normal dangers of the trade (Lubbock 1933).

It was only through the possession of such fleets and of a network of delivery sites that firms like Jardine, Dent and Russell were able to dominate the opium trade. So long as the trade remained illegal, the expensive infrastructure of clippers and delivery ships was a necessity of doing business. At the end of the Opium War, William Jardine expressed his satisfaction that the trade had not been legalized by the Treaty of Nanking. It would thus be possible, he wrote, to keep out "men of small capital" (Le Fevour 1968, p. 13).

However, even as the clipper ships were at their height, they were already being replaced by steamships. The first steam-powered vessels had arrived in China during the Opium War. By the late 1840s they became a regular feature of Asian commerce. Again, as in the case of the clippers, these boats were called into being because of the opium trade. The high value of the cargoes made it possible to initiate regular monthly runs between India and China occupying only 15 to 20 days each way. In 1852, the steamer *Ganges* sailed from Bombay with a cargo of 2,500 chests of opium, the largest quantity ever carried in one vessel (Allen 1853, p. 19). Because of their relative security, compared to clippers and other forms of sailing craft, the steamers now began to take over the opium trade, the mails, the passenger traffic, and it soon became possible to carry even greater quantities of cargo. The nature of Asian trade changed entirely.

Opium and the information revolution

Not only did cargo move faster, but information now moved faster and the traditional opacity that had characterized markets in earlier days began to dissolve. It was now possible to move not only drugs and money, but also market information between Canton and Calcutta in a matter of weeks. If the Chinese government launched a new opium suppression campaign, or if there was a sudden rush to buy opium in Canton, the news would be back to Calcutta within a month and would have an immediate impact on the prices at the next auction. This had the effect of adding to the volatility of the market, at least in the short run. Beyond this, however, it also tied the opium economy more closely to the global economy. As early as 1837, it was evident that the economies of Asia were linked to those of Europe and America. The crash in the opium market in early 1837 was, through global movements of silver, linked to roughly simultaneous financial panics in the United States and in Britain (Trocki 1990, pp. 59–61).

For firms like Jardines, information was almost as important as the movement of products and the accumulation of profits. One thing that emerges from the study of the firm's correspondence is the stress placed on market information. As brokers for a wide network of other traders, Jardine's took pains to collect information from their clients, or "constituents" as they were called, as well as to distribute it. Very often an inquiry from a prospective constituent about the market for some product in China would be rewarded with a detailed discussion of the state of the current market and possible future directions of the particular trade. In addition, the firm would include a copy of its current "Opium Circular" (Appendix 2).

Jardine triumphant

The 1860s saw the height of Jardine's success in the opium trade. Their system of clippers and steamers, their receiving vessels and their on-shore connections had given them a pre-eminent position on the China coast. In India their links with key firms in both Calcutta and Bombay made it possible for them to exercise considerable leverage at that end of the trade as well. Opium, which had dominated European commerce with China since the beginning of the century, continued to be the major import through the 1860s. With prices rising and output increasing, it perhaps seemed that legalization would bring even greater success to the European opium traders. That however, would not be the case. The very success of the trade and the improvements in European technology ultimately pushed even the Jardines out of the business. However, this was not the end for them, or for the trade. The firm went on to other pursuits and the expansion of the trade was left to other merchants.

The trade balance between China and the west had also been redressed. After lurching radically in favor of the west in the years immediately before and after the Opium War, China had once again regained its ability to attract import dollars. The growth of the tea and silk trade in the 1850s and 1860s brought fresh flows of cash back into China. Nonetheless, much of that was immediately turned around to pay for opium imports. On the other hand, China now began to "export" its own people on a massive scale. The collapse of civil order in south China that came with the Taiping Rebellion was an economic disaster for the region. Hundreds and thousands of impoverished Chinese now began migrating to the world which had been opened up to them by European commerce and shipping. So far as I know, no one has ever attempted to calculate China's trade balance by including the value of labor which she exported in the years between 1850 and 1930. Nor has the amount of money which these coolies remitted to their native villages ever been thrown into the balance. Nevertheless, the economic situation of China in the second half of the nineteenth century cannot be understood without some consideration being given to these factors. In terms of transfers of wealth, and the potential to produce wealth, China continued to undergo vast transformations. It is difficult to tell whether the migration of labor was a greater loss than could be recouped by the remittances. Nor is it possible to link, in any systematic way, the relationship between opium cash flows and migration flows, but it seems worth raising the issue. Finally, however much money they may have sent back to China, these laborers now became the largest consumers of opium in Southeast Asia, and because of their production as well as their consumption, were largely responsible for the beginnings of the capitalist transformation in the Nanyang. This question shall be addressed in Chapter 7.

6   In the hands of Jews and Armenians

The legalization of opium

The second half of the nineteenth century saw major readjustments in the opium trade. The legalization of the trade had two important results. First, it brought about the trade's "Asianization," and secondly, it gave great impetus to the domestic production of opium inside China. In some respects, these were the same things, but so far as the international opium trade was concerned, by the 1870s, opium had ceased to be a major concern for European trading houses in Asia. On the other hand, the process they had begun grew to unheard of proportions both in China and throughout colonial Asia. Despite the withdrawal of British traders, the British empire itself continued to rely heavily on opium profits. During these years, the political economy of opium moved into a new phase in which it functioned as a regular item of taxation and became a fiscal support for almost every Asian state.

The opium trade in China was legalized after the Second Opium War, or the Lorcha "Arrow" War of 1857–60, with the Treaty of Tianjin. This treaty, as Alexander Matheson had feared earlier, actually canceled out the factors which had given the Hong Kong agency houses their great prominence in the opium trade. As a result, merchants who had more intimate connections with both producers and consumers, and who could reduce the cost of doing business at the far upstream and downstream ends of the trade, gained the advantage. In India, this meant that control of the trade fell to merchants who could accept the risks of direct investment in commodity production and could thus guarantee their control of the drug at its source. On the other hand, those who had access to distribution networks inside of China and elsewhere, could monopolize or at least significantly control, retail sales of the drug.

As this happened, European middlemen were squeezed out, or at least marginalized, and the trade passed into the hands of locally based Asian traders. In India, where Parsi, Armenian, Jewish and Muslim firms had always played an important role in the opium trade, the competitive advantage of being white disappeared. In China, European involvement in the trade had never extended beyond the receiving vessels. Legalization may have opened the doors of China to British–Indian opium, but it was little help to British traders in the long run, and ultimately it fostered increased competition for Indian opium.

The legalization of the opium trade initially unleashed a wave of speculation and overproduction. Once all of the excitement and speculation related to the legalization itself died down and a crash had eliminated the unwise, much of the risk and volatility went out of the market. The monopolies took over. This took about five years. The British government in India had developed a systematic control of the production on both sides of the subcontinent. The management of the cultivation by the Opium Agencies in Patna and Ghazipur had become a tightly controlled regime. European agents and their Indian subordinates knew the potential output per *bigha* of virtually every village in every district of their regions. The costs of producing and delivering a chest of opium to Calcutta were calculated to the last *pie*. The annual reports of the opium agents for the 1870s show that detailed records were kept of the annual variation in the costs of poppy waste for packaging, and of mango wood for the chests, to say nothing of the costs of land, labor and of opium itself. In Bihar and Benares, it was possible, allowing for the vagaries of the weather, to carefully adjust the size of the crop and the number of chests reaching the market at any given time (India 1871).

While the size of the Malwa crop was not subject to similar controls, the Indian government could, through the "pass duty," manipulate the price of Malwa, thus ensuring that its price was always high enough to give the government a comfortable profit margin for Patna and Benares opium. The Indian government ultimately sought to stabilize the trade. The government did not relish speculation. After all, its revenue depended in great measure on the income from opium, and administrators preferred to have a revenue that was predictable. This did not stop them, nonetheless, from pushing the cultivation to its limits once the doors of China had been firmly beaten down.

The early 1860s was a boom period for Asian commerce. This was partly related to the demand for Indian cotton created by the American Civil War, and partly to the newly legal opium market in China, but most other products experienced a rising demand and increasing prices as well. To meet these demands, Indian cotton production rose along with that of opium. The government itself pushed Indian opium production to an early high of 92,131 chests in 1865–6. This figure included both Malwa and government opium. That crop, however, came in the year the bubble burst, and only 88,433 chests were actually exported. In the following year production dipped to just below 70,000 chests, but then went back up into the high 70,000s and 80,000s for the next twenty-five years. Between 1876 and 1885, Indian production hit its peak, never dropping below an annual output of 90,000 chests. In 1880, it reached the all time high of 105,000 chests, or well over 6,000 tons of raw opium. After 1885, Indian production gradually began to decline, but maintained an annual average of about 65,000 chests up until 1909, when international controls began to come into effect (Figure 6.1). By way of comparison, in the early 1990s, global output of all opiates, illegal and legal, was based on about 4,000 tons of raw opium. Modern opium production and consumption, despite the great attention given to illegal production and use of opiates such as heroin, has been far less than it was a century ago.

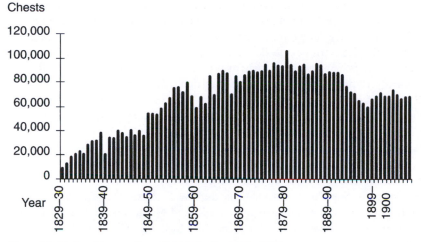

Chests

Figure 6.1 Opium Exports from British India, 1829–1906

The price profile of Indian opium shows that drastic fluctuations in the price of a chest of opium disappeared after 1866, nonetheless there were a few nasty bumps between 1860 and 1866. As the trade adjusted to the new conditions of legalization, prices fluctuated along with production levels. When the Indian output rose rapidly in the early 1860s, prices quickly fell, with the price of a chest of Patna opium falling from over $700 to only $415 between early 1860 and March, 1865 (Figure 6.2). As soon as Indian authorities reduced production levels however, the price moved back up to around $700. This shows that Chinese demand very quickly began to catch up with the expanding supply. The fluctuations in the price of Malwa are more reflective of the changing amount of the pass duty in these years than of the actual value of the product. But here too, production increased through the 1880s and then began to level out, and a relatively consistent quantity was produced until about 1893 and then production declined until it leveled out again at just over 50,000 chests per annum (see Figure 6.1). After 1865 the price too levelled out to just over $600 per chest and stayed there for the next forty years.

Withdrawal of British traders

Despite the great advantages that supported their position, the situation of European trading houses in China was never entirely secure. So long as the opium came from British-controlled territory, and so long as British traders possessed favorable access to the Indian opium market, British control of the international opium trade could be taken for granted. So long as opium was carried in British trading ships which were owned and controlled by the Hong Kong trading houses, they had an advantage. The infrastructure of clippers and receiving ships had been financed by opium profits and was vital to its continuance, so long as the trade remained illegal. The legalization of the opium trade now opened key aspects of the commerce to the Chinese, other Asians and to British companies based in the metropole. Shipping was a case in point. Although firms like Jardine Matheson made the move to steam as soon as it became practicable, they could not compete with firms such as the Peninsular and Oriental Steamship Company (P&O) which began operating regularly scheduled services to the China coast in the early 1850s. After the Treaty of Tianjin, anyone could buy opium in India and ship it via the P&O direct to Chinese buyers in any open Chinese port. In fact, Chinese buyers themselves could purchase opium in India through their own brokers. Jardine's and the other European firms lost most of their major advantages.

Thus, after 1860, European traders focused on developing stronger positions in the Calcutta and Bombay auction markets. Stiff competition during the 1860s drove out all but the most efficient and well-placed trading houses. The international trade in opium between India and China thus fell to large-scale, well-organized companies. By 1860, Jardine Matheson, of Hong Kong, and its Calcutta associate, Jardine Skinner & Co., had established a dominant position in the Calcutta market, giving them virtual control of the export of the Indian government production, a position which they maintained for the next decade. Likewise, through their informal, but well-established arrangements with the firms of Jamsetjee Jeejeebhoy & Co. and Remington & Co. in Bombay, Jardine's also enjoyed an important share of the Malwa opium trade. In fact, the three firms had joined together in an informal "Malwa Opium Syndicate" which functioned for thirty years. Through 1865, Jardine's handled close to £300,000 (about $1,200,000) worth of opium annually, on commission alone. In addition, they were investing heavily on their own account and in concert with their affiliated firms (Le Fevour 1968, pp. 19–26).

Their strong position and cozy arrangements however faced serious challenges in the late 1860s, and by 1871 Jardine's was forced to withdraw entirely from the opium trade except for minor commissions. The great rival of the Jardine's Malwa syndicate, by the middle of the nineteenth century, was the firm of David Sassoon & Co. of Bombay. Sassoon, a relative late-comer to the opium trade, had developed a more centralized form of business organization. Success in the Indian trade depended upon organization, and Sassoon's had made that one of their major strengths. "After 1860, all dealers in China, regardless of experience, faced the same tax and the growing competition of Chinese drugs, so that prices and costs in India became crucial to continued success in the trade" (Le Fevour 1968, p. 26).

David Sassoon, who belonged to a Jewish trading family which had long been established in Persia, had come to Bombay in 1832 and set up a business trading in cloth and hides. Later he moved into the trade in raw cotton and began shipping it to China, Manchester, and other ports as well as providing it to local weavers (Jackson 1968, pp. 22–3). Jardine's records show that Sassoon was shipping opium to Canton on his own account as early as 1834 (Le Fevour 1968, p. 27). It was natural that any ambitious trader would move into the opium trade, which was then the most lucrative business in the city. Commission merchants

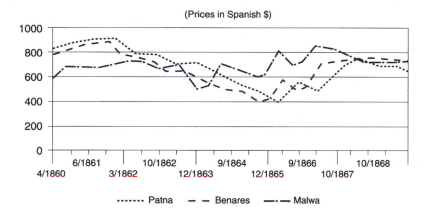

(Prices in Spanish $)

········ Patna   — — Benares   —·— Malwa

Figure 6.2 Hong Kong opium prices, 1860–1870

were said to be able to make £100 per chest on Malwa shipments. At the time, opium accounted for about one-third of the value of all Bombay's trade. In 1844, as soon as the dust from the Opium War had settled, David's son, Elias Sassoon, set up an affiliated firm first in Canton and then Hong Kong and converted some hulks into opium godowns. In 1850, Elias established a permanent base at Shanghai. Here Sassoon's went into direct competition with Jardine Matheson, building their own warehouses and developing the trade in silks, hides and textiles as return cargoes for their own fleet of opium clippers (Jackson 1968, pp. 22–4).

The Sassoons however, gained their great advantage by making advances to the Indian and Marwari dealers who controlled the production of Malwa opium. Those proto-capitalists of Ujjian, Indore and Madasaur, (see Chapter 4) now became part of a comprehensive system of advances that began with the Sassoons and ended with the ryots of Malwa (Farooqui 1995, pp. 469–71). The other Malwa opium merchants in Bombay had never risked making direct investments in the actual cultivation. They simply bought their supplies of the drug from the merchants and moneylenders in the provincial towns who controlled the production. During the first half of the nineteenth century, this was probably the most efficient way to conduct business. However, in the years after 1860, as the ground of the trade shifted, it was necessary to gain control of the crop at its source. Jardine's affiliates in Bombay were too slow off the mark. By the time they began to seek avenues through which to make advances to producers, Sassoon's had already pre-empted much of the crop. This put Sassoon in a position somewhat analogous to that of the Indian government in Bihar and Benares. The firm acted as the "banker" to finance the Malwa opium crop, making advances to an already established group of dealers and, in effect, purchasing the crop before it was even planted.

Sassoon's had already copied Jardine and its affiliates in forming combinations to control prices at the Calcutta auctions. Sassoon's had formed an association with the Calcutta brokerage firms of E. Gubbay and E. D. I. Ezra, and they were buying at high prices and then holding their stocks in China until prices increased. They also made bulk sales to Chinese dealers at a discount and were willing to offer substantial advances to their Chinese customers. These were the same tactics that Jardine's and Dent's had used earlier. Sassoon's tighter, family-based organization, together with their buying cliques in the Bombay and Calcutta bazaars, gave them an extremely strong position. By gaining control of most of the Malwa crop in the late 1860s, Sassoon's were in a position to use it as leverage to manipulate prices at the Calcutta opium auctions. This placed Jardine's and all other dealers at a permanent disadvantage. By 1871 Sassoon's took control of the opium markets on both sides of India. The firm was then acknowledged to hold 70 percent of the total of all kinds of opium both in India and China. It was the end of the opium trade for Jardine Matheson.

> Strict control of costs in India had allowed the [Sassoon] group to undersell all others in China for five years and against this organization Jardine's was defenseless; its withdrawal from the trade became inevitable as its partners realized that to stay would require a renewed concentration of resources and managerial skills which the firm could muster only by neglecting other interests, now of paramount importance.
>
> (Le Fevour 1968, p. 29)

As an alternative, Jardine's went on to expand their investments in the Treaty Ports. They developed interests in tea, silk, insurance and banking and got out of opium and shipping. Ultimately, the firm which had risen to prominence as an antagonist of the Chinese state, became a major supporter of the dynasty, acting as the agent for the Qing in their self-strengthening policies. Nevertheless, the firm's rise to prominence, in fact the overall creation of the western position in China, had been primarily a result of the opium trade.

> Opium had provided the capital reserve essential to survival and growth in a precarious economic environment, lubricated the export trade, stimulated the improvement of communications, and probably provided China firms with a surplus to invest in world markets. Decades of concentration upon the trade had conditioned the whole nature of Western enterprise in China.
>
> Profit from opium had averaged an estimated 15 per cent on the firm's own investments and a 4 per cent on agency business during the fifties and sixties. With these profits Jardine's had built the structure needed to sustain the trade to finance its investment in tea and silk.
>
> (Le Fevour 1968, pp. 29–30)

Jardine's also began to invest heavily in real property, particularly in docks, shore establishments and warehouses.

For David Sassoon and his sons, their opium investments had been equally lucrative. The 1870s and 1880s were boom times for the Sassoons.

This was harvest time for David Sassoon & Sons. The Yangtze mud glinted with gold as soon as they laid a brick on it. It was the same in all the Treaty Ports where land values bounded from year to year. Their wharves and godowns were bursting with opium, cotton goods, silks, spices, tea and metals. In the mid-seventies, when the rupee began to drop from its fairly stable value of two shillings through the demonetization of silver in various European countries, they could hedge or withstand any shock by swiftly moving goods to less sensitive areas. Conversely, in the later years they would buy heavily in silver when it soared in price, thus offsetting their heavy losses from a critical glut in piece-goods. As soon as opium sales dropped, the firm promptly scored compensatory gains in silver, sugar and dyes.

(Jackson 1968, p. 58)

Like the Jardines, the Mathesons and others that had become wealthy in the empire, David Sassoon's sons were able to move into the highest levels of English society at the end of the century. They had an "easier passage" to royal favor than did other Jewish families, such as the Rothschilds.

[They] enjoyed more immunity from the snobbery and racial prejudice that persisted towards that clan [the Rothschilds] in certain quarters. Opium trading was still considered unexceptionable and apparently less noxious socially than vulgar profit-making on the Stock Exchange. Besides, their mercantile eminence in India and the Treaty Ports lent them a semi-imperial cachet among the guardians of protocol at Buckingham Palace.

(Jackson 1968, pp. 68–9)

Even though the Anglo-Scottish merchant houses had lost control of the opium trade, it did not really slip away from imperial control. Most of the Sassoons moved to Britain and for all practical purposes became British. Identity, however, depended on location. This immunity from anti-Semitism may have protected them in the metropole, but among the British traders of Asia, the cachet of empire was no distinction and offered little protection against racist attitudes, particularly when economic considerations were thrown into the balance.

The 1860s and 1870s had been difficult decades for European traders in Asia. While it may have appeared that things were moving in their favor, not many of the original European agency houses in Hong Kong, Singapore and the Treaty Ports weathered the transition from opium-based "free" trade, to imperial trade based on commodity flows. There was thus a certain degree of resentment against more successful non-Anglo-Scottish merchants. A significant example was the collapse of the firm of John Purvis & Son in Singapore.

For nearly half a century John Purvis and then his son, had functioned as Jardine Matheson's agent in Singapore. The affiliation of the two firms, though largely informal, was quite significant. It went back to the early 1820s. Purvis had first gone to China on the same vessel as James Matheson, but had returned to seek his fortune in Singapore while the latter had stayed in Canton. (Buckley

1903, p. 76) The correspondence between the two firms is one of the most active in all the Jardine's India Letterbooks, as well as in the private letterbooks of William Jardine and Alexander Matheson after him.[1]

Jardine's partners were in the habit of investing tens of thousands of Spanish dollars annually with Purvis to speculate on their behalf in the Singapore opium market. While this was rather small compared to the $100,000 that was annually invested through Jardine Skinner in Calcutta, it was significant for such a small market as Singapore's. In 1842, for instance, Alexander Matheson sent Purvis $50,000 to buy opium for him in Singapore when the price there was $70 a chest lower than in Canton (C6/3 1/9/42). The following year he sent another $20,000, and again $20,000 the year after that. At the same time, Purvis was permitted to carry a large overdraft with Jardine's on his trade to China. Purvis regularly supplied Jardine's with market and political intelligence from Singapore and the Straits. He also found cargo for their ships; dealt with problems arising from European crewmen; managed the coal supply for their steamers; and looked after Jardine's wharf in Singapore. Singapore traders considered him to be Jardine's agent in that port.

On several occasions Jardine's partners made special efforts to rescue Purvis from financial difficulties. This was done with substantial advances, loans, useful investment advice on the Calcutta or Canton markets and by sending additional business opportunities in Purvis' way. We get some idea of their relationship in Alexander Matheson's response to Purvis' request for a loan in 1842.

> I have now to notice your application for an advance of cash for the purpose of speculating in the drug – & however reluctant we feel to make such advances after the severe lessons we have had, we would not hesitate to comply with your request, to a limited extent if we could see a chance of its benefiting you. Of this however, we have great doubts, in fact we feel certain that it would only plunge you into fresh difficulties. You tried it before and what was the result? What could you have done in Opium with borrowed Capital since January last? or, what are you ever likely to do in competition with the Jews in your settlement who are content with the smallest possible advance on cost & charges? It appears to me that the prospects are getting worse instead of better. Prices are likely to rule high in Calcutta for a long time to come.
>
> We have for some time past been putting a good deal in your way in the shape of commissions & I feel satisfied this is the surest way of saving you.
>
> (JMA, C6/3, 11/7/42)

This was not merely a polite demurral. Matheson in fact did lend Purvis $10,000 a few years later when he was convinced there was a much more certain chance of turning a fast 20 percent through speculation in "the drug." One also gets a clear sense of "us and them" in Matheson's remarks about competition from the Jewish traders in Singapore.

When old John Purvis retired in 1862, his business was taken over by his son, John Murray Purvis, who had been with him in the business since 1855. The relationship with Jardine's was maintained. Unfortunately, the younger Purvis was not as successful as his father. The details of his difficulties are not entirely clear. He apparently mismanaged the Jardine coal account. He also made some unwise investments in Straits produce and in the rice trade where he had to compete with Chinese dealers who could deliver produce far more cheaply. He also seems to have gone behind Jardine's back, as it were, and developed relationships with their competitors. In any case, his firm went bankrupt in the more general economic collapse of 1865. It is hard to say whether he also had difficulties in the opium trade, but it is clear that the involvement of European traders in the opium trade, as well as in the Southeast Asia-to-China trade (e.g much of the old country trade) was rapidly coming to an end.

Important sectors of economic life fell to more competitive Asian traders and as they did, an ethnic division of labor came to characterize the socio-economic relations of empire. Those Europeans who did survive now began to take a different view of the trade. By the 1880s, opium as an object of trade, had lost caste. It was no longer the sort of thing in which respectable (e.g. European) traders engaged. We catch a hint of anti-Semitism in Matheson's remarks above. It is much more explicit in the next quotation. Despite this attitude, it was still clear that European prosperity in Asia depended upon the trade. The remarks of Singapore merchant, W. G. Gulland are instructive:

> For the opium trade, pure and simple, in itself, I care nothing; it is wholly in the hands of Jews and Armenians, and I know little about its ins and outs: but there is no doubt that Opium enters largely into, and forms an important part of, the Native trade of this city, as of almost all other eastern settlements. All those prahus and junks which we see lying off Tanjong Ru are insignificant in themselves, but they are all small parts of one great trade. They come here to sell their produce and buy return cargoes: some buy one thing, some another; but they must all have Opium to a greater or lesser extent, and unless they get what they want without let or hindrance, I fear they will go another year to some of the neighbouring ports.
>
> (LEGCO 1883, p. 8)

The attitude which Gulland expresses here is notable for its combination of thinly disguised scorn, on the one hand, for the traders and the opium trade, and support on the other, for the continuation of the trade itself. The 1880s were a time when the voices in England raised against the trade itself were becoming more insistent and less easy to dismiss out of hand. For a number of years, both in Britain and to some extent, in Asia, physicians, missionaries and Quakers had been promoting the Society for the Suppression of the Opium Trade. In addition, since the late 1860s, the British government had begun to enact laws to control the use of opium among the British public (Berridge and Edwards 1987, pp. 113–209). This marked a real change of consciousness regarding opium and the trade within British culture. Gulland's remarks need to be seen in this context. The other actors in the trade, whose presence was so prominent that Gulland did not think it necessary to mention, were the Chinese. The shift in the trade now made it possible for the European imperial classes to distance themselves from direct responsibility while shifting the "blame" to the Asians. Empire was dirty business, he seemed to say, but somebody had to do it.

This was the period during which the young Joseph Conrad had gained his experience of maritime trade in Asia, and it was the era in which he set the tale of Jim. The romantic era of clippers, their daring captains and the Anglo-Scottish taipans had been enshrined among the myths of the empire. By the 1880s, however, their day had passed and they only survived in the romantic boys' adventure literature of Britain. Jim's "dream" was a mask for the dingy reality. Opium had ceased to be the stuff of legends and was no longer the source of super profits for the richest merchant houses. It was still the grease that lubricated the entire imperial machine and continued to be a part of the cargo of nearly every ship that plied Asian waters. These ships, however, were not dashing clippers racing across the seas under clouds of sail, but were rusty old steamers that were owned by "Arabs and Chinamen" making their tedious rounds from one steamy little river mouth to the next. Conrad seems to have had as little sympathy for the successful Asian entrepreneurs as the other Englishmen of his day. George Windsor Earl's comments on Arabs seem very close to some of Conrad's characterizations. According to Earl, there were two kinds of Arabs: the "genuine Arabs" who were "high-minded and enterprising men":

> but their half-caste descendants who swarm the Archipelago, comprise the most despicable set of wretches in existence. Under the name of religion they have introduced among the natives the vilest system of intolerance and wickedness imaginable, and those places in which they have gained ascendancy, are invariably converted into dens of infamy and piracy.
>
> (Earl 1836, pp. 68–9)

And while Jews, the Arabs and Armenians certainly had major roles in the trade, as it came from India, the downstream side of the trade, in Southeast Asia and in China itself was a little different. Here, the opium business was largely in the hands of Chinese. They paid for the dream.

Chinese domestic opium

Legalization of opium in China was not the great bonanza that many European traders had hoped for, rather it was the beginning of the end for the Indian opium trade. It was now possible for domestically produced Chinese opium to compete directly with the "foreign drug" as Robert Hart called it (Hart 1881).[2] It is perhaps a testament to the high reputation of Indian opium and the "taste" to which many Chinese smokers had become accustomed, that Patna, Benares and Malwa opium managed to maintain significant market shares throughout the nineteenth century. The Chinese demand for Indian opium appears to have remained relatively stable between 1870 and 1890. Thereafter, it finally began to decline, or at least, exports from India to China declined.

If European merchants had difficulty competing with Asian traders in India and Southeast Asia, where Europeans controlled the governments, they faced much greater disadvantages in China despite the unequal treaties. In the days before legalization, opium, by necessity, was distributed through wholly Chinese networks. So long as the trade was illegal, it was always possible for the East India Company, the British government, the American government, and even the European traders at times, to distance themselves from the trade. Once the trade was legalized, it was already too late for European trading houses to develop their own distribution networks into the Chinese market and to get around the Chinese brokers and middlemen who had established themselves at the gateways to China.

Try as they might, and some European traders did try very hard, it was not easy to crack the Chinese guilds that controlled local distribution networks in China. In the 1850s, Jardine's was able to send opium to the interior, but even at this, it was the Chinese merchant, their comprador, not the Europeans, who had access to the distribution network. Chinese domination of the inland market was evident in the attempt by a group of British traders to combat the power of the "Swatow Opium Guild," allegedly a group of Chaozhou traders.[3] They were said to have monopolized much of the opium trade on the Southeast coast of China, including that of Shanghai (Hamilton 1977). However, as Hamilton shows, there was no single corporate group that controlled the entire trade, but rather a more segmented affiliation of locally based cliques. Even their lawyers admitted that they did in fact, cooperate to keep Europeans out of the Chinese market, but that was just "business," and there was nothing illegal about it. With this kind of power, the "rationalization" of international commerce that began to occur after 1860 made it possible for such Chinese traders to either buy directly from the Calcutta auctions or to deal with firms like Jardine's and Sassoon's from a relatively strong position.

An extensive domestic trading network had been developed by Cantonese/ Shantou traders to bring the drug from Canton, to Hankou and from there to other interior locations. As the coast trade expanded after the Opium War, other networks were developed which reached inland from Shanghai, Shantou, Xiamen and other ports of entry along the coast. By the time the trade was legalized, there was little likelihood that Europeans could penetrate the Chinese market any further than they already had. It was, moreover, the established Chinese opium merchants who were best able to gain an advantage from the expansion of domestic opium production.

There was a three-tiered distribution system operating in China during the late nineteenth century. This was composed of a hierarchy of big wholesale dealers, large-scale retailers and local distributors. The wholesalers either bought the Indian drug from foreigners or purchased domestic opium in bulk from the producing areas in Sichuan, Yunnan or Guichou. These merchants were mostly from Shantou and Ningpo, and they seem to be the sort of people who were involved in the opium guilds.

> They were men of great wealth, and we can contrast the vast resources at their disposal with the scanty funds generally made available for "self-strengthening" or other enterprises. Thus in 1881 Li Hongzhang memorialized that a syndicate headed by the Cantonese Ho Hsien-ch'ih wanted to corner the entire Indian opium stocks through a company Ho would head in Hong Kong; they offered the Ch'ing government at least three million taels in additional annual taxation, in return for sole distribution rights in Chinese ports. Ho was going to capitalize the company initially at $Mex 20,000,000.
>
> (Spence 1975, p. 165)

Another of these was Sassoon's comprador in Chinkiang who reportedly had sold one and a half million taels of opium in a single year. These individuals were usually above police harassment and were treated with respect by officials.

The second group, the large-scale retailers, kept local shops and normally belonged to the local opium "guild." They usually refined the raw opium and sold chandu, the opium prepared for smoking. While some of their customers may have been wealthy users who bought large amounts for their home consumption, their major clients would have been those in the third category, the two types of local sellers: the operators of opium dens or divans and the itinerant peddlers who sold small lots of opium for immediate consumption (Spence 1975, p. 165–6).

There is no truly reliable information on the history or extent of the cultivation of opium in China. The growing use of Indian opium and the increasing imports in the 1820s spurred production of opium inside of China. In 1836, Su Naiji reported its cultivation in several southern provinces including Yunnan. At this time, the production of Yunnan alone was said to be several thousand chests annually (Benedict 1994, p. 6). By 1847, Jardine Matheson's agent reported that the production of Yunnan and Guangxi was in the neighborhood of 12,000 pikuls (approximately 12,000 chests). This information was offered with the caution that the Bengal government was "not disposed to put much faith in the reported cultivation" (JMA, C1/9, to C. B. Skinner, 23 June 1848, p. 351). Nevertheless, other contemporary estimates suggest that Jardine's number may have been on the low side. It was reported that 8,000 to 10,000 pikuls were being produced in Guangdong alone in 1847 (Spence 1975, p. 161). It may be that China was already producing around 20,000 pikuls of opium by 1850, a time when the opium trade was still illegal.

The cultivation of opium in Yunnan, Guangxi and Guangdong, seems to have fed right back into the Canton-based trading networks noted above. Carol Benedict has traced the internal trade routes through which the domestic Chinese opium trade flowed in the early nineteenth century. Never a very easy trek, the best routes into China proper from the Yunnan frontier led either southeast into Vietnam and down the Red River and then by sea to Hong Kong and Canton, or eastward through Bose and down the Yu and West Rivers to Canton. Later on, an alternative route opened up from Nanningfu to Beihai on the Gulf of Tongkin. These routes were little used before the early nineteenth century and only the development of the domestic opium trade made them viable avenues of commerce between the Yunggui and Lingnan macro regions. Cantonese merchants dominated this trade. Because the supplies of domestic opium flowed first to Canton and then into the same distribution networks that had been established for Indian opium it was probably natural that it too came to be controlled by the same group of wholesale merchants (Benedict 1994, pp. 6–10; Benedict 1996, ch. 2; Rowe 1984; Rowe 1989).

The domestic Chinese opium cultivation and trade grew rapidly in the years after the Opium War. The domestic product was also about half the price of the imported drug because it was generally considered to be of inferior quality. The elite market continued to favor Indian opium. Regardless of perceived quality, the increased supplies and the lower prices meant that opium was now moving even further down the Chinese socio-economic scale and being made available, in some form, to even the poorest of consumers. The world's first and largest drug plague had now reached epidemic proportions, and this was still only the beginning.

The only factor that slowed the progress of the drug epidemic in the years immediately following the Opium War was the traumatic series of upheavals that struck southern and western China. In addition to the Taiping Rebellion, there was the Nien Rebellion, the Miao Rebellion and the Muslim Rebellion, all of which deeply affected the vast hinterland of China's frontier provinces during the 1850s and 1860s. This was the area which Lin Man-huong has styled "interior China," the isolated western regions that were then underpopulated, or populated by minorities, and generally out of touch with the Chinese mainstream. These uprisings interfered with the opium trade, because the Taiping ideology included a strict ascetic code which banned opium smoking along with prostitution and alcohol consumption. The Muslims likewise banned opium use. Aside from such deliberate policies however, the sheer chaos which marked these uprisings and their subsequent suppression was a great hindrance to agriculture and commerce.

While Indian production figures continued to rise through the 1840s and 1850s, prices, particularly after 1845, tended to fall steadily until 1856. This suggests that the market was somewhat oversupplied. While these wars continued however, domestic producers were obviously hit harder than the importers of Indian opium. Since the shipping routes from Yunnan and Guangxi went through territory held by the Taipings, it was far more difficult for the domestic drug to reach Chinese markets. The Jardine Opium Circulars also show that the movement of opium from the coast to its interior markets was often disrupted by the Taipings. Even then, the rebellions only slowed growth rather than cause any measurable contraction in the trade.

Although these upheavals may have hindered the trade for a time, the poverty and disruption that they left in their wake created both an increased demand for opium as well as conditions which favored its cultivation. Loss, injury and the

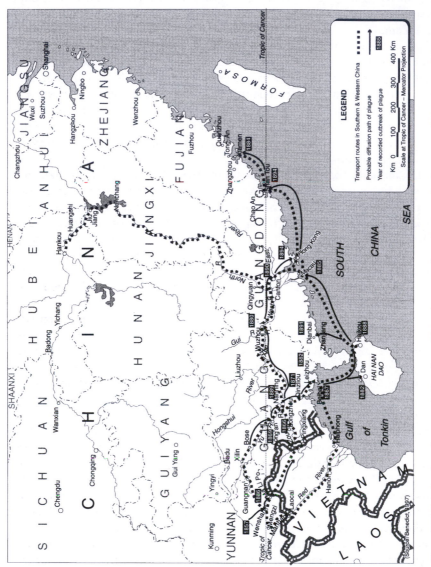

Figure 6.3 Overland trade routes in Southern China between the opium-producing areas of Yunnan and the southern coast. Bubonic plagues spread from Yunnan to Guangzhou and elsewhere along these routes

Source: Based on information in Benedict, 1997

trauma of life in the midst of civil war certainly must have driven many to seek comfort in the pipe. The wars had also mobilized millions of young men. The return of peace left tens of thousands of wandering "braves," who had been demobilized from the various armies. For them, opium may have become a way of life. At the same time, the prospect of rapid profits must have been a strong temptation to those impoverished by the wars and who were willing to cultivate or trade opium.

Although the dynasty had been saved, most historians date the creation of local militias, regional armies and other elements of regional autonomy from this period. These conditions are generally identified as the chronic weaknesses in the Chinese state which eventually brought about its downfall in 1911. It is important to understand that this new regionalism was very often intimately connected to the emergent opium economy. In fact, it is difficult to see how regional autonomy could have been maintained without the sudden availability of the new wealth that came from opium.

From the 1870s on, opium cultivation expanded at an extraordinary pace. By the end of the nineteenth century, opium had become an enormous enterprise in Sichuan, Yunnan and Guangxi, as well as in the coastal provinces of Zhejiang and Fujian and other parts of southern China. It may have become even more popular than grain as a crop. In the area around Hankou, opium was one of several cash crops that began to appear toward the end of the nineteenth century. Others included tea, cotton and tung seeds. Together they reduced the acreage of grain crops and by the 1890s caused a contraction in the city's grain supply (Rowe 1989, p. 210).

There is some uncertainty about the impact of these increases in opium cultivation on the production of food crops and the welfare of the peasants, at least in the short term. Lin Man-huong argues that as opium cultivation grew, it was largely taken up by people who had newly migrated from the densely settled regions of the coast and major alluvial plains, or "exterior China," to the relatively underpopulated and isolated areas of the interior. The opium crop was an expeditious way for them to support themselves. The opium economy actually financed the settlement of these regions. In particular during the period after 1870, migrants flocked into unsettled, hilly areas which were generally unsuitable for food crops, and there they planted opium. By 1879, the provinces of interior China (e.g. Sichuan, Yunnan, Guichou, Shanxi, Shenxi, Kansu, Honan, Guangxi, and Sinjiang) were producing nearly 90 percent of China's domestic opium crop. These areas maintained a similar share in national production for the next three decades until the 1911 Revolution (Lin 1993, p. 11).

Initially, this upsurge in Chinese opium production did not seem to decrease the amount of land, or effort devoted to the production of food crops. Not only was it grown on land that had been considered unsuitable for food, it was an autumn and winter crop, as it was in India. Thus it was planted in October–November and harvested in April–May. Finally, since it also used "surplus" labor, it had a minimal impact on the cultivation and production of food crops. In Manchuria, Sichuan and other important poppy areas, the cultivation, harvesting and processing of opium was the work of women and children. Lin generally supports Spence's conclusion:

> there were plenty of advantages in growing opium as a cash crop. It would yield at least twice the cash of an average cereal crop on a given acreage; it could be planted in the tenth month and harvested in the third when nothing else would grow; it could survive on very poor soil, as long as there was a reasonable amount of fertilizer; it could be interspersed with food crops such as beans or potatoes, or planted in alternate rows with tobacco. Winter growing was especially profitable to tenants holding lands on metayer tenure – that is, paying the landlord a fixed percentage of the yield of the *summer* crop. Furthermore, though the techniques for gathering poppy juice were labor intensive, they were very simple.
>
> (Spence 1975, p. 153)

Later on, the situation changed. Even Spence, reporting on the cultivation in Ningxia and Shenxi, notes that opium did cut into land and labor formerly used for food production (Spence 1975, p. 169). As time passed, poppies were increasingly grown on good soil. By 1880, in southwest China, opium came down from the hills to the valleys, and started to take over land formerly used for food crops.

Dr. J. Edkins, the American Presbyterian missionary who wrote a general history of opium in China at the end of the nineteenth century claimed that poppy cultivation was the root cause for suffering during famines in Shanxi. Opium cultivation had been started by the governor of Shanxi in 1852. During the famine in 1867–68 most of the deaths took place in the areas where poppy cultivation was the greatest (Edkins 1898, pp. 66–7). These are only incidental reports and it is still difficult to sustain any general conclusions about the impact of increased opium production in the nineteenth century. It is obvious that more data, and further study is needed to clarify the relationship between famine, food supplies, and opium cultivation at this period. One could also argue that opium cultivators would have been better able to purchase rice and other foods with their increased incomes.

For China in the twentieth century, the picture may be less ambiguous. Jonathan Marshall linked large-scale opium cultivation to a series of famines in the 1920s and 1930s including one in central China in 1925, in Shaanxi in 1928–33 and in Sichuan in 1934. The Shaanxi famine took an estimated 3 million lives during the five-year period. At the time about 32 percent of the fertile land in the province was devoted to opium (J. Marshall 1976, p. 24–5). Over the longer term, and particularly in situations where cultivators had little control over their choice of crops, it seems clear that opium had the capacity to drive out less remunerative grain cultivation. We might also ask the same questions with regard to famine and opium production in India. There does not seem to be a clear body of data on the two phenomena which would show a causal relation. By the late nineteenth century Indian officials were generally quite defensive about the opium business and would have been reluctant to offer information suggesting a famine in Bihar or Benares was the result of excessive opium cultivation.

The question of whether opium cultivation had a positive or negative impact on the peoples of China's frontier provinces is a complicated one. Clearly, it provided a much needed income for those who might otherwise have starved or been forced to migrate. It also provided an immediate income for new emigrants. It seems to have jump-started the economies of these areas after the devastation of the great civil wars of the mid-century. In conjunction with this, opium was the catalyst for trade and communication between China's interior and exterior provinces. We see a clear pattern if we look at the evolution of opium trade routes during the nineteenth century. In the early part of the nineteenth century, the Indian drug rode along established trade routes, moving from the Canton delta area, or the Lingnan macroregion, to the mid-Yangtze nexus of Hankou. After the mid-century, the drug began to create its own trade routes, its own settlements, and indeed, its own economy.

Benedict's study of the beginnings of opium cultivation in Yunnan and Sichuan shows that there was little regular communication between these provinces and the dense population nodes of coastal and central China, before the opium trade. The high value of the opium crop moving out of Yunnan and Sichuan financed trade along these routes. For some time, it appears that little other than opium moved along these routes, except for the secret outrider that accompanied it, bubonic plague. She shows quite convincingly that the spread of the plague, from Yunnan, where it was endemic, to the South China coast, occurred simultaneously with the activation of the opium trails running from Kunming to the various outlets of South China. The opening of regular traffic between the Yungui macroregion and the Lingnan area was made possible only with opium. The drug thus provided a vector whereby this new and virulent form of bubonic plague could escape to the outside world (Benedict 1994). Into the balance too must be thrown the fact that increased production of opium invariably led to increased consumption by those who grew it. In the 1930s, it was reported that Chinese peasants tended to consume about 25 percent of the opium which they produced (Spence 1975, p. 153).

The question of whether opium was a benefit or an evil may almost be an irrelevant one. Its impact was so multifarious and so profound that the question of the fate of individual human beings may seem insignificant. By the turn of the century, opium was the largest single item of Chinese interregional trade in domestic productions: e.g. rice, Ts100 million; salt, Ts100 million and opium, Ts130 million (Spence 1975, p. 154). Opium transformed China, economically, socially, politically and culturally.

The political economy of opium

All sources agree on one important fact, and that is that opium, no matter where it appeared, came to function as both a source of, and a substitute for cash. As the British, Dutch and other Europeans had discovered long before, and as many

Chinese already knew, opium was as good as money, and if it could not be spent, it could always be eaten or smoked. Ultimately everyone who could seems to have sought to reap a share of the increased bounty flowing from opium. If it enriched migrant peasants in the first instance, it was not long before landlords and tax collectors saw the possibility of added revenue for themselves. At all levels, it came to be an additional and important medium of exchange both in the Chinese private economy as well as in the fiscal support of localities, provinces and even the Chinese state itself. Income from the opium economy served the peasants, the landlords, the large and small traders, the magistrates and the tax collectors. Even though prohibitions against the cultivation of opium persisted in many localities after the legalization of opium imports, the laws were rarely enforced in any consistent fashion. Ultimately, most officials decided that money was better than morality.

Chinese domestic production probably did not surpass imports until about 1870. Between 1870 and 1906, domestic production of opium is estimated to have increased by five times. By the end of the nineteenth century China was producing nine times the total import from India (Lin 1993a). Available statistics from the period show staggering estimates ranging between 330,000 pikuls and 584,000 pikuls annually, in the years just prior to 1908 (Lin 1993a, Table 4, p. 42). It is probably safe to say that China was then producing between 30,000 and 40,000 tons of opium annually. China had become the largest producer of opium in the world. However, unlike India, little of this was exported. At the same time, China continued to import between 70,000 and 80,000 chests of Indian opium from 1870 to the early 1890s and between 50,000 and 60,000 chests thereafter until 1908. The Chinese also consumed significant portions of opium produced in Turkey, Egypt, Persia, the Balkans and that of a few other minor producers.

Opium smoking increased as fast as production. Nearly all of the opium produced in China was consumed in China except for some minor exports to northern Vietnam (Descours-Gatin 1992, p. 210).[4] This was an insignificant amount, however, compared to the spread of the opium epidemic throughout China. At the beginning of the twentieth century, China was consuming 95 percent of the world's opium supply. In Taiwan, under Japanese rule, only the Chinese were allowed to smoke. There was a population of 323,940 in about 1890, one-seventh of whom were opium smokers. In Taipei out of a population of 59,905, there were 13,299 smokers, and Tainan had 7,209 smokers in a population of 18,871 (Edkins 1898, p. 65). There are local estimates of as high as 60 to 80 percent of opium smokers in the populations of Shanxi and Kansu. None of these, however, are systematic or comprehensive estimates. Spence estimates that about 10 percent of the entire Chinese population were opium smokers of some regularity. In 1890, this very conservative estimate suggests that there may have been around 40 million actual opium addicts in China. This number must have increased considerably by 1908 (Spence, 1975).

In every city of China, opium dens, or divans, or shops, or whatever they were called, came to be the most common form of retail business. In Shanghai, in the mid-nineteenth century, opium dens were fashionable places frequented by

Figure 6.4 A Chinese opium den in Calcutta, 1946. This was quite similar to opium dens
  found throughout China and Southeast Asia during the nineteenth and early
  twentieth centuries
Source: Photo by Clyde Waddell. By permission of the British Library, Photo 934(52)

intellectuals, merchants, bureaucrats, artists and other Chinese of this rank. But,
as time passed and opium became cheaper, the ordinary people developed a taste
for opium and the dens spread. By the end of the century, "outside of these
specialized establishments, every section of the city had at least one salon reserved
for [opium] smokers" (Perrott 1992, p. 27). Random reports from the late
nineteenth century show opium shops numbering in the thousands in many cities
throughout China. Chongqing had 1,230; Chefoo (with a population of 30,000)
had 132; Wenchou had 1,130; and in Suchou there was a crackdown in 1869
which closed 3,700 opium shops and dens (Spence 1975, p. 166). By 1911, there
were 1,492 opium dens and shops in Hankou alone (Rowe 1989, p. 191). By
comparison, Hankou had only 286 wine shops and 696 tea shops, and even many
of these probably sold opium as well (Rowe 1989, p. 86).

> Teahouse operators . . . were sharply constrained by the modest buying
> power of their clients in the level of profit they could derive from the
> legitimate sales of tea, so in order to remain in business they were virtually
> compelled to supplement this with illegal activities such as sheltering refugees,
> running games of chance, distributing opium and staging pornographic
> shows.
>
> (Rowe 1989, p. 196)

Tea houses were also routine hangouts for criminal elements. During times of disturbance (e.g. 1850s, 1880s, and 1920s) these were frequented by "wandering braves" who also engaged in salt and opium smuggling (Rowe 1989, p. 225).

First attempts to end the trade

Opium had entered into the very fabric of Chinese life. It supported the state, it supported the economy and paradoxically, it undermined both. Spence and others make its importance clear:

> For at least the last fifty years of the nineteenth century, opium played an important role in the Chinese economy, and it did so in three major areas: it served as a substitute for money, it helped local officials meet taxation quotas, and it helped finance the self-strengthening program.
>
> (Spence 1975, p. 167)

And yet, despite its vital importance to the state, and despite the very weakness of the Qing political order, the Chinese government came very close to ending the opium plague. Before Sun Yat-sen and the republican revolution, before the warlords, before Chiang Kai-shek and before the Japanese and the Chinese Communist Party there was one final effort to undo the great harm done by opium. This began with the Sino–British treaty to stop the trade in 1906. Although largely forgotten today, or at least dismissed as a hopeless enterprise, it appeared at the time that the efforts of the SSOT and the anti-opium forces within China itself would prevail. Together with the Chinese and British negotiations came the American decision to outlaw opium sales in their newly acquired Philippine colony. This added pressure on the British and Indian governments to take steps to end or at least reduce, the opium trade. In 1906 the two countries signed a treaty which bound Britain to eliminate the opium trade to China, and bound China to stop opium cultivation and opium use. Both accepted a target of ten years for the achievement of these goals (Owen 1934, pp. 331–7). In the midst of these negotiations, a new Parliament took power in 1906, among whose numbers were 250 members of the SSOT. In May, 1906, the "familiar motion" condemning the opium traffic as "morally indefensible" and calling for the government to bring it to a speedy end, was introduced and finally passed without a division. In September, the Chinese government issued an imperial decree which commanded that within a period of ten years the evils arising from foreign and native opium would be completely eradicated. In the final agreement, a skeptical Indian government promised to reduce its export to China by 5,100 chests for each year for the period 1907–9,[5] provided the Chinese government was successful in reducing its production by 10 percent annually. If the Chinese demonstrated success and sincerity in carrying out this goal, then Britain would move ahead with compete elimination of the trade to China in the next seven years.

The Chinese embarked upon measures to eliminate opium consumption and production with unexpected enthusiasm and earnestness. European observers who "knew" China, were very skeptical of any possibility of success and most doubted Chinese sincerity. They assumed that as British–Indian imports declined, local production would increase to take up the slack. The American Consul in Sichuan, where in 1906, 40 percent of China's opium was produced, wrote: "To put the matter tersely, opium prohibition involves Szechuan in a commercial and fiscal revolution . . . Personally I do not consider that total prohibition is possible" (quoted in Wyman 1994, p. 1). By 1908, however, many of the doubters had become believers. Despite a range of regional variations in effectiveness, it appeared that the Chinese had achieved a fair degree of success in reducing both opium production as well as usage. In 1909, the British agreed that China had upheld its part of the treaty and now agreed to implement the rest of the agreement and continue to phase out opium exports to China at the same rate (of 5,100 chests annually) for the next seven years.

In Sichuan, Chinese officials, both at the provincial level as well as at the local level, undertook the elimination of opium cultivation as well as opium usage with considerable energy. Their success was no small thing in light of the extent of opium use in the province. Alexander Hosie, the British Commercial Attaché, estimated that there were nearly 2,800,000 consumers in a total population of 45 million (or 6 percent) and that 17 percent of the adult population were addicted (Wyman 1994, p. 4). Hosie, who had been sent around the Chinese provinces in 1910–11 to inspect the level of Chinese progress was deeply impressed. By 1911, hardly a poppy could be found in Sichuan.

> The 'turning point has now been reached in this question', he wrote to one of his colleagues in the Foreign Office; the eradication campaign 'has certainly been a marvelous piece of work which must raise China, with all her faults, in the estimation of the civilized world.'
>
> (Newman 1989, p. 548)

In fact, the Chinese were so successful that they pushed ahead of the schedule and Hosie saw that it was possible that the Chinese might succeed in stamping out opium completely by 1912 or 1913.

Chinese success in these measures placed the Indian government in a difficult position. By actually pushing ahead of the schedule, and by demanding that Britain respect provincial bans to further exports once opium had been eradicated, the Chinese precipitated a financial crisis among the opium traders in the treaty ports and in the opium-producing states of western India. Opium dealers, believing that Chinese prohibitions would drive up the price of opium had decided to hoard it. They also paid very high prices for the declining quantities of Indian opium. By December, 1912, there were 29,000 chests stockpiled in Shanghai. Prices in the Calcutta auctions were fluctuating wildly.

> In May, 1911, when the opium treaty had been signed, the price had been Rs 2,924 per chest; in October, on the eve of the revolution, it had reached Rs 6,015; it then fell back for several months, but by May, 1912 it had

climbed again to Rs 5,554. In June it suddenly crashed to Rs 3,878. It was not only the merchants who were alarmed at the accumulation of overpriced opium in their godowns; the Shanghai banks stood to lose millions of pounds which had been advanced to the merchants on the security of the stocks at their former valuation.

(Newman 1989, pp. 553–4)

These developments actually brought the Indian government to end auctions of opium and to bring the trade to a precipitous end. The last auctions were held in Bombay in the last month of 1912 and the last shipment of Indian opium destined for China sailed in February, 1913. That was the end of India–China opium trade.

The rapid reduction in Chinese opium production and consumption was largely due to the strenuous efforts of officials such as Zhao Erfeng who was governor-general of Sichuan from March, 1907 to June, 1908, and his brother Zhao Erxun who succeeded as governor-general from 1908 to 1911. They were able to virtually eliminate opium within a four-year period. Initially, Zhao Erfeng focused on distribution and consumption, by taking over most of the opium shops and dens and reopening them as government-run concessions. At the same time, smokers were given the opportunity to register. Then the government began to reduce the number of outlets while at the same time increasing the price. Initially, Zhao Erfeng made little headway in reducing production. It was not until 1909 that Zhao Erxun redoubled his efforts to end the cultivation. By the end of 1910, poppy cultivation in the province had been eliminated (Wyman 1994, pp. 13–20).

These accomplishments had not been without opposition. Many landlords and peasants were dependent upon rents and profits from opium sales. In 1907, a secret society known as the Hongdengjiao (Red Lantern Sect) arose and led an uprising against the government and the anti-opium policies. In 1908 and 1909, there had been organized resistance to prohibition measures and a resurgence of cultivation in some places (Wyman 1994, pp. 8–10). One of the main targets of these popular movements that sprung up to protect the opium cultivation, were the European missionaries and their Christian converts. This was rather ironic. Although the missionaries had been in the forefront of the anti-opium propaganda activities, in Sichuan they had been quite ineffectual in stopping the cultivation. The credit for really stopping cultivation and usage belongs to the efforts of the Zhao brothers and the local gentry leaders. The missionaries, however, shared in the blame. This was also the case in Fujian, where there was a similar, but unrelated uprising in 1912–14, the Sixteenth Emperor Rebellion, which was led by a man named Huang Lian. He too, defended opium fields and attacked Christians (Madancy 1994).

S.A.M. Adshead has theorized that opium use in Sichuan had developed almost as a fad or fashion. When opium cultivation began to expand rapidly in the province, many of the newly rich immigrants did not have anything better to do with their money or their leisure time. Henry Cockburn, a Chinese Secretary at the Beijing Legation told the 1895 Royal Commission: "The life of the better class

Chinese is a comparatively dull one -- he has fewer interests and far fewer recreations and distractions than the Europeans of the same class." Adshead concluded:"Thus it may be suggested that the disjunction of economic possibility and the social structure in provincial Szechuan produced opium addiction, a symbol at once of modest affluence and of the lack of adequate goals and foci" (Adshead 1966, p. 95). It is difficult to know whether this was so, nevertheless, it is true that opium cultivation did expand very rapidly in Sichuan and that it did make a great many people wealthy in a short period of time. It is also true, that during the years between 1890 and 1907, opium usage also expanded just as rapidly. The possibility of a causal relationship seems logical.

Adshead also offers another theory about the impact of the suppression campaign, and that is that the resulting economic uncertainty was an important factor in "preparing the ground for the revolution of 1911" (Adshead 1966, p. 98). There can be no doubt that the opium suppression campaigns of these years caused a great deal of economic disruption. Significant interests had come to depend on the revenues generated by opium. On the other hand, there is little evidence that the anti-Qing revolutionaries actively called for a return to the opium economy. It may be difficult to assume a cause and effect relationship between the anti-opium campaigns of the Qing government and the 1911 revolution, but it is clear that as soon as the Qing had passed into history, opium cultivation and opium usage immediately reappeared. And, as the power of the central government declined, the need for local governments to find ready sources of income strengthened the link between opium and the post-Qing political order, or perhaps, disorder would be a better word.

Those populations of young men, "wandering braves" as William Rowe called them, ultimately began to consolidate into the warlord armies that emerged following the overthrow of the Qing. Shen Congwen, one of the major writers to come out of this turbulent period of Chinese history, has written extensively of their lifestyle. By the 1920s, opium had become the economic mainstay of the warlords who now struggled with each other to control China. Within the warlord armies, soldiers found opium a major form of entertainment:

> The opium pipe was a standard social amenity . . . 48 of the 60 to 70 men he (Shen) served with in a secretariat in the 1920s were addicts. Opium was only 30 cents a liang (tahil), available to anyone who wanted it. And, there was social pressure to smoke. Since the drug was taken until late into the night, some of the officers slept part of the day.
>
> (Kinkley 1987, p. 48)

Shen was a clerk in a warlord army when he was a young man. His stories of military life tell how he cooked dog meat for his officers, played folk tunes for them on the flute, played cards, smoked opium and told stories and drank with them. Shen did not intend to write about opium, he was only interested in everyday life around him. Opium was simply an inseparable part of it. In one story, "A Night at Mallard Nest Village," Shen indicates that opium was a routine thing for the boatmen who stopped the night with the prostitutes of the village (Shen 1982, pp. 50–1). In the story "The Day Before He Deserted" he describes the head clerk who was a sympathetic character who tried to help him:

> yet his body was ravaged by opium. He has become a time server, like the bureaucrats from the end of the old regime . . . This good-natured man was completely beclouded by opium; but it had softened his heart and made him like a mother. Teaching him a joke was like telling a story to a child. This nonchalant disposition would forever limit him to the position he reached five years ago.
>
> (Kinkley 1987, pp. 49–50)

The soldiers did more than simply consume opium, it came to serve the same purpose for them as for the British, the other colonial powers and for the provincial Chinese authorities. Opium became the economic base for the warlord regimes. In places like West Hunan, where Shen served:

> the loss of subsidies from the national and provincial government was more than made up for by a new economic resource: convoys of opium going down the Yuan. The Sino-Miao Zh'enganese, long the object of Eastern colonialism, turned the tables and acquired economic as well as imperial sway over the lowlanders.
>
> (Kinkley 1987, p. 269)

Opium financed a major shift in the balance of power inside of China.

If at certain times Shen found some virtue in opium cultivation, ultimately he came to realize that it was opium itself that brought about the destruction of his homeland on the western Hunan frontier:

> Shen saw that social order was breaking down in West Hunan. Bandits swarmed in the no-man's lands between garrison districts; one militarist after another conquered the Yuan valley with guns purchased from opium revenues – then was cut down, often by his own troops.
>
> (Kinkley 1987, p. 65)

The combination of warlord armies and opium revenues became the great bane of China during the years from the 1920s to 1950. (Kinkley 1987, p. 251) We cannot really appreciate the power of the warlord regimes in China without factoring in the role of opium. It was clear that any political order, or proto-political order that could cultivate opium, or control its shipment or its marketing, could then rely on it as an economic resource. At this level there seems little difference between the joint-stock trading company, the established colonial regime, the ambitious mercantile house, the bandit-warlord army and, by extension, the Medellin or Kali cartels of today. An addictive drug was their ally and their fundamental resource. It was the quick and dirty fix, the short cut that could place one on the high road to political, economic and social power. In Asia east of Suez, opium paved the way. First by destroying the old order and then by financing the new, it laid the foundation for the coming of capitalism, for militarism and for the republics. Those who could harness the dragon could become the new ruling class.

The Chinese warlords adapted the pattern pioneered by the East India Company. They dragooned communities of peasants, or indigenous tribal peoples, into the cultivation of opium, so that the soldiers or officials could appropriate it and move it into the market and buy more guns. After 1927, Chiang Kai-shek, in his drive to unify China, embraced the warlords of Sichuan and Yunnan and did little to alter their economic resource base. In fact, when he took over Shanghai in 1927, he joined forces with the infamous gangster, Du Yuesheng. Not only did Du aid Chiang in his massacre of the communists and the Guomindang left wing, but he helped finance the fledgling Nationalist regime with his control of the area's opium revenues (Martin 1995, pp. 82–3).

The alliance between Chiang and Du's Green Gang was a most profitable one. In the very first year after the success of the Northern Expedition, the new Nationalist government gained $40 million in opium revenue and by 1933, the income had jumped to $30 million monthly (J. Marshall 1976, pp. 20–2). At that time, China was producing seven-eighths of the global opium supply, and both Du's "Da Kongsi" (The Big Company) and the Japanese in Tianjin had set up laboratories producing both morphine and heroin. In fact, the production levels of opiates now gave China a surplus that made it possible for China to turn the tables on the western powers and begin exporting drugs to the United States and Europe. American gangsters beginning with Arnold Rothstein and going on to Meyer Lansky, Charles "Lucky" Luciano, Louis "Lepke" Buchalter, and Jasha Katsenberg, forged links with Chinese drug lords, both in Shanghai and California to obtain supplies for the growing American narcotics market J. Marshall 1976, pp. 29–30).

Chiang, in fact went on to build his entire regime around the monopolization and protection of opium production and traffic. Jonathan Marshall's study on the connections between the Republican government and the opium traffic is a devastating critique of Republican China on the eve of the Japanese invasion.

> Chiang Kai-shek, who relished neither the traffic nor the disunity it brought China, came to power under such conditions. Refusing to break with the past or to challenge the pattern of dependence on foreign capital and the tra-ditional class structure, Chiang pragmatically forged alliances with provincial bosses and urban gangsters who demanded protection for their stake in the opium traffic. Chiang himself soon learned the political potential of the traffic and used it to finance his wars against the Japanese, Communists, and rival warlords. By moving to centralize the traffic under his personal control under the guise of "suppression," he sought to extend his regime's control. As a result, corruption and gangsterism, part of Chiang's unhappier inheritance, thrived as never before.
>
> (J. Marshall 1976, p. 19)

When Chiang was driven to Chongqing in 1939 by the Japanese, he became dependent upon the opium warlords of Sichuan and Yunnan. The best he could do was to displace them and attempt to control the opium revenues himself. Thus, the opium regimes continued to flourish in China through the 1940s. The system was only driven out of China when victorious Red Army forces finally expelled the last Guomindang remnants from southwestern China.

It should be understood, however, that there were few unambiguous "angels" in China. Even the Communist Party, up to and even after the establishment of the Peoples' Republic itself relied on opium revenues in certain areas. The Chinese Communists continued to produce and export opium from Shandong through the period 1927/52. Much as the other emerging powers in China, the Party used it as a source of profit and revenue to maintain their newly established political order (Devido 1996). On the other hand, it is also true that once firmly in power, the communists were able to eradicate opium cultivation and opium use within China almost completely by 1952 (Zhou 1997). However, even as they expelled the plague from China, the virus escaped to regain its strength and reinfect other populations.

As Alfred McCoy and his collaborators have shown, the system of "Opium Warlords" did not disappear, but was carried into the Shan Plateau and the inaccessible borderlands of Northern Burma and Laos. The warlord pattern today persists in the Golden Triangle. There was thus a direct connection between the Chinese warlord opium regimes of Yunnan and the global heroin traffic of the latter twentieth century. The heroin export traffic of the Shan Plateau was established by ex-Guomindang General Li Mi who, together with tens of thousands of troops, retreated from China in 1949. Because of the weakness of the Burmese military and with the support of the American Central Intelligence Agency's misguided anti-communist efforts of the 1950s and 1960s, this vagrant seed of the nineteenth-century opium regime struck root in the stateless land of the Golden Triangle (McCoy 1992, pp. 162–92)

The strange progress of opium

We see a rather intriguing transformation of the opium trade in the second half of the nineteenth century and early twentieth century. Legalization of the trade in China made it possible for Asian entrepreneurs to take control of the opium trade. As the English in Singapore and the port cities of China and Southeast Asia saw it, "Jews and Armenians" had seized control of the trade. While it is true that the Sassoons and the Chinese guilds had come to dominate the international trade in opium after 1870, it is clear that so far as distribution of opium was concerned, the Chinese alone dominated the domestic marketplaces. Part of the reason for this was because most of the consumers were Chinese, but then, the Chinese controlled virtually the entire retail structure of the Chinese and Southeast Asian economies at the turn of the century.

Within China, legalization of the trade was a green light for domestic cultivation of opium. Chinese opium cultivation appeared in response to the high demands of the 1820s, and by the time of the Opium War had already become well-established. The English had created a drug market in China, it seemed only natural that at some point the Chinese would begin an import-substitution industry in response to that market. For the rest of the century however, it was possible for British statesmen to point to this cultivation as an excuse for maintaining Indian production and continuing their exports to China.

Defenders of the opium trade continued to argue that Britain only sold opium because the Chinese demanded it, and claimed that if they withdrew, then someone else would take over. Nevertheless, the evidence indicates that at least until the 1870s, British Indian production drove the trade. The Indian producers consistently expanded their production during the nineteenth century, more as a response to competition within India, rather than as a response to the growth of the Chinese market. Indian production usually ran ahead of the Chinese demand during the years between 1820 and 1865. This is why there were so many crashes in the market and such a jagged price profile. Every spurt of production in India eventually brought a crash as it verged into overproduction and glutted the market. Prices would then fall, and as they did, new smokers were attracted to the drug. If Indian production was cut back for a time, then prices would begin to rise again, and the Indian government would attempt to maintain what it considered an optimum revenue. This, however, would last only until some other group of competitors saw the possibility of profit, and then further increases in production would follow. There was always competition, if not from Americans with Turkish opium, or British and Parsee traders with Malwa opium, then finally there was Chinese domestic production. On the other hand, as the supply of opium increased, so too did the number of smokers.

Ultimately, the trade was taken over by Asians. In Malwa, where "free cultivation" was permitted, the Sassoons came to dominate. In British India, the government Agencies continued to control production, but once it was auctioned, the Sassoons and other "non-Europeans" such as the Armenians, Parsees and Chinese took control of the drug and its distribution to the rest of eastern and southeastern Asia. This did not mean, however, that Europeans lost the advantage of opium profits. In India, the British government took its profit off the top in three ways: first by monopolizing the cultivation in Bihar and Benares and taking a direct gain at the Calcutta sales; second from the "pass duty" collected on Malwa opium before it was exported from India; and finally, from the monopoly of retail sales inside of India. This final category, the *abkari* system (as it was called in India) or the revenue farming system as was known in Southeast Asia, was a characteristic of all the colonial and quasi-colonial regimes of Asia during the nineteenth and early twentieth centuries. These systems will be examined in more detail in Chapter 7. The point here is simply that European rulers had once again managed to distance themselves from "the ins and outs of the trade" as Gulland called them, while at the same time, never letting go of the top level of profits from the traffic itself.

Thus, even though the entire imperial order in Asia was to some degree dependent upon opium revenues, Europeans themselves could adopt the attitude that opium was a weakness peculiar to Asians. Indeed, this idea became part of the virtual bedrock of the orientalist discourse. In particular, the practice of *smoking* opium was singled out as the most decadent, dangerous and depraved method of using the substance. A rather clear dividing line, that separated the "Asiatics" from the whites grew up around opium usage. Even Indians still tended to ingest opium rather than smoke it. And, when the habit of smoking did appear in parts of India (including Burma, during this period) and ultimately in Europe and America it was seen as an aberration and something to be eliminated or at least delimited to local Chinese consumers. In the final instance however, the appearance of opium smokers in these latter regions was usually the signal for the anti-opium movements to go into high gear and raise the specter of oriental decay seeping into Christian civilization.

7 A matter of considerably greater solicitude

Opium "farms" in Southeast Asia

The European position in China was reinforced by the colonial possessions in Southeast Asia. Initially, aside from spices and a few locally available products, Southeast Asia was important because it was a source of products which were in demand in China. Opium was often traded for these goods. Moreover, the region was strategically important for access to China from India, thus it protected the opium route. By the nineteenth century, Southeast Asia became valuable in its own right to Europeans because it provided important industrial and agricultural commodities to the west. These included timber, tin, rubber, tapioca, gambier, tobacco, sugar, coffee and pepper, most of which were produced by Chinese immigrant labor. Here too, opium had a role.

It is easy to conclude that the opium trade in Southeast Asia was strictly a British enterprise. Between 1750 and 1820, the British managed to gain effective control of the South Asian opium regions. British traders tended to dominate the carrying trade in opium to Southeast Asia as well as to China. Moreover, a great deal of opium was distributed to the region through the British ports of Singapore and Penang. Despite Britain's primacy in the opium trade however, other European colonial powers also participated in the trade throughout the nineteenth century and into the twentieth.

All of the colonial powers sold opium to their subjects in Southeast Asia. Every single Southeast Asian colony, and Siam as well, relied on some sort of opium farm or state monopoly for an important share of their revenue during the nineteenth and early twentieth centuries. These revenue-collecting institutions were at the heart of European colonialism in Southeast Asia (Butcher 1983). All needed opium to finance their colonial governments and many relied on the British to provide it. In regard to the opium trade, they were thus of one mind with the British. Perhaps the French or the Dutch would rather have had their own sources of opium, but they did not. They, like the Spanish, bought theirs from the British. At bottom, none could do without it. That is, they all agreed that it should continue and that, within their dominions, they should control it and profit from it. Although there was a high degree of strategic and economic competition among the European colonial powers, all collaborated in the opium regime until the early years of the twentieth century.

The farms and monopolies solved a crucial problem of colonial finance in that they were a supplement to colonial revenues. The Straits Settlements, for example were a case in point. Singapore was established in 1819, with the intention of avoiding the administrative costs that had undermined the Portuguese, the Spanish and the Dutch colonial establishments of earlier years. It was only to be a port and not a territorial empire. Unlike India, there were few peoples over whom to establish government, thus it was anticipated that the administrative and military costs would be minimal. Trade was to be free, and therefore could not be a source of taxation. With few inhabitants, not much agriculture, and no other products of the land, there was very little to tax. The situation stimulated commerce, but offered no means of paying administrative expenses. Even though the traders agreed that someone should suppress piracy and maintain lighthouses on some of the more dangerous reefs, they were unwilling to accept a tax on trade to pay for these things (Turnbull 1977). Raffles himself had left no clear guidance on exactly how the state was to be financed. Major William Farquar, Raffles second-in-command, took matters into his own hands in the latter's absence, and established the settlement's first revenue farms. Raffles later objected, but the farms stayed and were later placed on a more solid footing by John Crawfurd when he was Resident from 1824–8. The free trade regime was extended to Melaka and Penang in 1824 and the entire colony was from then on largely dependent upon the revenue from farms (Trocki 1990; Wong 1964–5).

The opium farm was the mainstay of Singapore's revenue, and the same was true for Melaka and Penang. In these two settlements, the farms were already well-established institutions well before the foundation of Singapore. For over a century, the income gained from selling opium to the inhabitants of these settlements regularly provided between 30 and 60 percent of the locally collected revenue (Trocki 1990). Other colonial settlements did not forego the taxing of trade, moreover they were sometimes able to tax land, agricultural production or other exports, or to collect a capitation tax. Even with these resources, they still had budget deficits which metropolitan governments were reluctant to cover. For all these other territories, the opium farm, together with a number of other farms, offered an important supplementary revenue.

It is one of the ironies of this age of high imperialism that these revenue farming networks were so vital to the fiscal stability of the entire European colonial enterprise. Most of the other major colonial territories derived from 25 to 30 percent of their revenues from opium farms or monopolies. At the end of the nineteenth century, in the Netherlands Indies, opium contributed about 35 percent to net revenues (Diehl 1993, p. 208). In the French colony of Cochinchina during the 1860s and 1870s, opium was the single largest revenue-generating operation (Nankoe 1993, p. 189). Between 1861 and 1882 the Cochinchinese opium farm contributed about 30 percent of the colonial revenues (Descours-Gatin 1992, pp. 100–1). Ian Brown has shown that the Siamese opium farm generated 5 million baht in 1901–2 out of a total government revenue of 36 million baht and by 1905–6 it had risen to 10 million baht in a total of 52 million (Brown 1993a, p. 233). These figures are typical of the entire period of colonial rule prior to 1920. While the opium farms provided smaller proportions of the revenue in places such as British Burma and the Philippines under Spanish rule, they were, nonetheless significant revenue generators (Brown 1993a; Butcher 1983; Le Failler 1993; Rush 1990; Wickberg 1965). Management of the farms tended to be relatively uniform across the region. Wickberg's description of the system in the Philippines, is typical of other colonies. There as in Burma, the consumption of opium was limited to the Chinese:

> In its final form the opium monopoly worked as follows: in each province where there were sufficient Chinese to make it worthwhile (non-Chinese were strictly forbidden the use of opium), monopoly rights were leased to a contractor on a three-year basis. He was to import opium, store it in a specially designated customs warehouse until ready for use, establish and supply as many government-licensed opium dens as the number of customers seemed to warrant, and prepare and sell opium to consumers. He might subcontract his monopoly as he wished, and was further empowered to select as many deputies as he needed to search out contraband. Furthermore, he had access to whatever law enforcement institutions were necessary to maintain his monopoly.
>
> (Wickberg 1965, p. 115)

The opium farm was a monopoly concession which the government usually auctioned to the highest bidder for a specific period of time. Three years for a specific territory seems to have been the standard period throughout Southeast Asia. The winning bidder gained the right to manufacture chandu, or smokeable opium from raw opium, as well as the right to retail chandu to the local population. There were also opium farms in British India and in most of the princely states of the subcontinent, where they were known as the *abkari* revenue. The opium revenue, as well as the revenue from liquor sales, coconut toddy, cannabis preparations, gambling, markets, pawnbroking, pork sales, prostitution as well as a number of other concessions were all farmed out at various places and times in Southeast Asia, Hong Kong and Australia during this period. This was usually labelled as the excise revenue in colonial budgets. Among all of the different types of farms, the opium farms were almost always the most lucrative.[1]

The opium farmers were invariably Chinese. To be successful a farmer needed several kinds of resources. In addition to processing the drug, for which some sort of building, equipment and trained personnel were necessary, the farmer also required either ownership or control of a network of retail outlets. These were opium shops where small quantities (anywhere from a "pot" of one or two tahils, to "tubes" of several *hoons*) of chandu were sold on a take-away basis; or divans or opium dens where the drug was smoked on the premises. Beyond these facilities, it was also necessary for the farmer to control a fairly large body of private security personnel. Part of the contract was that the farmer was responsible for the integrity of his monopoly. Even though the state passed laws to protect the revenue farming system, it was the farmer's business to police it.

The farmer thus controlled a private police force as well as a network of informers. In Singapore, the police were called *chintengs* or revenue peons, and in the 1880s a force of about eighty men were employed in this function. Very often these individuals were drawn from the local Chinese secret society or triad organization. In Java, the informers were called "mata-mata" or "eyes" and were often Javanese (Rush 1990). The major job of these police and informers was to prevent the smuggling of contraband opium into the farmer's territory. All of these facilities were part of the farmer's overhead. In addition, he had to purchase his stocks of raw opium on the open market and, of course, pay the government its monthly rent. What remained was his profit. It is clear that the profits could be immense, and normally the opium farmers were the wealthiest and most powerful Chinese in all of Southeast Asia. The evidence for this is quite compelling. Whether one looks at compendiums such as Song Ong Siang's *One Hundred Years of Chinese History in Singapore*, or more recent studies on Chinese economic leadership in colonial Southeast Asia, it is clear that opium farmers ranked very highly among the wealthiest, most powerful and most respected Chinese in the respective area. Finally, and most importantly, it was necessary to already have wealth, power and respect in order to become an opium farmer (Brown 1993b; Butcher 1983; Cushman 1991; Cushman 1993b; Godley 1981; Godley 1993; Le Failler 1993; Rush 1990; Song 1923; Trocki 1990; Wickberg 1965).

Although the sources usually speak of the farmer as an individual, by the middle of the nineteenth century, most opium farms were held by corporate bodies of investors, usually called a *kongsi* after the Chinese term for company. These were sometimes styled syndicates by contemporary Europeans. These *kongsi*, or syndicates, were generally run by cliques of the wealthiest merchants in the area. The farms always needed start-up capital and farmers had to put up security such as title deeds or other assets to cover defaults and other contingencies. Some members undertook the actual management of the farm while others simply invested money and held shares in the *kongsi*. The opium farming *kongsi* were probably the largest locally based forms of economic organization in colonial Southeast Asia until the twentieth century. At the time, the farms were responsible for the largest flows of cash in any given state. Literally hundreds of thousands, sometimes millions of dollars flowed through their coffers every month. For instance, in the Netherlands Indies alone, in 1895 the opium farm delivered ƒ17.7 million and in 1925, the government-controlled *régie* or monopoly, was worth ƒ41.9 million (Diehl 1993, p. 208).

By the late nineteenth century, many of the farms for densely populated territories, such as Singapore, Hong Kong, Saigon and even Shanghai, demanded such large investments that money was drawn from all over the region. As a result, it was common for wealthy Chinese from one colony to buy up or invest in the farms of another colony. As early as 1880, the Singapore farms had fallen under the control of a group of Penang merchants. At the same time, a one-time farmer from Singapore had interests in the Hong Kong opium farm. Even early in the nineteenth century, merchants in Penang and Singapore frequently held farms, or interests in farms in the Dutch territories of Riau and Sumatra. Later they also held interests in Javanese farms. In 1886, Lee Keng Yam, a Melaka Chinese, headed a syndicate which held both the Singapore farms and the Hong Kong farms, as well as farms in the Netherlands East Indies (Trocki 1990, pp. 194–5).

There are a number of important points here. The first is simply that the opium farms were large, complex enterprises that involved enormous amounts of capital. As a type of economic organization, they were found throughout Southeast Asia and the southern Chinese littoral. In fact, when we step back and look at it in its entirety, we see that the opium farming syndicates constituted a vast network of interconnected kongsis stretching from Burma to Shanghai and extending as far south as Australia. In most cases, the wealthiest local Chinese clique exercised a level of control or at least participated in the farms in their area, but almost all of them depended on outside connections that usually reached beyond the borders of their particular territory. The farms thus constituted a more-or-less separate economic system that was dominated exclusively by Chinese. It was, moreover, a network that integrated the opium economies of colonial Southeast Asia and connected them with those of southern China on the one hand and with India, on the other.

All of these opium farming systems depended on the Chinese. Chinese merchants were always the farmers and very often, Chinese laborers were also the major consumers. John Cameron's comment on the Singapore farm would deny this statement, but the evidence to the contrary is too abundant to sustain his assertion. He claimed:

> By greatly enhancing the cost to the consumer the consumption is kept within narrow bounds. To the labouring classes it is all but banned and forbidden fare, and even to the rich its indulgence to excess would be a serious item of expenditure.
>
> (Cameron 1865, p. 217)

While Cameron's remarks are generally quite useful, he seems to have been misinformed regarding the inability of the poorest consumers to obtain opium. Much of the evidence available indicates that the most reliable consumers were the poorest classes of laborers, the Chinese coolies. Indeed, it is hard to see how the opium farm could have paid half of Singapore's revenue if it did not sell opium to the greater portion of its population. In 1848, in one of the first substantial critiques of the opium farming system, Dr. Robert Little, the Singapore surgeon noted:

> Now certain trades are greater consumers of opium than others. Amongst the principal are carpenters, box makers, blacksmiths, barbers, hunters, coolies, boatmen, and gambier planters including gardeners. These trades seem almost entirely to be devoted to the drug. I should say fully 85 percent are opium smokers.
>
> (Little 1848, pp. 20–1)

Other comments on Chinese miners in the Malay or Siamese states indicate that opium was an absolute necessity for laborers. H. Warrington Smyth claimed that mining coolies would desert if there were no opium.

Chinese farmers and Chinese smokers

Before 1850, the development of the opium trade in Southeast Asia was limited because of the low density and the relative lack of affluence of the native population. By the middle of the nineteenth century, the weight of the Chinese migration to Southeast Asia had significantly changed this equation. Chinese had been migrating to Southeast Asia as laborers since the early eighteenth century and although initially they constituted one of several markets for imported opium, their numbers were relatively small. The growing opportunities offered by European settlements in Southeast Asia, together with the increasing population pressures in South China, the disruption resulting from the Tai Ping Rebellion and other factors caused a major explosion of Chinese migration to the region in the years after 1850. This migration began to burgeon at the same time that European merchants in Southeast Asian ports, such as Singapore, were coming to realize that they would not get rich by speculating in the opium trade to China, or in any branch of the China trade, for that matter. The advent of clipper ships and later of steam power, reduced the necessity for secondary opium markets in places like Singapore. The security that Chinese capitalists found in European settlements gave them the opportunity to dominate the trade in Southeast Asian commodities to China. There were thus relatively few opportunities for European merchants in Southeast Asia.

The "salvation" for European merchants in the region was the exploitation of local resources for shipment back to Europe and North America. The presence of Chinese merchants, laborers, craftsmen and retailers are what made this commodity trade viable. Success went to those European capitalists and local rulers who could exploit and profit from the services, the productions and the consumption of the Chinese. Perhaps John Crawfurd said it most bluntly: "I entertain so high an opinion of the industry, skill and *capacity of consumption* of the Chinese, that I consider one Chinaman equal in value to the state to *two* natives of the Coromandel coast and to four Malays at least" (Crawfurd 1854, p. 410; italics in the original). They were, however, a resource that Europeans found necessary to control, and the opium farms were the keys to that effort.

While there were opium farms in virtually every European colony and in Siam, there was a fairly high degree of local variation in the organization and scope of these farms. For the purposes of discussion, it is useful to recognize three different configurations of farms: the first, which might be called the Malayan pattern; the second, the Javanese pattern; and the third, simply the urban pattern. The primary differences between the first two systems relate to the ethnicity of the consumers and to the nature of the local economy. In the Malayan pattern, most of the consumers were Chinese, while in the Javanese, they tended to be Southeast Asians. Another distinction was that in the first type, the farmers were usually involved in one specific type of commodity production which also employed most of the Chinese laborers who were their consumers. In the Javanese pattern, the economic interests of the farmers and the general economy were far more diverse. The third type of farm could be found in all large Asian cities and served users of a variety of ethnic and economic backgrounds. Its special features arose from its urban base.

The Malayan system was found throughout the Malay world: that is, from the provinces of southern Siam and throughout the Malay Peninsula including Singapore. It continued into the Riau-Lingga Archipelago to the islands of Bangka and Billiton. It was also found in parts of Sumatra during the nineteenth century and in the settled parts of Borneo. Some variations of it seem to have existed in certain parts of Australia and the Philippines as well. The purest forms of the Javanese pattern were to be found on the island of Java and in the central plain of Siam. To some extent it also characterized the French systems in Cochinchina and Tongkin.

The Malayan system

In the Malay states, such as Perak or Johor, by the mid-nineteenth century, the picture was fairly simple. Virtually all of the opium consumers were Chinese coolies who worked in the tin-mining settlements, as in Perak; or on pepper and gambier plantations as in Johor. Generally these were financed by Chinese merchants in the Straits Settlements. For much of the nineteenth century, the Malayan farms can be subdivided by region and by type of industry. The merchants of Penang who invested in tin mining, controlled the farms of the Malay and Siamese states which were the centers of tin mining. The Singapore merchants, on the other hand, generally drew their income from the pepper and gambier agriculture which was based on Singapore Island, Johor and the Riau Archipelago.

The management of Chinese labor was common to both areas. Almost all the laborers were very recent migrants and were housed in "kongsi lines" or long attap sheds located near their worksites. The coolies had either migrated voluntarily at their own expense or had been imported from China as "piglets" under something like the "credit-ticket" scheme, in which the coolie broker who recruited them paid for their transportation from China. The laborers who came without debts usually had a bit more latitude in choosing their employers, but they often ended up in the same sort of situation as those who were already indebted. The coolie might begin his career in the mines or plantations of the Malayan jungle with a debt of about $15 to $20, or about six months' to a year's wages, thus most of the cards were already stacked against him.

At the time, wages were around $3 to $4 per month for mining and planting coolies. While expenses were fairly low, life was hard and lacking in virtually all amenities. Very often, the only form of diversion was the local opium shop. This too was usually owned, wholly or in part, by the same capitalists who held the coolie's debt. It was thus very easy for the coolie to slide deeper and deeper into debt and, in the process, become addicted to opium. Such an arrangement seemed central to the labor control system that existed in these parts of Southeast Asia.

Opium was not only useful for the capitalist, but despite its dangers, also offered certain benefits to the coolie in the jungle. The pipe in the evening served as his "rainy day woman," and was probably as close to sexual pleasure as he was likely to get unless he found it among his fellows, as many did. Swallowing a bit of opium in the middle of the day eased the pain in his muscles and made it possible to go on working through the heat. It also dulled the pain of standing for hours at a time knee-deep in bone-chilling jungle streams and mining sluices shovelling mud to separate out the ore. In contrast to the contemporary anti-opium propaganda, much evidence suggests that opium did not immediately turn its users into soporific vegetables, or sunken chested hulks. Some commentators report that coolies could work half the day, sit down for a rest, take a few puffs from an opium pipe, and then get up, "refreshed" and work for several more hours. This view was expressed by John Anderson, a Singapore merchant who was interviewed by the Royal Commission which investigated the trade in 1894.

> I have travelled on both sides of the Malay Peninsula, over tin mining districts, and have seen thousands and thousands of Chinese miners working in swarms at tin mines, displaying physical energy and endurance that the white man, under similar conditions, could not have and apply, and at the same time keep his full health . . . And when I have seen these Chinamen after working all but naked for hours together in water up to their knees, go back to their quarters, and either before or after their meal, or both, smoke a pipe or pipes of opium apparently without prejudicial effect, I have marvelled at the arbitrary inconsistency of some people in Britain who, with no true knowledge of the matter . . . would say to [a Chinese] 'Opium you shall not have.'
>
> (RoyComm 1895, v.5, p. 175)

There is no reason to doubt the sincerity of this and many similar observations. It can be argued, and indeed it was by many defenders of the system, that opium was a necessary work drug for the Chinese laborers. In addition to killing the pain of daily labor, opium was also the coolie's prophylactic against diarrhea caused by dysentery, bad food, and the range of intestinal parasites that plagued one in the jungle. It also reduced fever for those attacked by malaria, blackwater fever, dengue, typhoid and other ailments. In a world with virtually no form of medical care and in a climate which Europeans considered one of the unhealthiest in the world, opium appeared to solve many problems. Despite its baneful and intoxicating effects, opium was considered a useful medication for the numerous illnesses that are found in the Far East. Dumarest noted:

> And yet, opium constituted a precious medication for the numerous maladies one finds throughout the Far East. It can be, in its turn, and according to the dose, and the time, a stimulant, a relaxant, an analgesic or a sleeping drug.[2]

He too, notes its use against cholera, dysentery and malaria as well as beri-beri and neurasthenia. It was also a common element in many native and European remedies. The drug was often used locally by Europeans "who smoked a little to immunize themselves against 'la cochinchinette.'" ("La cochinchinette" was described as persistent intestinal "intoxications" caused by "salts of lead" and other impurities found in the drinking water of Saigon. See Dumarest 1938, pp. 32–3.) Actually, opium did not cure anything, it simply masked the symptoms and made it possible for an individual to ignore the messages of his body, and to go on working for yet another day. In all probability, opium made it possible for the coolie to wear out his body long before its time in a relatively painless fashion.

Other observers had a far more critical view of the impact of opium on its users. As early as 1809 a witness before the Penang Grand Jury claimed:

> The effects of the use of this drug are so injurious and destructive to the human constitution that the minds of those who use it are in a short time so debased as to become incapable of any exertion, and their bodies so debilitated as to be rendered totally unfit and unable to perform or undergo any corporal labour or fatigue, so that their services and industry are not only lost to the community, but it must be inferred . . . that they are under the necessity of resorting to robbery, plunder and depredation to enable them to procure . . . this pernicious drug.
>
> (Quoted in Wright 1961, pp. 167–8)

Those who follow the drug debates of the late twentieth century will realize that people have been saying some of the same things about drugs for the past two centuries. There is no need to discount this report any more than John Anderson's, but we do not have much clear evidence about how long it took for an individual to be transformed from the coolies that Anderson saw to those described by the Penang witness. There is also no reliable information on how long an individual could smoke opium before he became addicted, nor do we know for how long a habit could be maintained at a given level.

On the other hand, given the prospects of survival in the jungles, one might suspect that the coolies probably took the easiest way out. H. Warrington Smyth, an English mining engineer who worked for the Siamese government, estimated that the death rate for mining coolies in southern Siam was about 60 percent overall, and for new arrivals it was even higher. The main causes of death were fever and dysentery. Smyth's greatest concern was that word of an epidemic or the failure of the opium supply would cause the laborers to flee. A mine owner could lose 70 percent of his work force through desertion. This was the other great incentive to provide the coolies with a regular supply of opium. Without opium, coolies would desert. With it, at least they could forget their problems for a while (Smyth 1898a, pp. 20–1). Even Smyth, however, is not consistent in his views on the effects of opium. While on the one hand strongly recommending opium for the mining coolies, elsewhere he claims that it sometimes made Laotians unfit for work.

> The Lao of the Me Kwang struck us as, if possible much lazier than the Lao
> Pong Dam, and as having more vices. The men all smoke opium habitually,
> and though there is very little drunkenness, the people drink their full share
> of the native liquor, while theft is not entirely unknown. There is no doubt
> one cannot condemn Indo-Chinese mountaineers for smoking opium, for it
> is, in moderation, the best antidote that exists to the terrible fever bred in
> these hills by long marches, varying temperatures, and empty stomachs. At
> the same time, the Nan men do without it, and they are almost the only
> people of Indo-China of whom it can be said. My experience of opium-
> smokers was not, so far, a favourable one, as the majority of my escort were
> hopelessly addicted to it, and dreamed their way through life with as little
> exertion to themselves as possible; they were perfectly useless for any
> purpose whatever. A wider experience showed that the Shans, as a rule,
> do not take to the drug in excess, and that its use in moderation is certainly
> beneficial to them. This has long been maintained by Mr. Scott, whose
> opinion, based on long experience and careful observation is to my mind
> conclusive.
>
> (Smyth 1898b, pp. 194–5)

One could argue that although the coolie in the jungle faced suffering and a
dismal existence, his life in China would possibly have been even shorter and
more brutish had he not migrated. There he confronted unemployment,
landlessness, overcrowding, disease, warfare, and banditry as well as grinding
poverty. Moreover, he would not have been able to afford opium. In the jungles
of Southeast Asia, at least there seemed to be a chance that a coolie (if he could
resist the temptation of opium) could save his money, guard his health and
perhaps rise out of the muck. He could become, if not a wealthy taukeh himself,
at least possessed of enough money to come home with a small share of capital,
find a wife and have a better life than he might have had. Even if he was
unsuccessful, he might have passed his short life with the comfort of opium.
Dr. Little saw another possible future for these workers. His vision was the path
not taken in 1848.

> How different would be the condition of the people of this island if instead of
> spending on Opium $417,884 yearly, they knew not the vice; that money
> hardly and honestly toiled for would be spent in clothes, in food and better
> houses, the men could afford to marry, a taste would be formed for finery,
> and something more would be required, than bare rice the necessary of life
> . . . instead of 40 or 50 living under one roof, too often a mass of iniquity,
> a man and his family, or one or two single individuals could afford to live in a
> house of their own.
>
> (Little 1848, pp. 73–4)

Obviously an idealistic picture, and one, that would have been of little short-term
benefit to either the capitalists or the colonial treasury.

Opium was not peripheral to the system, as Dr. Little seems to have assumed, but rather it was central. Were it not for opium, there would have been little profit for the capitalist. His tin, pepper, gambier and even gold, would have been less competitive on the world market. If the cost of employing labor were not recaptured by the capitalist and recycled, as it were, there would have been no profit. This was certainly the case for the pepper and gambier economy that characterized all of the Chinese laboring settlements of Singapore, Johor, Riau, and later Negri Sembilan (Trocki 1979). Since the sale of gambier and pepper in the Singapore market could pay for little more than the cost of the labor, it is impossible to see how there would have been a profit, unless the investor could somehow recoup the labor costs. This was done largely through the mechanism of the opium farm. Smyth makes the point that the profits of the mining capitalist also depended on the revenues from opium as well as the other concessions that kept the coolie in debt:

> The Chinese "tauke" is in a position to work mines which no one else could possibly make pay. Very often he does not look to the actual mining for a profit but to the gambling, opium, and spirit shops attached to the "kongsi," and to the food and stores with which he supplies his coolies.
>
> (Smyth 1898b, p. 328)

All of the Chinese settlements in the jungle produced exportable commodities. The investors who hired the labor and financed the production also held shares in the opium farms. They could easily afford to "pay" their coolies $3 or $4 per month, partly because this was often only a bookkeeping transaction. Government officials in British Malaya not only understood the connection between opium farming and commodity production, but acted to facilitate it.

> Capitalists who already had a large stake in the country were in a strong position when it came to tendering for the farms, for a number of reasons; they were in a position to expand their enterprises if their applications were successful, and restrict production and immigration in an attempt to break the farm if they were not; and since their prosperity was of some importance to the state, there was an incentive to support them financially by giving them the farms.
>
> (Sadka 1968, pp. 333–4)

The amounts which the average smoker used were matters of speculation and incidental reports. J.D. Kerr, said that in China, the largest opium smokers consumed between 16.2 and 90 grams per day. S. Laurent said that a large smoker consumed 20 to 40 grams a day, while a Singapore doctor had a patient who used 243 grams daily. Various reports suggest that it was common for an average smoker to consume about one to two tahils or 30 to 70 grams a day. The price of opium in Singapore stayed below $1 per tahil (37.6 grams) until 1862. By 1864, it had risen to $2, while at the same time, rice was $2 per pikul (60 kilos).

Descours-Gatin argues that in 18 days an ordinary smoker spent as much on opium as he would to feed himself for two months. Thus, a worker who made $5 per month could spend $3 in one day on opium or 60 percent of his wage (Descours-Gatin 1992, p. 103–4). Of course, if the worker were willing to smoke dross, or the remains left from a previous smoker, he could economize.

That the system was designed to get coolies into debt seems obvious. Even more so is the proposition that it depended on most of them never getting out of debt, and on a significant proportion of them being permanently trapped by opium in the cycle of labor, indebtedness, addiction and ultimate death. There are indications that in some places and certain times, Chinese laborers could bargain with their employers from positions of strength (Pasquel 1895–6). There was a labor shortage in Southeast Asia which they alone seemed capable of filling. It was easy enough to slip off in the middle of the night or even during the day, into the jungle and to turn up, unencumbered by debt, at another mine or another plantation where labor was needed and few questions would be asked. This was particularly easy in Malaya and Siam where the governments made few efforts to restrict the movement of labor. It was much more difficult in Sumatra where the Dutch colonial government imposed a penal sanction for runaway laborers and an arrestee could be forced to return to work, in chains. The Sumatran plantations between Medan and Deli had a very bad reputation among Chinese laborers (Stoler 1985).

Opium thus served a number of purposes among the Chinese in Southeast Asia. In the first instance, it filled what may seem the misguided, but very real physical and psychic needs of the users. This is why there was a demand. Because they earned a cash income, they could afford to buy opium. They paid the long-term costs of satisfying those needs both in terms of contracting a chemical dependency as well as in whatever damage was done to them physically by the difficulty of their labors. Perhaps more important, opium also left them in debt and deprived them of their wages. In this respect, opium served the colonial state and provided an easily collected revenue from those who could least afford it and who were least likely to protest the exaction. It also served the Chinese entrepreneurs by giving them a large cash flow together with the means of continually compounding their profits through the relationship between opium farming and commodity production. It was thus possible to bring important commodities to market at lower prices. This factor served the needs of European capitalists and, by extension, European industry which was thus able to procure strategic commodities at rock-bottom prices. Finally, it served the capitalist system in Asia by providing an easy avenue for rapid accumulation. It seemed the perfect system for the rulers of the Southeast Asian colonies.

The problem, however, was in the fact that the different mining and planting zones were not coterminous with political or administrative territories. For instance, the pepper and gambier area around Singapore included the Dutch territories in Riau, the Malay state of Johor and the other British territory of Melaka. This meant that each of the farms for these four territories were leased separately. As a result, the holder of the most valuable farm, such as that of

Singapore, often needed to buy all of the other farms in surrounding territories in order to prevent smuggling. If he did not, then competing syndicates would buy farms in adjoining territories and work to undercut the Singapore farmer. The rulers of these other territories, such as the Maharaja of Johor or the Resident of Riau, could demand premium prices for their farms simply on the basis of their nuisance value. There was, thus, every incentive for farming syndicates to transgress political boundaries and to become truly "international."

Because of the potential for smuggling and violence, the opium farms were almost always connected to the secret societies that flourished in Chinese communities throughout Southeast Asia. The historical development of the societies was largely affected by their relation to the farms. Initially, perhaps in the early nineteenth century, the societies seem to have been simply ritual brotherhoods which underlaid the partnership agreements that bound together the mining and planting kongsis. These appear at first to have been partnerships between laborers, planters and capitalists. These societies also provided self-defense forces for settlements in the jungle which were far away from colonial protection. As time passed, the societies became the muscle for the planters and taukehs. They became gangs of toughs who intimidated the coolies and protected the other economic interests of the shopkeepers and merchants. In particular they were necessary to protect the opium farms, or conversely to attack the farms of rival syndicates. This was their role in places like Singapore, Penang and the tin-mining states of western Malaya and southern Siam during the mid-nineteenth century.

In the years when competing opium syndicates fought for control of the various farming territories, the secret societies flourished because they had direct access to the major economic institutions of the region. By the late 1860s, however, their influence began to wane. One cause for this seems to have been the efforts by the moneyed interests of the Straits Settlements to reach compromises in controlling the opium farms. In 1870, the "Great Opium Syndicate" (Trocki 1987; Trocki 1993) was formed in Singapore which represented the combined capital of both Hokkien and Teochew merchant cliques in the settlement. It also united the opium farms of Singapore, Johor, Riau and Melaka (Trocki 1990). This reflected a natural tendency toward industry-wide monopoly combinations. Unfortunately such combinations worked against the fiscal interests of the colonial governors who hoped that competition would increase their revenues. It was only when the value of the urban farms outweighed those which serviced the coolies in the jungles that colonial governments were able to gain a measure of control over their opium farmers.

The Javanese system

The other type of opium farm was found in areas, such as Java, where there was a fairly large population of Southeast Asia peasants. In these places the indigenous people made up a significant proportion of the consumers. The central plain of Siam, Cochinchina and Tongkin were similar situations. In these areas, the proportion of Chinese to native consumers varied considerably. In some places, while there were still many Chinese consumers they did not always make up a majority of the user population. As in the other areas however, the farmers were always Chinese. In Java, the smoking of opium had been practised since the seventeenth century. By the nineteenth century, the economies of the business had changed significantly. Every regency had its own opium farm and the business was highly competitive. One account described the opium farm auction as the "battle of kings" where the wealthiest, most powerful Chinese in the regency gathered to outdo one another in their fight for the concession. Each bidder sought to increase his prestige by outbidding his rivals (Rush 1990, p. 41).

Two important factors distinguished these farms from the Malayan type of farms. Since many consumers were members of the indigenous population, the governments had to be a little more circumspect about the farming system. Particularly toward the end of the nineteenth century, when colonial governments felt the need to justify their existence by claiming that they were working for the welfare of the natives, it was difficult to explain the opium farms. The Dutch "Ethical System," the French *Mission Civilisatrice*, and even the benevolent despotism of Siam's King Chulalongkorn all drew considerable fiscal support from their opium farms. In Malaya, Burma and the Philippines the farms could be justified on the ground that they merely served the "sojourning" Chinese. It was claimed that if they did not get their opium, then they would not remain and the work would not be done.

The opium farms often placed colonial governments in French Indochina or the Netherlands East Indies at a rhetorical disadvantage before metropolitan moralists. They too, however, tried to claim that opium-smoking was primarily a Chinese vice. In Cochinchina, they could point to the fact that the average Chinese smoker consumed 1.4 kg. annually compared to only 200 grams for the average Vietnamese smoker. Moreover, while nearly 40 percent of the Chinese population used opium, only 2 percent of the Vietnamese used it. Of course, these statistics need to be understood in light of the circumstances. The Chinese population was overwhelmingly young and male and were gainfully employed. They were, moreover, far outnumbered by the Vietnamese. The latter population showed a much more balanced age and sex distribution; and most did not participate in the cash economy. Among the Vietnamese, the French claimed that only the very rich or the very poor smoked opium. Those who had long hours of nothing to do, *les personnes oisives* (the idle rich) or *l'oisivete* (the unemployed) (Descours-Gatin 1992, p. 213–14).

In Siam, after several decades of unsuccessfully attempting to ban opium in the kingdom, a farming system was finally permitted and opium sales were legalized. This took place on the eve of the Bowring Treaty which opened Siam to European commerce. Here too, it was claimed that the opium was for the Chinese:

> In 1851 . . . Rama IV set up an opium farm for the exclusive benefit of the Chinese. This came about after certain Chinese petitioned the king to

appoint them farmers to manage opium strictly among Chinese in Bangkok and provincial towns, for which they would pay an annual fee of 10,000 taels Siamese (£5,000). In addition to the right to import opium for local consumption, the farmers could also export it to China.

(Viraphol 1977, p. 234)

Therefore they too could argue that opium was really only a Chinese vice and one that did not affect a significant portion of the indigenous population And, since the Chinese were merely sojourners, their behaviour really did not reflect adversely on government policy. Chinese, it was claimed, were inveterate opium smokers and it was not the job of the state to change their character. It therefore only made sense to tax opium since that would prevent "excessive indulgence."

This discourse was mirrored in some way, in almost all Asian colonies, and generally can be read as an effort to blame the victims. In Indochina the anti-Chinese rhetoric also became part of the government's campaign to take over the farms and organize a government monopoly or a *régie*. Use of opium by the Vietnamese population was portrayed as a result of the greed of the Chinese opium farmers.

> In a real sense, this political debate over the creation of the opium régie illustrated a much deeper structural reality. Vietnamese representatives on the Colonial Council claimed that the local Chinese merchants abused, mistreated and exploited the Vietnamese population. They sought the assistance of the French colonial administration to break the Chinese monopoly over trade in Cochinchina. For their part, the colonial administration used this ethnic antagonism to divide and rule.
>
> (Nankoe 1993, pp. 190–1)

It should come then as no surprise that the farms in the French and Dutch territories were taken over and turned into government monopolies far sooner than those in the British Malaya.

Despite these protestations about Chinese usage it seems clear that in both Java and Indochina, natives formed an important group of users. Cochinchina represented the largest opium-consuming area in the colony while Tongkin, in the north, was the second largest consuming area. Here, as in Java, farmers prepared several grades of opium. These varied in quality. The first grade was *chandu*, a preparation which has already been described. This was made from good quality Bengal opium. In Java, the second quality opium was *cacak*, intended for the "mass market," which was made with cheaper Turkish opium and adulterated with burnt sugar, lemon juice and *jijing* or opium dross, (the burnt remains of good opium). Jijing was also sold as yet a cheaper grade to poorer smokers. Finally, there was *tiké*, made from *cakal*, or chopped leaves, and other adulterants. Similar cheap grades also existed in Indochina. These were sold to the less affluent natives and often represented even greater profit for the opium dealer, since these preparations were little more than recycled opium.

The other major difference between these farms and those in British Malaya was that the farmers, if they were to succeed, found it necessary to form patronage relationships with the existing Southeast Asian power structures. This was most important in Siam where patronage was at the heart of the entire political economy, but it was also true in Java (Brown 1993a; Rush 1990; Wilson 1993). In Java and Siam, members of the local aristocracy received substantial "gifts" from opium farmers who operated in their territories. The farming system was thus more deeply entrenched than elsewhere. In Siam, the influential Chinese gained titles and many of them intermarried with the Thai elite, both in the court and among the provincial elite families. By contrast, the appearance of such alliances was far less welcome in the Netherlands Indies where the Dutch rulers discouraged such informal linkages.

Urban farms and the end of the farming system

In the long run, both types of farms got progressively larger and more valuable. Not only did revenues grow, but so too did the number of users and the amounts of opium consumed. Farms that included large urban areas grew the fastest, and it seems possible to conclude that there was a direct ratio between the modernization of the economy and the increase in opium smoking. Again, it is difficult to draw conclusions about cause and effect. On the one hand, we might conclude that as people got more money, they tended to spend it on opium. On the other hand, perhaps the need to satisfy a habit gave people an incentive to work for a cash income. Wherever there was cash, there was opium to soak it up.

Another thing happened as the size of the farms grew and became more urbanized. The connection between the farming system and one particular productive industry tended to become less and less important. Until the middle of the nineteenth century, a majority of Singapore's opium users, for instance, actually resided in the rural parts of the island and made their living as pepper and gambier planters. By the 1880s however, many of the planters had moved on to Johor and Riau and the urban area had grown, both in physical size and in influence. The Singapore farm thus became a truly urban farm, serving a variegated population of coolies, craftsmen, dock laborers, rickshaw pullers, and the entire range of city-based occupations. This level of variety meant that a link to the gambier industry was much less necessary for success in revenue farming ventures. Similar trends occured in other large Southeast Asian cities such as Batavia, Penang, Saigon, Bangkok and possibly Manila. Control of the farms no longer demanded control of a particular commodity production system. It was now possible for the colonial government to seek bidders from a wider group of capitalists, even those from outside the colony. Anyone would do, so long as they had the money and the will. Coupled with this was the fact that the colonial police forces had enhanced their ability to control the population. All of these factors tended to increase the power of the government vis-à-vis the farmers and the partnership between revenue farmers and colonial states began to be seen as less and less necessary (Trocki 1990). The development of farms in large urban areas was thus the first step in the elimination of farms altogether.

The farming system was always a partnership between the colonial state and the Chinese, and despite occasional differences, it reflected a relationship built upon a certain degree of trust. The French and the Dutch, in their colonies in Indochina and the Netherlands Indies were far less trusting than the British. Very soon after establishing themselves in Cochinchina, the French attempted to do away with the opium farms and tried to place them under a government monopoly, or at least give the farms to European investors. Neither alternative succeeded and by 1864 the colonial government once again gave the farms to a Chinese syndicate in Saigon. First it went to a group of Cantonese and later a Hokkien merchant clique formed the "Banhap" kongsi to bid for the farms themselves. This group held the farms until 1881, but there were continual squabbles with the government over the terms of the contract (Dumarest 1938, pp. 44–5; Nankoe 1993, pp. 184–6).

The Banhap clique was known for its methodical organization of the farms. In each district they set up a central trading post for opium. They also named a European agent in each district who had charge of relations with the French colonial authorities. These agents also had extensive powers to pursue smugglers. They were called the first "douaniers Cochinchinois" or Cochinchinese customs agents. This gave them a great deal of power which they quickly misused to enrich themselves and to gain commercial advantages (Dumarest 1938, p. 45). Abuses such as these made it painfully obvious that the farmers had gained an excessive amount of power within the colony.

After 1881, the French again attempted to organize a government monopoly. The French government abolished the farming system in 1883 and created a government monopoly (*régie directe*) but it was still under the control of the same Chinese who had previously run the opium farm.

> A special colonial agency was granted a monopoly over the importation of raw opium, the refining process and sales. However, Chinese businessmen still exercised considerable influence and control over the opium trade. The staff of this newly established agency consisted exclusively of Chinese merchants who had previously dominated the buying, refining and selling of opium. A refining plant was established in Saigon, and a well-to-do Chinese merchant was put in charge of preparing the final product. In the provinces this colonial agency distributed fixed quantities of processed opium to private warehouse owners who, after successfully bidding for the concession, in turn, enjoyed exclusive rights over sales within a determined area in return for the payment of a fixed fee . . . In short, despite the formal introduction of the opium régie, the colonial administration still maintained many features of the farm system.
> (Nankoe 1993, p. 191)

The Dutch had been in the habit of farming opium revenues to the Chinese for a very long time, in fact most scholars believe they were the first to do so (Rush

1990). Both opium farming as well as opium smoking may have originated in Java. By the 1890s, however, even the Dutch began to worry about their "partnership" with the Chinese and, when the French *régie* in Indochina appeared to prove successful, the Dutch were quick to emulate it in Java, and established their own monopoly.

In Java, the move toward eliminating the farm was also spurred by its increasing value and the increasing level of competition that now appeared in the bidding process. While such a development was one which colonial governments generally welcomed, they found that the Chinese were often willing to bid far more than the farms were worth. Once gaining the contract, the farmers would petition for relief and attempt to renegotiate the contract on more favorable terms. The government was often at a disadvantage in such situations. If the farmer went bankrupt, it would be difficult to re-auction the farms. Chances of receiving equivalent bids, particularly after one farmer had gone broke, were unlikely. The value of the farm was diminished in everyone's eyes. Often the government found it best to accept a deal with the current farmer, but such compromises were costly, both in pride and in anticipated revenue. There was thus, a growing dissatisfaction with the farming system in Java, which came to a head in the mid-1890s following a wave of bankruptcies and spectacular failures among some of the more prominent farming syndicates (Rush 1990).

Even within the British colonies there had always been a certain level of debate regarding the morality, usefulness and appropriateness of the farms. All could agree, however, that they were profitable. A typical comment was that of John Cameron, the editor of the Singapore Free Press, who in 1865, published his classic description of the Straits Settlements (*Our Tropical Possessions in Malayan India*) and left a lengthy discussion of the opium farming system.

> I cannot go the length, as I notice some local writers on this subject have gone, of saying that the main object of the farm at its establishment was the restriction of opium consumption. With the East India Company revenue was a matter of considerably greater solicitude than the moral condition of the large populations under their rule; and there can be very little question that the opium farm had its origin in the necessities of the local exchequer.
>
> (Cameron 1865, p. 217)

The British in the Straits Settlements and Malaya, despite frequent disagreements with Chinese farmers maintained the farming system longer than others, only abolishing it in 1909. Here too, it was the appearance of significant financial troubles that led to the abolition of the farms. In the years between 1907 and 1909, Southeast Asia was hit by one of its periodic economic crashes. Commodity prices in the Singapore market fell precipitously in mid-1907. This occurred shortly after a syndicate of Penang Chinese led by Khaw Joo Choe, a member of the powerful Khaw clan, had just offered an enormous increase in the annual opium farm rent. The same syndicate had currently acquired the farms for Penang, Sumatra, southern Siam and for Bangkok itself. The collapse of this syndicate was taken as a major wake-up call by the British and Siamese governments. This financial crisis, together with a new wave of pressures against the opium trade generated by events in the Philippines and in China now led the British government in Malaya to completely abandon the farming system. The Siamese government, whose farms were closely integrated into the financial systems of the Straits Settlements, also abolished their farms at that time (Brown 1993a).

In the Philippines, the farming system ended slightly earlier than in British Malaya and Siam, but no opium monopoly was erected to replace it. Rather, the Philippines were the first Asian possession in which opium was forbidden altogether. Following the annexation of the islands by the United States in 1899, the U.S. Congress, under pressure from missionary interests and other groups in the country, sent a commission of inquiry to the new colony. The Philippine Commission investigated the opium farming systems, not only in the Philippines, but travelled throughout Asia, including Japan and Taiwan, and gathered comparative statistics on opium farming throughout the region. The result of their mission was the decision to completely prohibit opium smoking in the Philippines. This was the first instance in which a major Western power had moved decisively to ban opium in any part of Asia. It was the first step in the process of banning the opium trade on an international level (Owen 1934, pp. 327–8).

The American policy in the Philippines led the British and Chinese to agree to their 1906 treaty ending the trade in China, but its effect in Southeast Asia was limited. At most, it can be seen as having eliminated the final objections to the abolition of the opium farms in British Malaya and Siam. Both the Siamese and the British now followed the French and the Dutch and replaced the farming systems with government-run monopolies. For the British in Singapore, this shift led to a decade of enormous profits from opium. In 1909, the year before the opium farms were abolished in the Straits Settlements, the Singapore farm brought the government just over $2.5 million, which was actually $400,000 short of the contracted amount. Most of the major revenue farming cliques in British Malaya had gone bankrupt. In 1910, the government shifted to a state monopoly, and although profits for that first year fell back to only $1.8 million, the situation quickly improved. In 1911, the government netted $3 million and by 1914, net profits from opium sales were in excess of $5 million annually (Trocki 1990, p. 203–4). Profits continued to rise until 1920 when Britain was finally forced to take action to effectively restrict opium use in its Malayan colonies, but in that year profits from opium sales netted the three Straits Settlements the all time high of over $20 million. However, even after a decade of restrictive measures, net profits for the Straits opium monopoly were still in excess of $8 million in 1929. One could probably argue that opium profits and actual usage only declined in a serious way with the onset of the global depression and the slump in trade.

The results of the opium empire

The opium farming system not only paid for free trade (at least in the Straits Settlements), and made a few Chinese businessmen very wealthy, it also had a few important structural results. The creation of commodity-producing settlements also created Southeast Asia's first class of wage-earners. Opium turned the Chinese coolies into wage-spenders, or what we now call consumers, where only self-sufficient peasants had previously existed. These coolies now produced for a market, sold to the market, calculated the value of their labor in the market and bought from the market. Even though they lived in what we would consider "company-store" economies, their economic situation was not unlike that of "modernized" humanity living in the late twentieth century. There appears to be a close connection between the mass marketing of addictive drugs and the creation of a consumer consciousness. Although today, we consume "useful" things such as soft drinks, cosmetics, video games and clothing with designer labels, the Chinese coolies of nineteenth century Southeast Asia at least understood that the opiate of the masses was the real thing. In these respects, the opium farming system had a similar impact on the peasant economies of Java, Siam and Vietnam. It brought them into the cash economy as consumers of vital non-necessities.

The opium farming system also was the primary vehicle of capital accumulation for the Chinese during a large part of the nineteenth century. The revenue farms were their cash cows, providing large amounts of capital which could be freely redirected into an array of investments. While we do not know the average interest that could be earned from a share in the opium-farming kongsi, we do know that it was not inconsiderable; moreover, in a largely unregulated economic environment, the opium farms were relatively secure (Trocki 1990; Trocki 1993). The farmers were men of substance who had the confidence of the government. They had to put up security and could thus be trusted to make good their debts. Shares in the revenue farms were something like shares of stock: that is, they were negotiable and could be bought and sold, and they could be expected to pay dividends and to rise in value (Trocki 1979). Thus, in addition to providing liquid capital which was available for investment in other enterprises, but especially in commodity production, the opium farms also served as a vehicle for attracting and accumulating savings from within the community. It is no accident that the first Asian banks in the region were organized by revenue farmers.

One can get some idea of the role which opium farms played in providing a springboard for Chinese capitalism in Southeast Asia in Jennifer Cushman's account of the rise and fall of the Khaw/Na Ranong dynasty (Cushman 1986; Cushman 1991). This was the family group headed in the late nineteenth century by Khaw Sim Bee. Together with his brothers, cousins, in-laws and other affiliates, at the beginning of the twentieth century, Khaw controlled vast holdings of tin mines, both in British Malaya and in southern Siam. In addition to the family base in Penang, Khaw Sim Bee was also the Siamese governor of

Ranong province in southern Siam and held a number of revenue-farming concessions, government positions and other honors from the Thai government, including the NaRanong surname. The family controlled tin smelting works, steam dredges, owned the Eastern Shipping Company and had its own insurance company. At the core of this empire was the revenue farming syndicate mentioned above. It was an extensive, interlocked amalgamation of revenue farms which included Singapore, Melaka, Penang, southern Siam, Sumatra and Bangkok. These were linked through various members of the Khaw syndicates under the leadership of Khaw Joo Choe. It seems that the opium farms were expected to play a vital role in providing a source of ready cash for the other enterprises in the empire. Unfortunately, when the farming syndicate collapsed in the economic downturn of 1907, the entire corporate construct began to disintegrate.

Although European merchants and speculators found much to criticize in the opium farming system, it was actually of great benefit to them. Since it was so closely tied to commodity production by the Asian masses, whether Chinese coolie, Javanese or Vietnamese peasant made no difference, opium farming had the effect of bringing products to the market far more cheaply than they might have been. This increased the marketability of colonial products in the west. It also saved the Europeans in the colonies from taxation themselves. Every tax dollar paid by opium smokers was one dollar that was not taken from the European merchant or producer. In this way, opium paid for free trade and the empire itself.

If the Chinese opium farmers got rich and Chinese capitalists in general found the farms useful, it was the colonial governments that reaped the greatest benefit from the opium farming system. The farms supplied the hard currency for day-to-day operations of colonial administration. The statistics show that the opium farms, and later the state monopolies, were among the major props of the colonial states. This was even more the case in Siam. Wilson makes the point that throughout most of the century, the collection of taxes from traditional sources (e.g. the land tax and others which came through the *krom*, or government divisions) were highly irregular. On the other hand, the revenue farming income was a dependable and never-failing source of revenue for the state. This was particularly true during the period when King Chulalongkorn undertook the modernization of the Siamese governmental structures.

> The administrative reorganisation of the 1880s and 1890s was a major act of statecraft, one that created a viable modern state, recognised as such by all outside observers and other nations. The role of the tax farms in all of this was to provide a basic level of revenue stability that made it possible for the restructuring of the administrative system to take place. At some point – it is not clear when – the payments of suai [traditional taxes] must have dropped to very little. The imposition of a capitation tax must have taken some time to implement and enforce.

> (Wilson 1993, p. 161)

In fact, herein lies one aspect of the real importance of opium and the opium farming system. It supplied the necessary framework within which the new state structures of Southeast Asia were erected. There can really be no serious argument with the proposition that the farms served a similar function in British Malaya, in the Netherlands East Indies and in French Indochina. It is difficult to imagine how colonial administrators could have raised sufficient revenue to support their new establishments without opium. It may be that empire could have been constructed by other means and financed from other sources, but the fact is that it was not. Without opium the process would have been slower and would have offered fewer advantages to the emerging capitalists both in the metropole and in the colonies.

The revenue farms, and in particular the opium farms, were analogous to the bamboo scaffolding one sees on the construction sites of the modern skyscrapers of Hong Kong, Southeast Asia and China. It looks messy, is incredibly low-tech and seems very much out of place in a modern urban setting. And yet, it does the job cheaply and effectively where almost nothing else could substitute. If we push the metaphor one step further, the opium farms were like scaffolding, in that they marked the boundaries of the new political–administrative structures. This drawing of boundaries was one of the main legacies of the European empire in Asia. The territorial boundaries of the opium farms marked and affirmed the very arbitrary administrative boundaries of the new political units. In most cases, the opium farmer's chintengs, mata-mata or revenue peons, were the first customs agents of the colonial states. In the act of policing the borders, they defined them and made them real. Even though Chinese revenue farmers held farms in a number of different territories, the fact that they themselves recognized the sovereignty and legitimacy of the new colonial order that laid claim to the areas, was an important step in the revolution of meaning that was taking place in the region. When it was no longer necessary to hold up the edifice, the farms were pulled down and discarded, revealing government monopolies, colonial police forces and the more prosaic structures of state bureaucracies which had been constructed underneath.

One may question whether the elimination of the farms really improved anything other than the revenues. As Thomas Braddell once quipped: "In a state of society where so large a proportion of the public revenue are derived from the encouragement of opium and baang smoking and the drinking of spirits, the public does not expect perfection" (Braddell 1857, p. 78). Indeed, public expectations counted for nothing in a colony. On the other hand, it is worth considering the fact that the structure of empire really did very poorly without its opium revenues. Once opium was forbidden, the empire was indeed, like the *Patna*, a rusting hulk heading off into oblivion waiting only for the first minor tempest to send it to the bottom.

The final point is something of a paradox, and that is that the farms were often controlled by financial groups who resided outside the colony. Colonial territorial boundaries, although enforced by Chinese revenue farmers, were no obstacle to the flow of Chinese capital throughout the region. Already, by the 1880s, Chinese capital in Southeast Asia had begun to exhibit those transnational leaps which continue to characterize overseas Chinese economic life today. The colonial powers felt threatened by this development. Ultimately there came a time when such a "compromise" of administrative integrity and economic security would no longer be tolerated, but for most of the nineteenth century this partnership between Chinese capital and European colonialism was a successful and profitable one.

8 The most long-continued and systematic international crime

The shame and the blame

When Joseph Conrad wrote, he wrote *for* the English. He took aim at their inflated sense of pride in the empire, and, by extension, at those pretensions of heroism and honor that he saw as essentially hypocritical, given the empire that he knew. His use of the Frenchman as the hero of the Patna episode is a case in point. It seems doubtful that any other English novelist would have dared present such a characterization to his audience at that particular time. The very idea of introducing an off-the-shelf French naval officer to rescue the Asian passengers whom Jim had abandoned seems something quite beyond the pale of British imperial discourse. It is difficult to imagine Kipling presenting such a situation. Conrad had no particular brief for the French, nor is this particular Frenchman shown as a great hero. He just followed orders and did his job. As such, his very ordinary nature made him the perfect foil for Britain's imperial fantasy.

Conrad sought to awaken contemporaries from their delusions, but how are we to view them? Especially, how are we to view those who promoted, perpetuated and defended the opium trade, denying to themselves and the world that there was any impropriety in the enterprise? In their dream, the empire, the Raj, was a great and glorious enterprise. It was also a global drug cartel which enslaved and destroyed millions and enriched only a few. The image of the Raj was itself a delusion created by opium. If there is to be any long-term evaluation of the empire, the opium trade must be reckoned in the equation.

It is always easy for historians to see the contradictions and failings of their predecessors. It is equally easy to condemn the past by the standards of the present. In what way can we judge eight to ten generations of men who built the empire around the opium trade? The enterprise had very deep roots, growing out of the traditional long-distance trade in exotic chemicals and being further developed by the Portuguese and the Dutch. Markets were developed in Southeast Asia and China and a new culture of drug use was created. English involvement began with people like Alexander Hamilton and Peter Floris in the seventeenth century and involved an entire succession of empire-builders. This included Robert Clive, Warren Hastings and Lord Cornwallis in the eighteenth century; Thomas Stamford Raffles, Alexander Matheson, David Sassoon, and

Frank Swettenham in the nineteenth and even Victor Purcell in the twentieth, among many others. None of them started the trade, and only put their hands to situations which already existed, yet each left behind an enhancement of the trade. All seem to have collaborated in some way or other, in assuring that the opium business was either promoted or at least protected.

Purcell, who finished his career in Malaya as the Protector of Chinese, probably knew better than anyone what opium had done to the Chinese. He did as much as anyone to dismantle the empire. Despite his various roles, his closing remarks on the demise of Malayan opium farms and the opium monopoly seem defensive:

> All that need be stated here is that in 1907, a Commission on Opium was appointed which made its report the following year, that at midnight on 31 December 1909 the opium farms in Singapore, Penang and Malacca suspended business and the Government Monopolies Department entered into possession of the premises and reopened them for business as usual the following day; that a policy of gradual suppression of opium-smoking was followed for many years, and that His Majesty's Government on 10 November 1943 adopted a policy of total prohibition in British and British-protected territories in the Far East then in enemy occupation.
>
> (Purcell 1965, p. 275)

More than three decades passed between the elimination of the Straits Settlements opium farms and the prohibition of opium in the British colonies. There is no record of any serious attempt at suppression between 1911 and 1920. This was a period during which opium revenues in the Straits Settlements soared, from $3 million to $20 million annually. It seems an overstatement, to call the next twenty-three years a period of "gradual suppression." It is even more ironic that Britain did not adopt total prohibition until their entire empire, east of Bengal, was actually in Japanese hands, at a time when British law and authority were literally dead letters.

In 1931, R .N. Walling wrote an essay called "House of the Tiny Tin Tubes." It was his name for the opium processing plant of the Singapore Opium Monopoly, then located on Pasir Panjang Rd (Walling 1931, p. 33). The factory produced a million tahils (about 4 tons) of *chandu* each year, and in addition to supplying all of Malaya, it also provided smokeable opium for the Siamese government monopoly. Walling described its modern machinery in glowing terms. It was perhaps one of the first modern mass production facilities of any kind in Singapore and probably all of Southeast Asia. It had a counterpart in the Netherlands East India as well that produced even more (Rush 1990). The Singapore plant had been designed to turn out 450,000 two-hoon (.752 grams) tin tubes of chandu each day.

> The machines which do this are beautiful, highly technical and impossible for me as a layman to describe. After sealing, they [the tubes] are weighted by delicate, automatic, weighing machines, and packed in small boxes,

two hundred at a time. They rest there like so many miniature Sainsbury's cooking eggs.

(Walling 1931, p. 36)

The morality and sensibilities of the past were different, as were the legal structures. Nevertheless, on one level and in some part of their public lives, the captains of the empire were always dedicated to the promotion or defense of the opium trade. For that, they, and thousands of others, whether English, Dutch, French, Spanish, or American, would by today's standards be considered criminals. And, at least in China and a number of other Asian states, those who dealt in opium broke the law. As we have seen, the opium trade was illegal in China from 1725 until 1860. It was also forbidden in parts of Java, Sumatra, Vietnam, Burma and Siam at the beginning of the nineteenth century. Where such laws existed, Europeans applied pressure to force open the door for the opium trade. Each of these areas, as they fell victim to European colonization or were, like China, forced to sign unequal treaties, found their country open to the opium trade and the government coming to depend on opium revenues for a significant part of its taxes.

Opium was sold in order to make a profit. Those profits went first to the institutions which promoted and protected the trade, including the East India Company, the government of India, the Colonial Office, all the colonial governments of Southeast Asia and even the British government itself. John K. Fairbank has written in uncompromising terms regarding the trade:

> The trade, constantly supplied by the British government opium manufacture in India was to have a life of more than a century, until given up in 1917. The most long-continued and systematic international crime of modern times, it provided the life-blood of the early British invasion of China.

(Fairbank 1978)

The provisions of the Treaty of Nanking, which stripped China of tariff autonomy and laid the foundation for the entire system of unequal treaties, left China without a credible defense against the opium traders. Lord Elgin defeated the Chinese in the Arrow War of 1858–9, often known as the Second Opium War. He also negotiated the Treaty of Tianjin, in which the Chinese government agreed to legalize the opium trade. He was, nevertheless, outraged at the activities of his countrymen in China.

> I have seen more to disgust me with my fellow-countrymen than I saw during the whole course of my previous life, since I have found them in the East among populations too weak to resist and too ignorant to complain.

(Owen 1934)

Much of the evidence shows that many nineteenth-century Englishmen had a sense of moral discomfort over the trade. Despite frequent defenses of the trade, despite protests that opium was rarely used to excess and that it was a necessary product for the Chinese, despite all the rationalizations and excuses, Europeans and the others who traded in opium were well-aware of the dangers of opium use. They knew it was addictive and that it was a poison. Even though the chemical nature of addiction was not fully understood at the time, the phenomenon was well-known. The effects of opium had been understood by generations of European medical men and scholars well before the nineteenth century. The argument that they did not know the damage they were doing is hardly credible.

As early as 1849, someone like Donald Matheson, a young partner in Jardine Matheson, felt he had to resign from the firm in order to register his objection to the opium trade: "It was intolerable to me to continue in such a business, and I sent home my resignation to the senior partner who was in this country. I left China finally in 1849" (Foster 1899, p. 19). Despite the increasing waves of criticism, British and American traders continued to deliver ever larger amounts of opium to China between 1840 and 1880. Except for minor readjustments in production, the totals of opium imported to China progressively increased year-by-year, rising from just around 35,000 chests at the time of the first Opium War to over 95,000 in 1876. It peaked at over 100,000 in 1880. By 1890, the quantity gradually began to decline so that by 1905, the annual export of Indian opium to China stood at about 51,000 chests, but India was still producing about 70,000 chests. The other 20,000 were distributed within Southeast Asia.

The reasons for the decline in Indian production are not entirely clear, but in general they reflected calculations about the absorptive capacity of the China market and the productive capacity of the Indian peasants. The decline was in no way related to qualms of conscience about the morality of the opium trade among those who profited from it, and profits were the most important thing. By the 1890s there were also other sources of profit in the Asian empire that did not depend on opium. Nevertheless, so long as there was considerable profit in the drug, the enterprise was protected and given a safe haven in British India.

It seems clear that so long as there was a legal "base" where opium could be produced, processed, and sent into the market as a commodity, then it was impossible to stop the trade in other jurisdictions, especially in China. Certainly the United States today spends a great deal of its drug suppression budget in seeking to stop drug trafficking "at the source." During the nineteenth century, the continued legal production of the drug in British India effectively prevented the eradication of drug use elsewhere. So long as European traders (particularly the British and Americans) refused to suspend their opium shipments to China, it was impossible for the Chinese government to control opium production and use within the country. The accomplishments of the anti-opium campaigns in China during the years 1908 to 1912 seem to validate this argument. So long as China had a government that could actually control the country, and so long as foreign states would agree not to support or carry on the trade to China's shores, then consumption could be checked. The success of the Peoples Republic in eradicating opium cultivation and usage after 1950 is further confirmation of this proposition.

The Japanese example offers some support for the argument that the British government alone had the power to end or prevent the opium trade at any time it chose to do so. In Japan, the government was committed to an anti-opium position from the time of its first treaties with Europeans in 1854. By a quirk of history, Japan was able to sign its first unequal treaty with American officials who agreed to ban the trade. American negotiators had been willing to ban the trade to China in 1842, but British and American trading interests had prevented any such undertaking. This international commitment, in 1854, to forego the trade to Japan by the United States gave Japan the confidence to insist on similar commitments from other European powers. With these agreements and the will of the Japanese government, the opium trade never got started in Japan. Ironically, in 1855, the very same year that Japan signed its first treaty with the British, John Bowring signed a similar treaty with Siam, with the singular distinction that the latter contained a clause requiring Siam to legalize its opium trade. The key variable was the commitment of the British government to either accept a ban or permit the trade. Where the British allowed it, no domestic government could effectively stop it, and where Britain agreed to ban it, the trade usually faltered. Britain's constant defense, that if they did not reap a profit from the trade then others would, seems difficult to sustain. On the contrary, the opposite contention, that if Britain did not provide a safe and legal haven for the trade, it could not flourish, seems possible to demonstrate.

The records show that the Indian government and the Colonial Office were constantly at pains to maximize profits and to protect, at almost any cost, the opium revenue of India. Even Sir William Muir's mild suggestion in 1880 that the Indian government might consider abandoning its monopoly on opium production and simply collect a tax on Patna and Benares opium as it already did on Malwa, was strongly opposed by Indian authorities. British authorities fought tenacious battles throughout the 1890s and into the twentieth century to preserve the opium system against reformers or opponents. So long as the British government profited from and perpetuated the opium industry, there could be no stopping it. It was the persistence in protecting the trade and preserving the revenues that seems the most reprehensible element of British policy during these years.

The "oriental vice"

In the defense of European traders, we should at least acknowledge that when the opium trade began, the drug was legal in Britain and the United States, and it remained so until quite late in the nineteenth century. At the time of the Opium War, opium was commonly available throughout the British Isles, the rest of Europe and the United States without restriction. It is noteworthy, however, that in the west, as in India, the drug was almost invariably ingested. In the west, the smoking of opium initially was confined to the Chinese population, who at this time were mostly laborers on the railroads and in the mining fields, as well as a few seamen. It was not until the practice of smoking opium began to spread beyond the Chinatowns of London, New York, New Orleans and San Francisco, that opium came to be seen as a drug worthy of legal restriction. Virginia Berridge has surveyed the social forces behind the anti-opium movement of the nineteenth century and found a complex alliance of physicians, temperance crusaders, church-people, and racists. Each group had its own agenda, but all seemed to converge around that strain of middle-class morality which recoiled at the prospect of the "oriental vice" of opium smoking spreading amongst Christian Europeans. This was linked to a concern that the working class might be made unsuitable for labor. By the end of the nineteenth century, opium was on its way to becoming a banned substance throughout the west no matter how it was used (Berridge and Edwards 1987, pp. 197–201).

Despite these qualifications, what is to be made of the unchecked spread of opium throughout China in the second half of the nineteenth century? Clearly a complex group of forces was at work, some external to China, but many internal. Opium moved down the social scale; from the luxury of a narrow elite in the 1820s, it became a drug for the masses by the 1880s. While the British and Americans brought opium to China and sold it to the Chinese, they did not distribute it to Chinese consumers. Chinese wholesalers, Chinese distributors, Chinese dealers and most of all, Chinese officials all took part in the trade. Indeed, they made it work, not only in China, but also throughout the European colonies. There, the wealthiest Chinese capitalists got rich by selling opium to their own countrymen. Moreover, once the market for the drug had been established, many Chinese were quite willing to develop the domestic opium industry to a scale far beyond that ever imagined by Europeans. By the beginning of the twentieth century, China may have been producing anywhere from six to ten times as much opium as she imported from India. Understanding the Chinese demand for opium and the facility with which it was served remain the unsolved problems.

There were strong forces that led the Chinese to consume the drug. Among them was the simple fact of the Chinese innovation of smoking the drug. This reduced the danger of overdosing and at the same time produced a much more immediate and intense high. It is also a mark of the creation of a specifically Chinese culture of opium use in which the drug found a context. The nineteenth-century crisis of Chinese culture also had a part in the drug epidemic. The intellectual and moral bankruptcy of Confucianism; the failure of the Chinese state to combat the western incursion; the chaos of domestic upheavals and finally the simple struggle to stay alive in a world that was collapsing; all of these factors lay behind Chinese drug use. They seem to have left many Chinese with little more than a desire to escape what appeared a hopeless situation. In that way, our own drug plagues in Europe and the United States at the end of the twentieth century may seem to parallel China's situation at that time.

Despite its dangers, it is clear that opium had other properties and uses. It was very often taken for its medicinal as well as for its psychotropic properties. At least some of the users saw it as a convenient method of self-medication for a wide range of complaints. Some of these, no doubt, used it only so long as they needed it and stopped when they decided they no longer had a need. In the case of the coolies and peasants and others who used very small amounts of highly adulterated opium, it is difficult to get an accurate idea about how many were actually addicted and how many could have been classed as "moderate" users (Kramer 1979).[1] It is probable, however, that many Chinese users were aware of its dangers when they began smoking it. They were willing, however, to take the risks. Many in our own society take such risks as well. While there were many moderate users there were probably many who could not stop. Impressionistic reports from the nineteenth century suggest that a significant number of smokers were in fact addicted to the drug, and that a considerable number of lives were ruined as a result of that addiction.

There is a problem here however, in estimating the long-term cost of that addiction. There is no historical evidence that sustained drug use destroyed Chinese civilization, nor is there a case that I know of where any civilization has been seriously or decisively weakened because of the drug-induced demoralization of the population. While we should not dismiss the individual human cost of drug addiction, it seems that most reasonably healthy social formations can tolerate a certain level of drug addiction without serious consequences, so long as that phenomenon is not accompanied by economic and legal complications. Indeed, it may be a powerful force, but the enormous swings that appear in the import and apparent consumption levels in nineteenth-century China suggest that in times of scarcity, many addicts did without the drug. Many others seemed quite capable of stopping altogether when circumstances required. Still others seem to have maintained habits for decades without self-destruction. There is, it seems, much more to be learned about the phenomenon of addiction. We still know little of its long-term social and historical effects. Existing accounts of nineteenth-century China show that Chinese civilization was already in decline at the time opium use became a drug epidemic. Perhaps opium use hastened the decline, but even this is not clear.

The political economy of drugs

The real damage which the drug did to China was economic and political, and to some extent these were self-inflicted wounds. The fact that the drug was a foreign import, meant that money flowed out of the country and thus impoverished certain sectors and caused dislocations in rates of exchange, inflation and similar difficulties, but these problems seem to have been temporary and rather limited in scope. On the other hand, even this ill-effect could have been prevented had the opium trade been legalized. It was the illegality of the trade for nearly a century of its remarkable growth (from 1760 to 1860) that did the real damage. That damage was both to the legitimate economy and the legal political system. A great deal of "new wealth" suddenly appeared in China and it did not always flow into the hands of those who were already wealthy. It must have provided much in the way of new opportunities, but in most cases those opportunities were there for those who were willing to overlook or break the existing laws. It is necessary to ask: Where did the money go? Who got rich? Who got poor? What social and economic and political institutions were corrupted? What really changed?

From the late eighteenth century until the middle of the nineteenth, opium was the major commodity of the Asian trade. It was the single most valuable export from India for many of these years. It was the single most valuable commodity which China imported. Opium also flowed to all of the ports and states of Southeast Asia. Wherever people had cash to buy it, or wherever a valuable commodity could be offered in exchange, opium was sold. Opium pushed old commodities, such as Indian cloth, out of the market, and at the same time, brought new ones into the market. Opium seems to have supplied an irresistible incentive to produce, or at least to make others produce. In China, it was not long before others began to produce opium themselves.

Opium became new money and thus a new form of exchange medium as well as a consumer commodity. As appears typical of newly established drug trades, the opium trade created massive transfers of wealth, new accumulations of capital and new owners of capital. As an aside, if we look at current global conditions, we can make some rather sobering conclusions about the direction of the current global economy. The annual turnover of the world drug trade (the illegal one) in 1997 amounted to $US400 Billion or 8 percent of the value of world trade. That was more than the global trade in iron and steel or in motor vehicles. In the decade between 1986 and 1996 opium production tripled, from about 2,000 tons to about 6,000 tons. Coca leaf production doubled over the same period (Taylor 1997). There appears an enormous potential for the further growth of legal and illegal drug trades in the future. Their potential for further undermining and influencing the non-drug economy is also even greater.

The rise of a drug trade does not mean, however, that everybody in a drug-using country loses out. Looking at nineteenth-century China, we can see that there were many Chinese who benefited. Beyond the stereotypes of Chinese users and European dealers, there is the fact that so many other Chinese were willing to produce and trade in the drug at the expense of their fellow countrymen. The entire distribution network inside of China, as well as those in the various European colonies of Southeast Asia and in Siam, were all entirely managed by the Chinese. Ultimately the largest and most pervasive system of opium cultivation was the one in China. Perhaps there might be some justification for the perception that opium was something that belonged peculiarly to the Chinese. If we look closely at the new Chinese power configurations of the late nineteenth and early twentieth century, it seems that many of them were related, in some way or other, to the trade in opium. The new merchant classes, the provincial powers, the warlords, the Qing state, the new political parties all relied on opium incomes to some degree. Most of the new Southeast Asian state structures were built on opium profits as well. The new nations of Southeast Asia began as colonial states and inherited their administrative and economic structures from the colonies which preceded them. These were significantly influenced by the Chinese opium farmers and opium capital.

A question that arises from this study is the role that commodification played in the opium trade. If we compare the opium commerce of the eighteenth and nineteenth centuries, it seems to be similar in structure to the trades in the "softer"

Figure 8.1 Opium Smokers in Yarkhand in Sinjiang province, China, 1873
Source: Photo by Francis Edward Chapman. By permission of the British Library, Photo 997(62)

drugs that swept into Europe during the eighteenth century. These "excitania" as Jordan Goodman has called them exploded into the European market and became true mass market commodities (Goodman 1995). The opium economy of nineteenth-century Asia does not seem terribly different from those of coffee, tea, tobacco, chocolate and even sugar. Of course, we do not label these economic developments "drug plagues" or epidemics, because they were not illegal. Nevertheless, the purely economic phenomena are similar. It is also true that these commodities were controlled by European capitalists, not foreign ones.

In many respects, opium was the first mass-produced commodity in Asia. The British takeover of the commerce had led to well-organized production systems, standardized packaging, portioning and pricing. The British created a regular supply that was carefully adapted to suit what were perceived as the current tastes of the market. Behind these developments lay the creation of vast enterprises. These included the considerable agricultural preserves in Bihar, Benares and the Malwa states, together with their large indentured labor forces. The infusion of significant amounts of silver into the hands of these agriculturists sustained entire classes of tax and rent collectors in India, not to mention the revenues of the colonial and Asian governments which ultimately got the taxes. There were also extensive collection, administrative and industrial processing facilities for the opium itself, which were embodied in the organization of the Indian Opium Monopoly. The next link in the chain were the extensive shipping, wholesaling and financial networks. To a certain extent, the creation of all of these were financed by the accumulations of capital generated by the opium trade. Even such innovations as the clipper ships and certain Indian railroad lines appear, at least in the first instance to have been wholly dependent upon the opium commerce to underwrite their cost.

These developments matched changes in China itself. Chinese culture had already developed many of the aspects of a consumer society even before the opium trade took off. This is another reason why opium moved into China so rapidly. It is quite clear, however, that opium made a very big place for itself in the consumer economy. Opium shops and divans had come to outnumber every other form of retail establishment in most Chinese cities by the end of the century. The opium trade restructured the Chinese economy and political relations in much the same way that the "soft" drugs had affected Europe and America.

Even though it was a "foreign" commodity, the Chinese themselves developed an entirely new relationship with this product and created a subculture and rituals to accompany its use. This process paralleled the acculturation of foreign drugs such as tea, coffee, tobacco and chocolate in Europe and America. Europeans created their own specific rituals and artifacts around which the consumption of their drugs was built. So too did the Chinese. Opium was different because it was illegal. It also came from foreign sources beyond Chinese control. It was also highly addictive and was a powerful and dangerous poison. Because of all these things, opium brought a new dimension to the drug commerce, the drug plague. Like these other substances, opium became a market commodity, but it became a true "drug on the market" in that it not only created a market where none had previously existed but it glutted the market in such a way that it seemed at least for a time to drive other commodities out of the market.

The impact of the drug on Southeast Asia, was even more dramatic. This had been an area where the cash economy hardly existed before the nineteenth century. The majority of the population lived on a subsistence economy and most exchanges were cloaked in ritual. When a commodity such as opium was introduced into these traditional, or pre-modern economies, it had a volatile transformative effect. From the first, when British country traders began to carry the drug throughout the archipelago, the traditional balance of power was upset. Not only did the opium trade undercut the Dutch position in the region, it provided wealth and prosperity for new states or for the refurbishment of old ones. Aceh, Riau-Johor, Palembang, Selangor and Sulu all flourished as they gained access to the wondrous new commodity which the British placed in their hands. Opium enabled the rulers of these states to begin the extraction of reliable supplies of valuable trading commodities from their subject populations. Their prosperity was even more spectacular since the British country traders brought arms as well as opium. At the same time, other states and other ports faltered. They did not have the commodities which drew English traders. Brunei lost ground to Sulu; Palembang grew at the expense of Jambi; Riau prospered to the loss of Trengganu and Siak; and Aceh's gain was Kedah's loss. This prosperity and the accompanying wave of state-building led to a great deal of indigenous military activity, which Europeans came to label as "piracy." It was cut short when the British established permanent bases in the Malay world and began to create their own empire. Among their initial moves was the suppression of "piracy," a policy which cut the ground out from under the traditional maritime polities of the archipelago. As the European empires expanded in Southeast Asia, opium was still the main force driving the engines of change (Trocki 1979). The new century saw the colonial states use opium to capture the fruits of Chinese labor and to extract cheap industrial commodities for little more than the cost of keeping the laborers stoned (Trocki 1990). Those Asian states that were able to muster a Chinese labor force and a corps of Chinese merchants to exploit them also prospered. Here, the Chinese opium farms were the crucial institution. Siam and Johor managed this combination, as did Selangor and Perak, for a time. Controlling these forces was an unpredictable enterprise.

Like drug consumption in Europe, opium consumption in Southeast Asia flourished as an adjunct to new forms of labor organization. It is probably necessary to qualify the claims of the prohibitionists that opium destroyed the laborer's will to work. In fact, it seems the reverse was true, at least initially. Opium consumption seems to have facilitated labor. One might hypothesize, although it would be difficult to prove empirically, that because the conditions of labor under early capitalism in Asia were so inhumane, only opium could provide the necessary relief to get the job done. Rather than destroying one's power to labor, opium made continued labor possible by killing the pain of exhausting toil, by dulling the hunger pangs, and soothing the mental and spiritual anguish of those trapped on an endless, hopeless treadmill. If some became so addicted that they were destroyed by the drug before the labor itself killed them, that was an unfortunate side-effect, and one that probably only affected a minority of the work force. But, again, it would be difficult to demonstrate this hypothesis. In the case of many Southeast Asian natives who used opium, their consumption levels were so low, that it is doubtful they consumed sufficient amounts to create an addictive syndrome.

Ironically, it was the combination of opium and warlords which on the one hand destroyed the Qing, but on the other sowed the seeds for the next opium plague, one which would sweep out of Asia and wreak a kind of poetic justice on the former colonial powers. Even as the twentieth century opened, Yunnanese opium was leaking into French Indochina where it was undermining the finances of the colonial state. The cultivation itself had already moved into the Shan Hills and the parts of northern Siam and Laos which we today call the Golden Triangle. By the end of the Chinese Civil War in 1950, opium cultivation would be there to support yet another rogue political order in the shape of the runaway Guomindang warlords. Already past masters at financing a renegade military with opium profits, they fell on the Shan Plateau and found a weak and divided people in an inaccessible refuge.

With help from the American Central Intelligence Agency, the Opium Warlords of the Golden Triangle prospered during the global Cold War and the Asian hot wars in both Korea and Vietnam. So long as they were ostensibly anti-communist, the US supported them, thus the Guomindang military, the Shan warlords, the Thai generals, the Hmoung chiefs, and the South Vietnamese leaders all profited from regular American support and encouragement throughout the Vietnam War era. No small part of their profits came from the drug trades they controlled. When the Vietnam War ended and "native" warlords such as Khun Sa rose up to take the poppy fields from the likes of General Li Mi and Lo Sing Han, a new source of legitimization was found in Shan nationalism. The entire enterprise, however, continued to be a drug regime, now with the capability of transforming the raw opium into heroin, a commodity more readily transported and marketed.

Opium thus created a succession of new political and economic orders in Asia during the past two centuries. These included the state of the East India Company itself, the new Malay polities of island Southeast Asia, the colonial states of nineteenth-century Southeast Asia and the warlord regimes of post-Qing China as well as the Guomindang and communist states that arose out of that milieu. At the same time, the economies of the entire region were radically reoriented, or perhaps "re-occidented" would be a more appropriate word. India's opium production was brought under western control while China's domestic economy was opened to the west. Southeast Asia was first opened to western traders and then to western control. With the migration of Chinese labor, Southeast Asian economies were transformed into commodity-producing regimes focused on exporting to the industrializing western powers. Underlying all of this, opium rearranged the domestic economies and pushed them down the path of mass consumption, which together with mass production, typified the "modern" economic order.

Figure 8.2 A Kachin woman of northern Burma tapping opium in the 1920s. In the
          1950s, their opium fields would begin supplying the world's heroin market
Source: By permission of the British Library, Photo 830(4)

It is possible to suggest a hypothesis that mass consumption, as it exists in
modern society, began with drug addiction. And, beyond that, addiction began
with a drug-as-commodity. Something was necessary to prime the pump, as
it were, to initiate the cycles of production, consumption and accumulation that
we identify with capitalism. Opium was the catalyst of the consumer market, the
money economy and even of capitalist production itself in nineteenth-century
Asia. This is why it seems appropriate to use the image of Conrad's *Patna* as the

symbol of the European empire in Asia. Whether it was British, Dutch French, Spanish, Portuguese or even American, the white man's domination of Asia rose and fell as a more-or-less unified enterprise. And, before the onset of wide-scale industrialism, it was always a "drug" enterprise beginning with spices and ending with opium. In 1900, as the industrial century opened, the rusting, decrepit *Patna* was gliding off into the silent sea to some uncertain demise, loaded with hapless Asians engaged in their own pilgrimage, and piloted, so long as it seemed secure, by a crew of weak, deluded and unreliable fools. The idealistic Englishmen, whom Conrad admired, believed they had made something great and glorious, which would last for ages. Conrad's message was that the reality of empire was far less uplifting. The parasites of the empire, as Conrad saw them, the self-serving Europeans, the Chinese, the Arabs, the "half-castes" and the corrupt Malays were the only ones who managed to profit. In the end, something quite different and extraordinary was created, something not even Conrad could have imagined.

Opium was vital, both to the capitalist transformation of the local economies as well as to the finance of the colonial administrative structures which protected those economies. Opium was also important because it speeded those vital changes in the relations of production that were necessary for capitalist-style growth. Opium was the tool of the capitalist classes in transforming the peasantry and in monetizing their subsistence lifestyles. Opium created pools of capital and fed the institutions that accumulated it: the banking and financial systems, the insurance systems and the transportation and information infrastructures. Those structures and that economy have, in large part, been inherited by the successor nations of the region today.

Appendix 1 The literature of the opium trade

The literature of opium, and with it, of drugs and "narcotics" is extensive. The starting point for most of the scholarly work on opium is David Edward Owen's pioneering work, *British Opium Policy in China and India* (Owen 1934). Owen has provided the essential background of British trade between India and China and traced the development of British policy both in the Indian subcontinent and on the China coast in regard to the opium trade. He was the first to bring together much of the partisan literature generated by the anti-opium movement of the late nineteenth century, with the information from the British colonial archives, and finally, the large body of English-language works of travel, description, and history dealing with nineteenth-century Asia. Crucial to Owen's work was the publication in 1926 of Morse's *The Chronicles of the East India Company Trading to China* (Morse 1926–9). Until much more extensive research is done on sources in South Indian languages and in Chinese, Owen will remain the standard work on the subject.

There is, to supplement this, extensive writing on three related areas: the economy and administration of British India; British trade with China and Southeast Asia; and British and other European relations with China.

Owen's work subsumes two themes that may also be seen as different bodies of scholarship that have, in subsequent years, grown more distinct from each other: studies of the China trade and of European relations with China on the one hand; and studies of British India on the other. Oddly enough, the two areas of study have come to focus on relatively distinct sets of questions. The literature on India deals largely with administrative issues and the policies of the Indian government as well as a fairly narrow range of commercial considerations. On the other hand, the literature on the China end of the opium trade has been essentially interested in diplomatic and commercial issues. Even the two areas of commercial interest are only occasionally congruent, while the political and administrative studies seem to inhabit entirely separate universes. There are however, certain unifying threads in much of this literature. These are the issues that concerned the European traders and administrators at the time: free trade and monopoly. These were the two great engines of the British empire: carefully administered monopoly in India, paired with fiercely prosecuted free trade in China and Southeast Asia.

In the case of the early period of the India–China commerce, the era of the "country trade" scholarly study begins with C. Northcote Parkinson's *Trade in the*

Eastern Seas (Parkinson 1937), which further expanded the story of British trade in China and to some extent in Southeast Asia. The discovery of a large collection of letterbooks and other materials which now constitute the archives of Jardine Matheson & Co. opened up yet another area of study, that of the individual European firm operating in China. These have added an important dimension to the information in the India House Records and those of the Colonial Office. The first product of these papers, and certainly one of the best, was Michael Greenberg's *British Trade and the Opening of China, 1800–1834* (Greenberg 1951). In the 1960s, Greenberg's work was supplemented by Edward Le Fevour who completed the nineteenth-century history of the Jardine Matheson firm with his *Western Enterprise in Late Ch'ing China: A Selective Survey of Jardine, Matheson and Company's Operations 1842–1895* (Le Fevour 1968). An important addition to works on British trade in China was also provided in the 1930s by Charles Stelle with his study of American involvement in the trade, *Americans and the China Opium Trade in the Nineteenth Century* (Stelle 1938). Together, the four studies tell us a great deal about Anglo–American trade and commerce on the China coast.

Regarding the history of the drug in India, much of the most useful work on opium deals with the eighteenth century and early nineteenth century. The landmark work here was Holden Furber's, *John Company at Work* (Furber 1951). Furber focused more exclusively on commercial concerns in India and adopted many of his assumptions from the views expressed by British administrators in Calcutta. The Indian side of the equation has been more broadly developed by H. C. R. Wright who has exhaustively examined the Indian economy in crucial years of the late eighteenth and early nineteenth century, when the opium trade was developing.

Since the 1950s, beginning with the work of John K. Fairbank (Fairbank 1953), China scholars have turned their attention to the opium trade and its impact on diplomatic relations between China and the west. Much of this literature has focused on the issues relating to the Opium War of 1839–1842 between Great Britain and China. Since Fairbank, this literature has also benefited from the use of Chinese sources (Waley 1958; Wakeman 1966; Collis 1968; Fay 1975). Although it may seem strange, many of the more general studies of China from this era appear to lose track of the opium question after 1842 and occupy themselves with more general issues relating to the modernization of China, the Taiping rebellion and other western encroachments. Until quite recently, little attention has been paid to the impact on China of the great expansion of the opium trade after the Opium War. There had been little systematic study of opium use in China and the domestic cultivation of opium until the 1980s and 1990s. Aside from works which focus largely on the early twentieth century and issues related to the end of the trade and the opium suppression movement, much remains to be done on the impact of opium in late nineteenth-century China.

The same might be said of the opium business in India. Scholars seem to have expressed little interest in questions related to opium cultivation, opium revenue management and the growth of opium-based capitalism toward the second half of the nineteenth century. In works on the economic history of India such as those by

Wright, Marshall, and Nightengale and a few others (Philips 1961; Wright 1961; Nightengale 1970; Marshall 1976; Waung 1977) the primary interest is on the period of Warren Hastings, Cornwallis and Wellesely, and events of the period 1770 to 1830. Possibly because it was a government monopoly, and not considered as part of the private economy of India, narratives of Indian economic history after 1830 on the whole ignore opium altogether or give it only cursory treatment at best (Philips 1961; Metcalfe 1979; Richards 1981). The "standard" Indian university textbooks today, can neglect the issue completely (Desai 1968). Even the *Cambridge History of India*, has little of substance on opium and the *New Cambridge History of India* has even less (Bayly 1983; Bose 1993; Tomlinson 1993). Works such as that by Narayan Prasad Singh, which treat the administration of the Indian opium monopoly, stand out as exceptions (Singh 1980).

Another area delineated by Owen and which has some momentum in scholarly, or semi-scholarly work, is what might be termed the "end game" of the colonial powers. This is the literature on the movement to suppress the opium trade in the early twentieth century. Much of this literature has its roots in the anti-opium polemics of twentieth-century missionary and medical activists, but it evolved into important administrative studies and reports which give the later productions of this genre more scholarly credibility (Rowntree 1906; Commission, International Opium 1909; Great Britain 1921; Lo 1933; Great Britain 1974). This literature was the starting point for Owen and Furber. By the 1970s, however, the global movement to suppress the trade could be seen as a "forgotten crusade" by Bruce Johnson (Johnson 1975). Besides these works, there has, until quite recently, been virtually nothing of substance on the opium trade in general and even less on opium use in Southeast Asia, in particular.

Since the 1970s, scholarly work on drugs and on opium has taken a number of different directions. In particular, with the increase in drug use in the west and the development of what might be termed "drug epidemics" or "drug plagues" among users of substances such as heroin, cocaine and even alcohol and tobacco, there has been a great deal more study of the medical, social and cultural constructs of addiction and its history in the west. Scholars such as Kramer, Warner and Parssinen have re-examined both the notion as well as the physiology of addiction in ways which require a re-examination of earlier literature (Kramer 1979; Parssinen and Kerner 1980; Courtwright 1982; Berridge and Edwards 1987; Warner 1992; Warner 1993a). The appearance of publications such as the *Journal of Drug Issues*, as well as studies such as those by Berridge and Courtwright on opium use in nineteenth-century England and America, provide a comparative field against which to re-examine the Chinese phenomenon. It is one aim of this study to bring together some of the insights derived from this literature.

Another area of study which bears on the nineteenth-century trade in drugs is the work done on the pre-British drug trade, in particular that of the Portuguese and Dutch in Asia during the seventeenth and early eighteenth century by Charles Boxer, Om Prakash, Leonard Blussé, Barbara Andaya and others (Boxer 1962 (reprinted, 1976); Lewis 1970; Wills 1974; Andaya 1979; Boxer 1979; Wills 1984; Prakash 1985; Prakash 1986; Blussé 1988; Andaya 1989). Their work throws new light on British trade in the nineteenth century and its relationship to the general pattern of European trade in Asia.

In addition to the opium trade of the nineteenth century, opium was quite important in colonial finances outside of the profits gained by the Indian government for the sale of its own opium. An important element in every Asian government, colonial or indigenous, during the nineteenth century were the opium revenue farms which contributed significantly to the maintenance of these pre-modern states. My own work on Singapore and Johor (Trocki 1979; Trocki 1990; Trocki 1993) has been complemented by James Rush (Rush 1990) and by the more comprehensive collection of studies edited by John Butcher and Howard Dick on revenue farming in Asia (Butcher 1993). These studies need to be examined in the context of the Asian opium trade as well as in the overall picture of the development of global capitalism because they show a clear link between the evolution of capitalism, European empire and the opium trade.

Another area that has benefitted from recent scholarship has been work on the domestic opium industry of China itself, particularly in the years after the legalization of opium. Most significant have been the writings of Lin Man-huong, Paul Howard, Joyce Madancy, Carol Benedict and Judith Wyman who have made more extensive use of Chinese language materials, in particular those of provincial authorities in China (Lin 1989; Lin 1991; Lin 1993a; Lin 1993b; Benedict 1994; Madancy 1994; Wyman 1994; Howard 1997).

Another area that needs some further comment is the discussion of opium use in the pre-modern era, particularly prior to the sixteenth century. One of the more important works here is Mark David Merlin's *On the Trail of the Ancient Opium Poppy* (Merlin 1983). This, together with other studies that examine the great shifts that have taken place in the patterns of drug use and long-term changes in human culture provide an important historical dimension that has heretofore been lacking. We have yet to confront the question of why drug epidemics, as we have seen them in China and as we experience them throughout the world today, seem to have no historical precedent. I believe that this question is, in some respects being approached by studies of drug economies and the development of capitalism. Such books as that by Sidney Mintz on sugar and capitalism provide a model that may equally be applied to studies of tobacco and opium.

Finally, just a word on all of the writings about drugs as "narcotics." Very little of the general literature is at all objective, although much of the above is among the least "tainted," it too is still locked into a rather limited discourse. Many historians, not to mention sociologists, criminologists and medical researchers come to their studies with a great many assumptions and beliefs which are not based on any solid fact or observance. Information on the effects of drugs, on the nature of addiction, the extent of drug use among any given population at any given time is often impressionistic at best, and outright propaganda at worst. Much of the literature is emotional, uninformed, highly prejudiced and intended to persuade rather than to inform. In particular, since the mid-nineteenth century, at any rate, the business of manufacturing and selling certain types of addictive, mind- or mood-altering substances have been classed as immoral and usually illegal activity. Thus, the pronouncements and "facts" presented by politicians, law enforcement officials, clergymen and other religious leaders, as well as by many physicians and scientists should be viewed with skepticism. Much should be seen as the work of "moral entrepreneurs" who have sought to make social and political capital out of drug use and drug trafficking. While it is tempting to assert that they are without much credibility, it would not be entirely true. There is much in their publications that deserves study. This study too has a point of view and a frame of discourse that some will find problematic, but if I can make a contribution to the understanding of drugs in modern history, then I will be satisfied.

Appendix 2 A Comment on the Jardine Matheson "Opium Circulars"

The Jardine Matheson Archives contain copies of the firm's "Opium Circulars." These appear to have been mimeographed (or reproduced by some other means) reports which Jardine Matheson sent to each of their "constituents, or clients, during the period between the 1830s and 1860s. Generally, they were issued on a monthly basis, but were sometimes more frequent if circumstances required. They generally reported on market conditions in China, giving prices current of the various kinds of opium (e.g. Patna, Benares, Malwa, and sometimes, Turkish and Persian). Occasionally, prices for old and new varieties of Patna and Benares were also given, although this was usually at the beginning of the season when remaining supplies of the previous year's crop were still unsold. Circulars also reported on the size of the supply of opium and provided inventories of what was on hand in Canton and later in Shanghai as well as what was known to be in transit. The prices were given separately for Shanghai and were often quoted in Taels rather than Spanish $.

Circulars also reported on any current events likely to impinge on the opium trade. There were thus regular notes and comments on the progress of the Tai Ping rebellion, comments on the Chinese government's policies regarding opium and other trade policies. There were also notes on wrecks or delays of ships carrying opium. The arrival of a new shipload of 100 or more chests of opium could often have an impact on Canton prices.

The economic information in the Circulars was not confined to the opium trade but also touched on cotton prices, sugar prices, and sometimes rice. They also commented on the general state of the market for "Straits Produce" generally, meaning tin, pepper, rice and some "forest produce" such as rattans, betel nut, etc. In addition to imports, some of China's major exports, such as tea and silk were also given some space. Overall however, the principal focus of these Circulars was always opium. It was this possession of the best and latest possible information on market conditions, together with the prognostications of the company's senior merchants on future trends in the trade that gave the Jardine firm its preponderance in the market during most of the nineteenth century. Gaining this sort of information and making it available to their constituents gave JM their great edge in a market environment that was at once very opaque and at the same time highly competitive.

There are mentions of Circulars being enclosed with correspondence in the early 1830s, but copies of these have not been preserved in the India Letterbooks (C10 series). In the 1820s one could find similar information in the regular correspondence with their constituents. In many cases, letter after letter to different individuals or trading firms would contain exactly the same paragraphs on, for example, the state of the Malwa trade, or the prospects for legalization, or the viscissitudes of the Coast trade, etc. It is difficult to get regular reports on the state of the market from this correspondence during the early 1830s because of the institution of the Opium Circulars about that time. The information is not in the letters and the Circulars have not been preserved. The letters, from this period are much more personal and specific to individual clients and for matters of prices simply refer the reader to the enclosed Circular. Only in the later 1830s do we find copies of these bound into the ILB ledgers according to their dates. It appears that they were not originally a part of the ledger. They are reproduced on thin (onion-skin type) paper while the original was hand-written. These are "press" copies of those originals, perhaps some sort of early carbon copy. One assumes that the firm sent out at least 200 or 300 of these each month. By the mid-1870s the Opium Circulars disappear and are replaced by a range of other, more specialized market reports, such as those covering Japanese cotton, or tea or some other specific product.

Appendix 3 Englebert Kaempfer's comments on opium from his *Amoenitatum Exoticarum*

The ingestion of the poppy is another example of Kheif use. The Indians and Persians gather it from gardens and fields by slicing the heads so as to produce a milky sap. This juice is called opium in Europe, in Asia and Egypt, Afiuun and Ofiuun. The Persians, out of reverence, call it Theriaki (i.e., Theriacum), inasmuch as it confers those qualities lauded by the poets, namely, Galene, Hilare and Eudios, that is to say, the medicine Andromachus described in verse that lends to the soul serenity, joy and tranquility. In Persia the custom is that at the onset of summer, when nearing ripeness, the skin of the heads [of the poppies] is wounded cross-wise. A sharp knife with five cutting edges serves the purpose, so that with a single slice, five long parallel wounds are made. The next day the juice exuded from the wounds is wiped off with a knife and collected into a small vesssel bound around the waist. Then the other face of the head is wounded in like manner to bring forth an equal flow of the liquor. With a view towards increasing production, side branches and smaller heads are removed, so that the remaining heads grow larger and produce more copiously. The first collection, called Gobaar, is of superior quality, with greater virtue to sooth the brain. It exhibits a whitish to saffron-yellow color, becoming darker as it dries in the sun. Secondary collection produces a juice inferior both in potency and in value, the color for the most part being dark to reddish black. A third tapping renders a sap even more darkly colored and of little strength.

The most potent opium is produced in the following manner: the collected juice is moistened with a little water while being pounded and stirred with a wooden spatula in a shallow wooden bowl until it achieves the consistency of tar, sticky and reflective. After long kneading [several days?], the product is rolled into short cylinders and put out for sale. Pieces are snipped off with forceps [shears?] according to the need of the individual buyer. The opium thus painstakingly produced is termed Theriaak malideh, i.e. theriac produced by grinding, or also Theriaak afiuun, i.e., opiated theirac to designate [or distinguish it from] the therian of Andromachus, which they called Theriaak Faruuk. The preparation is the work of the vendors who are termed Kheifruus, or as you might say in German, Trunken Kraemere, apothecaries, druggists. These men sit out in public squares and at cross-roads manipulating lumps of opium, often using honey instead of water to temper the dryness and bitterness of the drug. This specialty is called Baebrs. A more remarkable preparation is one that calls for nux Myristica to be added, along with cardamom, cinnamon and mace ground fine. The preparation is believed to produce an opium suited to [or especially good for] the heart and brain, and is known as Polonia, or as some pronounce it, Felonia, for Philonium Persicum, or Mesue. Others, omitting the aromatic spices, add only saffron and ambra [ambergris?]. Each apothecary perfects his own special recipe, and it is not unlikely that many [customers] are cheated by greater or lesser amounts of opium in proportion to other materials. Aside from this triple-prepared opium in the form of pills to be swallowed, there is a much touted liquor called Coconar, in Greek Mekonion (i.e. laudanum, juice of poppy) the Nepenth of Homer, which establishes health when drunk in measured doses at hourly intervals. Some [others] produce a liquor by steeping the leaves for a short period of time, others use the macerated and bruised heads, placing them in a filter and pouring plain water over them seven or eight times, mixing the drug to individual tolerance. I might mention here a third kind of especial inebriatory and heartening electuary prepared by unguenters, each according to his talent, variously elaborated with different ingredients for uplifting the spirit. There are different descriptions, the first and most famous being that attributed to the invention of Hasjem Beg, which is said to inspire the soul with great joy and to sooth the mind with magical and voluptuous apparitions.

While a dose of as little as a single grain may prove fatal to a European, those long accustomed to the use of opium may consume as much as a drachm (of the drug) without harm. Yet many injure themselves through abuse and long use, as a result of which the body becomes emaciated, virility slackens, the spirit grows gloomy and the intellect dull. One may see the opium-eaters sitting mute and somnolent in the midst of their companions. I have often been offered a reward of as much as a hundred pieces of gold to cure men of this addiction this side of death. I refrain from adducing here examples of the ravening after opium of which the medical texts are replete. A few heads of poppies soaked in vinegar for two months are made into pills or sipped in a drink, according to the desire of the user.

(Kaempfero, 1712, pp. 642–645)

Kaempfer's report of opium smoking in Java:

[There is] also [another] strange use of opium among the *nigritas* [Javanese(?)] for they mix with it, tobacco diluted with water so that when kindled the head spins more violently. In Java, I saw flimsy sheds [made of] reeds in which this kind of tobacco was set out [for sale] to passers-by. No commodity throughout the Indies is retailed with greater return by the Batavians than opium, which [its] users cannot do without, nor can they come by it except it be brought by ships of the Batavians from Bengal and Coromandel.

(Kaempfero 1712, p. 650)

(Translated by David J. Trocki)

Appendix 4 The economics of Malwa opium cultivation

Expenses and profits of cultivating one bigha of opium in a good, tolerable and a bad season extracted from Sir John Malcolm's *A Memoir of Central India* etc.

Good Season

Expenses	Rs
5 seers of seed	0.9
Manure	2.0
Watching expense	4.0
Weeding, plowing,etc	6.0
Cutting & gathering	4.0
Watering (9s)	6.0
Linseed oil	1.0
Rent (to govt)	6.0
Total	29.9

Receipts (Good year)	
5 seers (pukka)	40.0
Sale of seed (3 M.)	4.0
Total Income	44.0
Exp	−29.9
	14.7
Village dues	−1.8
Net	12.15

Tolerable season

71/2 seers (kutcha)	30.00
Seed	2.11
Total	32.11
Exp.	31.10
Net.	1.01

Using the same scale of values, in a bad year the gross would only be 5 seers kutcha (second grade opium) for Rs20 and seed for Rs.2 leaving a loss of Rs9.

But, in a bad year, opium would probably be worth more so the loss may turn out to be a little less.

(Malcolm, 1823, pp. 359–60)

Glossary

Abkari In India, a revenue or tax farm, or monopoly concession. Usually involved the right for an individual to monopolize the trade in some product or service in exchange for a periodic rent to the government.

Betel The name given to the combination of substances chewed together with parts of the nut of the areca palm, sometimes known as betel nut. It was usually consumed by most Southeast Asians prior to the nineteenth century, and included a kind of leaf, some lime, and sometimes some tobacco, together with some shavings from the areca nut.

Bigha In India, a land measure, corresponding to about 2/3 acre or about 2700 sq. metres. (i.e. 2697.96 sq. m.)

Banian Indian merchant, often a Guzerati, but in Calcutta the term was applied to Hindu brokers who worked for private European traders.

Chandu The Malay term normally used for opium which has been prepared for smoking.

Chee Chinese weight, equivalent to 1/10 of a tahil or about 3.76 grams.

Chin-shih The rank of one who has passed the provincial level in the traditional Chinese examination system. This was the rank at which one could be appointed to an official position.

Chinteng The Chinese term used in Malaya and Singapore to describe the security personnel who worked for the revenue farmer, particularly the opium and spirit farmer, and assisted in the policing of his monopoly.

Dadni An advance made to a craftsman or weaver. Also, dadni merchants, usually in Bengal, who worked as go-betweens, making advances to Indian producers and on behalf of European merchants and their companies during the seventeenth and eighteenth centuries.

Gomastah An Indian agent or representative. Often involved in delivering advances to peasants who were contracted to cultivate opium for the British East India Company and later for the Indian Government.

Hoon Chinese weight, equivalent to 1/10 of a chee, or 1/100 of a tahil, or .376 grams.

Kongsi Chinese term for a company, a syndicate. Also often used for secret societies or triads.

Krom A government department, more or less equivalent to a ministry, in the traditional Siamese state.

Mahajan In India, a banker or "great merchant."

Mato A minor Indian functionary, usually an agent or go-between.

Maund Indian measure of weight equivalent to about 76–80 lb. or about 40 kg. Divided into 40 seers.

Pangeran Traditional Malay territorial chief, usually in Borneo.

Panseri Indian measure of weight, equivalent to five seers or 9.5–10 lb, or slightly less than 5 kg.

Pie (pice) The smallest copper coin of the Anglo-Indian currency. Worth 1/12 of an anna and 1/192 of a rupee.

Pikul A weight derived from the Chinese standard of measures, although the word itself is of Malay origin. It is equivalent to about 133.3 lb. or about 60 kg. It is comprised of 100 catties.

Rabi An Indian term referring to crops grown in the cooler months, e.g. between November and April.

Régie French term for a government opium monopoly in Indochina.

Sahukar An Indian banker or money lender.

Seer Indian measure of weight equivalent to 1.9–2 lb. or just under 1 kg.

Sudder Indian term meaning chief, or main or principal: e.g. the sudder factory, the sudder court.

Tael Derived from the term "tahil," but when spelled in this fashion, it normally refers to the standard unit of traditional Chinese silver currency. In the nineteenth century, was often figured at 4s.6d, and was notionally divided into 1000 copper cash, but this fluctuated.

Tahil Weight derived from the Chinese standard of measures, but the term itself is of Malay origin. It is equivalent to 1.3 oz. or 37.6 grams. It is a sixteenth part of a catty.

Theriaca Greek term for various medicinal concoctions considered to be panaceas, or cure-alls. Normally made of considerable portions of opium.

Vis Measure of weight. The term is of unknown origin, but it is generally used for opium. It is the standard weight for a ball, or cake of opium, and is equivalent to about 3 lbs or 1.5 kg.

Notes

1 The dream of empire

1 Patna opium was the produce of Bihar state which was gathered and processed at the town of Patna, hence the name. Benares opium was the produce of the state then known as Benares (Varanasi) and was gathered and processed in the town of Gaziphur.

2 (Darras 1982, pp. 4–5, fn 10). Conrad wrote to Henry Darvey explaining why he felt that foreigners would find more enjoyment in Kipling than in his writings: "Il parle de ses compatriotes. Moi j'écris pour eux. Donc lui peut très bien intéresser les étrangers – pour moi, c'est bien plus difficile – peut être impossible."

3 Fernand Braudel, the great historian of consumption, commodities and capitalism has virtually nothing to say about opium, which gets only three passing mentions, one in each of his massive volumes in *Civilization and Capitalism*. Two other fairly recent books that make much of the impact of commodity trade in certain drugs on the course of European empire and the capitalist economy have relatively little to say about opium. James Walvin in *The Fruits of Empire*, (Walvin 1997) has virtually nothing to say about opium. Granted he is writing about British consumption, but the topic barely rates a footnote. In *Seeds of Change*, Henry Hobhouse, has decided that tea is more important than opium and has only had room for five pages of commentary on opium in his chapter on tea (Hobhouse 1985, pp. 115–120).

2 All the drowsy syrups of the world

1 Merlin suggests that it is possible that *Papaver somniferum* may have developed as a result of artificial selection from "wild" *Papaver setigerum*, but the chromosomal evidence is inconclusive (Merlin 1983, p. 72).

2 Although the opium poppy's association with the Great Earth Mother Goddess continued down through the epic, archaic, and classical periods of ancient Greece, it did not begin until the Mycenaean civilization emerged and the shamanistic influences of the patriarchal Indo–European culture had entered into the Greek realm. When these influences arrived in Greece, in the Late Bronze Age, some were synthesized with the indigenous traits of the matriarchal culture dominated by the Earth Mother Goddess. Thus I believe that the opium poppy may have been introduced into the Greek realm by shaman seers who utilized this species (as well as other hallucinogenic plants) for ecstatic, divinatory (and/or medicinal) purposes. This could explain why there is no confirmed evidence for the opium poppy in the available written records of the Mycenaeans.

(Merlin 1983, p. 20)

3   I think both the capsules and the seeds of the opium poppy probably had a role
     in the mystery rites of Eleusis. In fact, I would like to offer what I believe is an
     original suggestion concerning the possible connection between the drug plant and
     the Eleusinian initiation. I have found evidence indicating that opium and/or
     opium poppy seeds may have been mixed with another drug plant derivative and,
     for precautionary purposes, either added to a ceremonial drink containing the
     psychoactive alkaloids of an ergot, or taken after the ergot-based concoction was
     drunk: 'Two of the most useful drugs to offset ergot poisoning are papaverine, one
     of the alkaloids of opium, and atropine, derived from belladonna or henbane.'
     (Taylor 1965:65; Emboden 1979a:82) In other words, since both the seeds and the
     capsules of the opium poppy contain papaverine, either could have been part of an
     antidotal safeguard against the possible effects of the toxic ergot alkaloids.

                                                                 (Merlin 1983, p. 229)

4 Although it is a very minor point, perhaps it should be noted that this is the passage
   which Owen, (1934, p. 15, n 45) and other writers have quoted regarding the
   smoking of opium with tobacco in Java in the 1680s. The reference on opium
   smoking in Java is further along in his text, on p. 650, (see Appendix 3, pp.
   181–2).
5 According to the Royal Commission of 1894, India, including both the Malwa states
   of western India as well as the government monopoly areas of Bihar and Benares,
   exported just over 100,000 chests of opium in 1880. At an average of 130 lb or 60 kg
   per chest, that works out to 6500 tons or 6000 metric tons. Assuming that only about
   80 percent of that went to China (the rest went to Southeast Asia, where probably
   much of it was consumed by resident Chinese), China itself imported and consumed
   5600 tons of opium in 1880. By the most conservative estimate, in the 1880s, the
   Chinese were also producing an amount equal to what was imported, and they were
   consuming all of that (Hart 1881). Other estimates that seem more reliable than
   Hart's, indicate that domestic production was at least two or three times the quantity
   imported. Be that as it may, an estimated 12,000 to 15,000 tons, does not seem an
   unrealistic figure for the annual consumption of China at that time. By contrast, in
   1983, the estimated global production of all opiates was based on about 2000 tons
   production of raw opium. If we assume that figure to have been more or less constant
   through the decade, then we can see that at the very least, the Chinese consumption
   level of a century ago, would have serviced all the opiate requirements of the entire
   world for certainly six or seven years and possibly even for the entire decade of the
   1980s.

3 Cleverer than alchemists

1 "Bengal opium" was the eighteenth-century term for opium from Bihar and Benares
   (Varanasi), as well as Bengal itself.
2 I have found no mention of opium being traded to Taiwan or China either by the
   Dutch or the Chinese junk traders visiting Batavia at this period. Neither Teijiro
   Yamawaki nor Leonard Blussé mention opium in the cargoes of the Dutch ships nor
   even in those of Cheng Cheng-kung (Koxinga) who traded widely in Southeast and
   Northeast Asia during the mid-seventeenth century (Blussé 1988, pp. 116–20;
   Yamawaki 1976, pp. 111–15). Owen points out that when Manchu forces took Fujian
   and ultimately conquered Taiwan itself in 1683, there was no mention of the drug,
   nor was there any prohibition of the drug by the Chinese government until 1729
   (Owen 1934, pp. 15–16). Thus, while it may be possible that opium was being used
   in Taiwan and in Fujian as early as the mid-seventeenth century, it does not seem to
   have been perceived as a problem until sometime later.

3 The Sumatran Malays in Bengkulu, described by William Marsden around 1800, still seemed to follow nearly the same method as that described by Kaempfer. They mixed the opium liquid with tobacco. Marsden described the method of preparing it:

> The raw opium is first boiled or seethed in a copper vessel; then strained through a cloth, to free it from impurities; and then a second time boiled. The leaf of the TAMBAKU, [*sic*, tobacco] shred fine, is mixed with it, in a quantity sufficient to absorb the whole; and it is afterwards made up into small pills, about the size of a pea, for smoking. One of these being put into the small tube that projects from the side of the opium pipe, that tube is applied to a lamp, and the pill being lighted, is consumed at one whiff or inflation of the lungs, attended with a whistling noise. The smoke is never emitted by the mouth, but usually receives vent through the nostrils, and sometimes, by adepts, through the passage of the ears and eyes. This preparation of the opium is called MAADAT, and is often adulterated in the process, by mixing jaggri, or pine sugar, with it; as in the raw opium, by incorporating with it the fruit of the pisang, plantain.
>
> (Marsden 1811, p. 277/-8)

4 The Dutch guilder (florin) was worth roughly half a Spanish dollar or about 2 shillings sterling at this time. Thus, 400 million guilders was equivalent to about Spanish $200 million or £40 million and 590 million guilders equaled about $295 million or £59 million (Furber 1976, pp. 386–7).

5 Straits produce was the general term used in the nineteenth century to refer to the vast array of items from the forests and seas of Southeast Asia and included such things as: rattans, sappanwood, other types of tropical timber, rhinoceros horn, ivory, buffalo horn, hides, birds' nests, dammar, camphor, sea slugs, pearls, mother-of-pearl, birds feathers, betel, gambier, tapioca, sago, coconuts and rice, to name some of the major ones.

6 For example, the VOC spent in excess of 2.75 million guilders between 1783 and 1793 in policing the seas in the Straits of Melaka. Even this was not the full cost of the three naval squadrons that were sent from Holland in those years. The national government bore most of the cost of building, equipping and manning the fleets, which was much higher still. The lesson was simple. Empire, as the Dutch were attempting to manage it, did not pay. No amount of profits made on the eastern trade could recover that kind of overhead (Vos 1993, p. 187).

7 The Dutch regularly imported silver bullion and first used it to pay for their opium and saltpetre investment before the Battle of Plassey, for example in 1755–7 the Dutch imported 3,168,681 guilders and the total export to Europe and Batavia was 4,219,737 guilders (Sinha 1956, p. 57).

8 Its major export components were British woollens (75.8 percent), metals (14 percent) and miscellaneous (0.2 percent) totalling ninety percent of their imports to China. The rest, from India and Bengkulu, was made up by pepper (4.7 percent), cotton (3.5 percent), opium (1.2 percent) and sandalwood (0.6 percent). This, of course, did not include opium and Straits produce carried by the country traders (Pritchard 1936, p. 154).

4 In compassion to mankind

1 McNeill, applying ecological and biological principles to "the human condition" notes that all species have been limited in their expansion by both macroparasites (bigger things that eat them) and microparasites, (smaller things that live off them, or their food supplies). Homo sapiens, having risen to the top of the food chain ceased to have any serious macroparasites. McNeill argues that this function was then taken over by other human beings: bandits, outlaws, governments, etc.

2 In 1773, the first contract was let to Meer Muneer who was to deliver an unspecified

amount of opium at a cost of Rs320 per maund or about 80 lbs (40 kg). At about two maunds per chest, that was quite generous (Owen 1934, p. 24 fn 14). Later, in 1775, contractors received only Rs190 per chest, or about Rs95 per maund! They also received a 2.5 percent commission on the proceeds of the Calcutta auction, which in 1775 netted the EIC £56,255. We may estimate this would have probably given the contractor something like an additional £1,200 or Rs12,000 (Owen, 1934 p. 30, fn 23). However, Owen also notes that, by the time he delivered the opium, the contractor had probably already paid out about Rs100 per maund.

3 Flour was considered the worst adulterant because while most of the other substances were a nuisance, they could be removed and it was possible to salvage some of the opium. Flour, however ultimately fermented thus contaminating the entire ball in which it was mixed (India 1871, p. 25).

4 In 1860, the government raised the price to Rs4 per seer, and then to Rs5 in the following year, but then it dropped back to Rs4.8 the next year. From then until 1882, it fluctuated between Rs4.8 and Rs5 (India 1883, p. 37). There were 40 seers in a maund and about 2 maunds to a chest, this would suggest that Crawfurd's estimate that the "natural cost" of Rs112 per chest is in error. In 1821, Rs 112 was the price per maund, so it should have been about double that per chest. At Rs3.5 per seer, a chest would cost around Rs250/280.

5 It may be that the Malwa peasant had to put more labor into the product since Malwa opium was soaked in linseed oil and had a much lower water content than did Bengal opium which was usually 70 percent "consistency" or 30 percent water; while Malwa opium was close to 100 percent consistency.

6 In the eight years between 1814 and 1822, I have calculated from the figures in the Letters from the Court of Directors that the government's profit per chest varied between a low of ten times the cost of production in 1818 and twenty times the cost in 1821.

7 Personal communication.

8 In his annual report, R.L. Mayles notes that the average production per bigha in Bihar in 1867/8 was 4 seers 15 chuttacks; while in 1866/7 it had been 5 seers, 6 and 2/3 chuttacks (India 1871, p. 1). In his section of this same report, C. F. Carnac, the Benares Opium Agent reported that the average land area per cultivator was 14.16 bighas and the rate of production was 3 and one-half seers in 1867–8 (India 1871, p. 124).

9 The opium districts in Bihar were: Tirhut, Hajipur, Chupah, Alligungi, Mutihari, Bettiah, Shahabad, Gyah, Tehta, Patna and Monghyr (India 1871, p. 13). In Benares, just over 260,000 bighas were under cultivation. Each cultivator had an average of 14.16 bighas under opium. There the opium districts were: Benares, Ghazipur, Azimqurh, Gorukpur, Busti, Cawnpur, and Fyzabad (India 1871, p. 23–5).

10 Informers received Rs100 per conviction and Rs200 for a particularly large seizure. Offenders normally received a prison sentence of about two months. In 1869, two newly employed European assistants in the Opium Department were sharply criticized for failing "to detect even a moiety of the adulterations that passed through their hands." In 1867, over 52 maunds of adulterated opium had been confiscated while in the previous year, only 26 maunds were found (India 1871, pp. 1 and 26).

11 By the 1880s Indian government officials were beginning to complain about the difficulty in getting wood for the chests and about the disappearance of the large mango orchards which had once dotted the Indian countryside (India 1882, p. 11).

12 It was largely in defense of this "peaceful trade" that a succession of American administrations waged war against the "Barbary pirates" of the north African coast between the late eighteenth century and 1815.

13 In 1826, in Canton, when Patna was selling for $1050 and Benares was at $1060, Turkish opium was only $540. At the same time, Malwa was selling for $880.

14 For the period 1831 to 1890, pass duty rates were as follows:

1831	Rs.175	1861	Rs700
1835	Rs 125	1862	Rs600
1845	Rs 300	1877	Rs650
1847	Rs 400	1879	Rs700
1859	Rs 500	1882	Rs 675 (at Ajmere) Rs 650 (elsewhere)
1860	Rs 600	1890	Rs 625 " Rs 600 "

15 The names of the Bombay firms are scattered throughout the India Letterbooks of the JMA and included: Agha Mohammad Suastry, Ameerchand Sukurchang, Cursetjee Ardaseer, Cursetjee Cowasjee, Framjee Cowasjee, Hormasjee Dorabjee, Jamsetjee Jejeebhoy, Madowwdas Ransordass, Motichand Amichand, Mohammad Ali Rogay and Nanjee Sescurn. The names of the European firms included: the Jardine affiliate Remington and Crawford, as well as Forbes & Co., T. Crawford, Alexander and Mackintosh, Leckie, Ritchie Stewart, Roger de Faria and J.F. Pereira, as well as the firm of David Sassoon.

5 The most gentlemanlike speculation

1 Steinberg *et al.* (p. 233) estimate the total population of Southeast Asia in 1870 at about 55 million. While this figure had tripled by 1940, it should be understood that much of the increase, was the result of extensive immigration from China. China's population at the beginning of the nineteenth century was already close to 400 million.

2 Greenberg's figures are based on the Jardine Matheson Archives, and I have supplemented his with additional data from those sources. Starred (*) items indicate sums which I have calculated from other sources rather than figures actually given in the records and should thus be treated as only approximations.

3 The only possible exception to this might have been in the instructions given to the two eighteenth-century British missions to China in 1787 and 1792. Both Lt Col. Charles Cathcart and Lord Macartney were authorized to promise that "if necessary, the company would prohibit the export of Indian opium to China" (Owen 1934, p. 76). But, such a proposition was never actually put to the Chinese government. The Cathcart mission was lost at sea on its way to China, and Macartney never truly engaged the Chinese authorities on these issues.

4 Prinsep's paper on this subject is: "Note on the Condition of the Opium Trade," Ft. William, 9 August 1837, no. 5, India, Separate Revenue Proceedings, Range 208, vol. 19.

5 According to a comment by Alexander Matheson, the Chinese government may have come up with the money to pay the $5 million indemnity by confiscating the wealth of one of the Hong merchants, Howqua, who died in 1843, leaving a fortune estimated at around 20 million taels (C6/3, PLB, A.M. to J.A. Smith, 10 September 1843).

6 Greenberg shows the "genealogy of the firm from 1782 to 1832 (Greenberg 1951, pp. 222–3, Appendix II). The firm changed its name as partners came and went over the first half-century. First it was Cox & Reid, then Cox & Beale, later Reid & Beale and then Beale & Magniac. The major partner in the firm which James and Alexander Matheson joined in 1827 was Charles Magniac. William Jardine joined in 1825, and in 1832 it took the name of Jardine Matheson & Co. which it has retained to the current day.

7 A brigantine, or brig, is a two-masted vessel which is square-rigged on both masts. A bark, or barque, has three or more masts which are all square-rigged except for the aftermost which is rigged fore-and-aft.

6 In the hands of Jews and Armenians

1 The JM–Purvis correspondence is scattered through the C10 series of India Letterbooks in the JM Archive at Cambridge. Virtually every one of the 50 or 60 volumes covering the years between 1820 and 1865 contains about ten or more letters to Purvis. The Private Letterbooks of William Jardine (C5) and those of Alexander Matheson (C6) likewise contain many letters to Purvis.

2 "How Many Smokers Does the Foreign Drug Serve?" was the subtitle of Robert Hart's 1881 report "Opium" (Hart 1881).

3 The actual ethnic identity of the Chinese opium dealers is not exactly clear from the sources. Many sources indicate that the opium traders were "Cantonese," but since Swatow or Shantou, is within Guangdong province, the term was often used, by the Dutch and sometimes the English, to refer to the Teochews, the Min speakers of that northeastern part of the province. At other times, however, it seems clear that "Cantonese" refers to people from the Pearl River delta area (i.e. Taishan, Zhungshan, Guangchou, Hong Kong, etc.).

4 Initially opium was smuggled into northern Vietnam, or Tongkin as it was then called, but later on the French began to purchase Yunnanese opium for local sale. By 1907, opium smokers, principally in Tongkin (many of whom may have been Chinese immigrants) were consuming over 75,000 kg of Chinese opium (Descours-Gatin 1992, p. 210).

5 This figure was based on the calculation that the average annual export of opium from India during 1901–5 had been 67,000 chests, of which 51,000 went to China. Thus, 10 percent of that which would have been exported to China was to be cut each year.

7 A matter of considerably greater solicitude

1 Singapore did have a gambling farm for a short period during the 1820s and early 1830s and for about three or four years it earned more than the opium farm, but the Indian government, under pressure from Parliament, decided that it was immoral to encourage gambling and so it was abolished. The ruler of Johor maintained a gambling farm as did many other Malay rulers, the Dutch, and the Siamese, but none of these earned more revenue than opium.

2 Et, cependent, l'opium constitué un médicament précieus pour de nombreuses maladies que l'on trouve surtout en Extrême-Orient. Il est tour a tour, selon la dose et le moment, excitant, calmant, analgesique, somnifère (Dumarest 1938, p. 32–3).

8 The most long-continued and systematic international crime

1 Dr. John Kramer has determined that one needs to consume at least 30 milligrams of opium daily for at least 30 consecutive days before physically measurable withdrawal symptoms are evident. This includes such phenomena as changes in body temperature, heart rate, observable trembling, sensory disorientation, etc. Even though most nineteenth century users smoked far more than 30 milligrams a day, it is doubtful that their body actually absorbed much more than ten percent of what was smoked. In any case, it is really impossible to get any exact measure of how much opium is actually absorbed by a smoker since so much of it goes up in smoke or is exhaled (Kramer 1979).

Bibliography

Archival Sources

1. (NAI) National Archives of India: Secret Revenue consultations, Letters from the Court of Directors to the Governor-General (SRC, LCD).
   8 April 1821, 30 Jan. 1822, and 11 July 1827.
   24 Oct. 1817, para. 77.
   24 Oct. 1817, para. 85.
2. (JMA) Jardine Matheson Archives: Cambridge University Library.
   A7/231, Log of James Innes, "Jamesina," 1832.
   C1/9 Private Hong Kong and India Letterbook.
   C5 Private Letterbooks of William Jardine.
   C6/3 Private Letterbook of Alexander Matheson.
   C10/1/67 India Letterbooks.
3. US Consular reports.
   William Stewart, US Consul, Smyrna to SoS, 25 April 1803.
   David Afflee, US Consul, Smyrna to SoS, 31 Dec. 1824.

Published Sources

Adshead, S.A.M. (1966) "The Opium Trade in Szechuan, 1881–1911" *Journal of Southeast Asian History* 7, no. 2, Sept: 93–9.

Allen, Nathan (1853) *The Opium Trade: Including a Sketch of its History, Extent, Effects as it is Carried on in India and China.* Lowell, Mass.: James P. Walker.

Andaya, Barbara Watson (1979) *Perak, The Abode of Grace: A Study of an Eighteenth-Century Malay State.* Kuala Lumpur: Oxford University Press.

—— (1989) "The Cloth Trade in Jambi and Palembang during the Seventeenth and Eighteenth Centuries." *Indonesia* no. 48, October: 26–46.

—— (1993) *To Live as Brothers: Southeast Sumatra in the Seventeenth and Eighteenth Centuries.* Honolulu, HI: University of Hawaii Press.

Bayly, C.A. (1983) *Rulers, Townsmen and Bazaars: North Indian Society in the Age of British Expansion, 1770–1870.* Cambridge, England: Cambridge University Press.

Benedict, Carol (1994) "The Development of the Yunggui-Lingnan Domestic Opium Trade and the Spread of Plague." A paper delivered at the Association of Asian Studies, Annual Meeting, March 24–7.

—— (1996) *Bubonic Plague in Nineteenth Century China.* Stanford, CA: Stanford University Press.

Berridge, Virginia and Griffith, Edwards (1987) *Opium and the People: Opiate Use in Nineteenth Century England.* New Haven and London: Yale University Press.

Blue, Archibald Duncan (1982) "The China Coast: A Study of British Shipping in Chinese Waters 1842–1914." Ph.D. Thesis, University of Strathclyde.

Blussé, Leonard (1981) "Batavia, 1619–1740: The Rise and Fall of a Chinese Colonial Town." *Journal of Southeast Asian Studies*, 12, no.1 March: 159–78.

—— (1988) *Strange Company: Chinese Settlers, Mestizo Women and the Dutch in VOC Batavia*. Dordrecht, Holland; Providence, RI: Floris Publications, 1988.

Bose, Sugata (1993) *"Peasant Labour and Colonial Capital: Rural Bengal Since 1770."* In *The New Cambridge History of India*, vol. III, part 2, ed. C.A. Bayly, John F. Richards and Gordon Johnson. Cambridge: Cambridge University Press.

Boxer, C.R. (1962) "The Dutch East-Indiamen: Their Sailors, their Navigators and Life on Board 1602–1795." Greenwich: National Maritime Museum, reprinted, 1976.

—— (1979) *Jan Compagnie in War and Peace 1602–1799*. Hong Kong, Singapore & Kuala Lumpur: Heinemann Asia.

Braddell, T. (1857) "Gambling and Opium Smoking in the Straits of Malacca." *Journal of the Indian Archipelago and Eastern Asia* 1 (new series): 66–87.

Braudel, Fernand (1979a) *The Structures of Everyday Life: Vol. I, Civilization and Capitalism 15th–18th Century*. Translated by Siân Reynolds. New York: Harper & Row.

—— (1979b) *The Wheels of Commerce: Vol. II, Civilization and Capitalism 15th–18th Century*. Translated by Siân Reynolds. New York: Harper & Row.

—— (1984) *The Perspective of the World: Vol. III, Civilization and Capitalism 15th–18th Century*. Translated by Siân Reynolds. New York: Harper & Row.

Brown, Ian (1993a) "The End of the Opium Farm in Siam 1905–7." In *The Rise and Fall of Revenue Farming: Business Elites and the Emergence of the Modern State in Southeast Asia*, ed. John Butcher and Howard Dick, 233–45. New York: St. Martin's Press.

—— (1993b) "Imperialism, Trade and Investment in the Late Nineteenth and Early Twentieth Centuries." In *The Rise and Fall of Revenue Farming: Business Elites and the Emergence of the Modern State in Southeast Asia*, ed. John Butcher and Howard Dick, 80–8. New York: St. Martin's Press.

Buckley, Charles Burton (1903) *An Anecdotal History of Old Times in Singapore* (1967 Reprint). Kuala Lumpur and London: University of Malaya Press.

Butcher, John (1983) "The Demise of the Revenue Farm System in the Federated Malay States." *Modern Asian Studies*, 17: 387–412.

Butcher, John and Howard Dick (ed.) (1993) *The Rise and Fall of Revenue Farming: Business Elites and the Emergence of the Modern State in Southeast Asia*. New York: St. Martin's Press.

Cameron, John (1865) *Our Tropical Possessions in Malayan India: Being a Descriptive Account of Singapore, Penang, Province Wellesley, and Malacca; their Peoples, Products, Commerce and Government*. (Reprinted 1965 by Oxford University Press, Kuala Lumpur.)

Cao, Xueqin (1973) *The Story of the Stone*: Vol. 1, The Golden Days. Translated by David Hawkes. Harmondsworth, Middlesex, England: Penguin Books.

Chang, Hsin-pao (1964) *Commissioner Lin and the Opium War*. Cambridge, Mass.: Harvard University Press.

Chauduri, K.N. (1971) *The Economic Development of India under the East India Company 1814–1858: A Selection of Contemporary Writings*, Cambridge: Cambridge University Press.

Collis, Maurice (1968) *Foreign Mud: The Opium Imbroglio at Canton in the 1830's and The Anglo-Chinese War*. New York: W.W. Norton & Co. Inc.

Commission, International Opium (1909) *Report of the International Opium Commission*. Shanghai, China: *North China Daily News & Herald*.

Conrad, Joseph (1986) *Lord Jim*. New York: Penguin.

Courtwright, David T. (1982) *Dark Paradise: Opiate Addiction in America before 1940.* Cambridge, Mass: Harvard University Press.

Cranmer-Byng, J.L. (ed.) (1963) *An Embassy to China Being the Journal Kept by Lord Macartney During His Embassy to the Emperor Ch'ien-lung 1793–1794.* Hamden, Connecticut: Archon Books.

Crawfurd, John (1820a) *A History of the Indian Archipelago Containing an Account of the Manners, Arts, Languages, Religions, Institutions, and Commerce of the Inhabitants,* Vol. III. (Reprinted 1967 by Frank Cass and Co. Ltd, London.)

—— (1820b) *A History of the Indian Archipelago Containing an Account of the Manners, Arts, Languages, Religions, Institutions, and Commerce of the Inhabitants,* Vol. 1. (Reprinted 1967 by Frank Cass and Co. Ltd, London.)

—— (1837) "A Sketch of the Commercial Resources and Monetary and Mercantile System of British India, with Suggestions for Their Improvement, by Means of Banking Establishments." In *The Economic Development of India under the East India Company 1814–1858: A Selection of Contemporary Writings,* ed. K.N. Chauduri, 217–316. Cambridge, UK: Cambridge University Press.

—— (1854) *Journal of the Indian Archipelago and Eastern Asia,* 10 new series: 410.

Crisswell, Colin N. (1981) *The Taipans: Hong Kong's Merchant Princes.* Hong Kong: Oxford University Press.

Cushman, Jennifer Wayne (1986) "The Khaw Group: Chinese Business in Early Twentieth Century Penang." *Journal of Southeast Asian Studies* 17, no. 1, March: 58–79.

—— (1991) *Family and State: The Formation of a Sino-Thai Tin-mining Dynasty, 1797–1932.* Singapore: Oxford University Press.

—— (1993a) *Fields from the Sea: Chinese Junk Trade with Siam during the Late Eighteenth and Early Nineteenth Centuries.* Ithaca, New York: Southeast Asia Program, Cornell University.

—— and Michael Godley (1993b) "The Khaw Concern." In *The Rise and Fall of Revenue Farming: Business Elites and the Emergence of the Modern State in Southeast Asia,* ed. John Butcher and Howard Dick, 267–71. New York: St. Martin's Press.

Darras, Jacques (1982) *Joseph Conrad and the West: Signs of Empire.* Translated by Anne Luyat and Jacques Darras. Hong Kong: Macmillan.

Desai, T.S. (1968) *Economic History of India 1757–1947.* Bombay: Vora & Co.

Descours-Gatin, Chantal (1992) *Quand l'opium financait la colonisation en Indochine: l'elaboration de la régie generale de l'opium (1860–1914).* Paris: Editions L'Hartmann (Ouvrage publie avec le concours du Centre National des Lettres.)

Devido, Elise Anne (1996) "The Making of the Communist Party-State in Shandong Province, 1927–1952." Ph.D. Thesis, Cambridge, Mass: Harvard University.

Diehl, F. W. (1993) "Revenue Farming and Colonial Finances in the Netherlands East Indies, 1816–1925." In *The Rise and Fall of Revenue Farming: Business Elites and the Emergence of the Modern State in Southeast Asia,* ed. John Butcher and Howard Dick, 196–232. New York: St. Martin's Press.

Dumarest, Jacques (1938) "Les Monopoles de l'opium et du sel en Indochine." Lyon, Doctorat en Droit, Université de Lyon, Faculté de Droit.

Earl, George Windsor (1836) "Narrative of a Journey from Singapore to the West Coast of Borneo in the Schooner Stamford in the Year 1834, with an Account of a Journey to Montradoh, the Capital of a Chinese Colony in Possession of the Principal Gold Mines." *Journal of the Royal Asiatic Society 3,* no. v: 1–24.

—— (1837) *The Eastern Seas: or Voyages and Discoveries in the Indian Archipelago in 1832–33–34.* Kuala Lumpur: Oxford University Press. (Oxford in Asia Historical Reprint, 1971.)

Edkins, J. Dr (1898) *Opium: Historical Note on the Poppy in China.* Shanghai: American Presbyterian Press.

Fairbank, John K. (1953) *Trade and Diplomacy on the China Coast: The Opening of the Treaty Ports, 1842–1854*, two vols. Cambridge, Mass.: Harvard University Press.

—— (1978) "The Creation of the Treaty System." In *The Cambridge History of China*, vol. 10, ed. John K. Fairbank, 213–63. Cambridge: Cambridge University Press.

Farooqui, Amar (1995) "Opium Enterprise and Colonial Intervention in Malwa and Western India, 1800–1824." *The Indian Economic and Social History Review* 32, no. 4: 447–73.

Fay, Peter Ward (1975) *The Opium War.* Chapel Hill: University of North Carolina Press.

Fields, Albert and Peter A. Tararin (1970) "Opium in China." *British Journal of Addiction* 64, nos 3/4: 371–82.

Fitch, Ralph (1583) "Voyage of Ralph Fitch to Goa and Siam." In *Richard Hakluyt: Voyages and Discoveries: The Principal Navigations Voyages, Traffiques and Discoveries of the English Nation*, ed. Jack Beeching, 252–69. New York: Penguin Books, 1990.

Foster, Arnold (1899) "The Report of the Royal Commission on Opium Compared with the Evidence from China that was Submitted to the Commission: An Examination and an Appeal." In *Reports of the Royal Commission on Opium.* London: Government Printing Office.

Frank, Andre Gunder (1979) *World Accumulation, 1492–1789.* New York and London: Monthly Review Press.

—— (1998) *Re-Orient: Global Economy in the Asian Age.* Berkeley, Ca: University of California Press.

Furber, Holden (1951) *John Company at Work: A Study of European Expansion in India in the Late Eighteenth Century.* Cambridge, Massachussetts: Harvard University Press.

—— (1976) *Rival Empires of Trade in the Orient 1600–1800, Vol. II: Europe and the World in the Age of Expansion.* Minneapolis, Minn.: University of Minnesota Press.

Godley, Michael R. (1981) *Mandarin Capitalists from Nanyang: Overseas Chinese Enterprise in the Modernization of China, 1893–1911.* Cambridge: Cambridge University Press.

—— (1993) "Thio Thiau Siat's Network." In *The Rise and Fall of Revenue Farming: Business Elites and the Emergence of the Modern State in Southeast Asia*, ed. John Butcher and Howard Dick, 262–6. New York: St. Martin's Press.

Goldsmith, Margaret (1939) *The Trail of Opium: the Eleventh Plague.* London: Robert Hale Ltd.

Goodman, Jordan (1995) "Excitantia: Or, How Enlightenment Europe Took to Soft Drugs." In *Consuming Habits: Drugs in History and Anthropology*, ed. Paul E. Lovejoy, Andrew Sherratt and Jordan Goodman, 126–47. London and New York: Routledge.

Great Britain, Foreign Office (1921) *Correspondence Respecting the Cultivation of Opium in China.* London: Government Publishing Office.

—— (1974) *The Opium Trade 1910–1941.* London: Facsimile Reproduction of Foreign Office Collection, F.O. 415.

Greenberg, Michael (1951) *British Trade and the Opening of China, 1800–1842.* Cambridge: Cambridge University Press.

Hamilton, Alexander (1727) *A New Account of the East Indies*, Vol. 2. London: Argonaut Press. (William Foster ed., 1930 reprint of 1727 edition.)

Hamilton, Gary G. (1977) "Nineteenth Century Chinese Merchant Associations: Conspiracy or Combination? The Case of the Swatow Opium Guild." *Ch'ing-shih wen-t'i* 3, December: 50–71.

Harrison, Brian (1953) "Trade in the Straits of Malacca in 1785, Memorandum by P.G.

De Bruijn, Governor of Malacca." *Journal of the Malayan Branch of the Royal Asiatic Society* 26, no. 1: 56–62.

Hart, Robert (1881) *Opium*. Shanghai: Imperial Maritime Customs, special series, no. 4.

Heilbroner, R. L. G., John, K. (1987) *The Economic Problem*. Englewood Cliffs, NJ: Prentice-Hall.

Hobhouse, H. (1985) *Seeds of Change: Five Plants that Transformed Mankind*. London: Sidgwick & Jackson.

Howard, Paul W. (1997) "Opium Suppression in Late Qing China: The Limits and Possibilities of Social Reform." A paper delivered at the Conference on Opium in East Asian History, University of Toronto, York University, May 9–10.

Hunter, William C. (1882) *The Fan Kwae at Canton before Treaty Days, 1825–1844*. London, 1911 edn.

India, Government (1871) *Behar and Benares Opium Agencies Reports 1870–71*. Calcutta: Department of Revenue.

—— (1882) *Report on the Administration of the Opium Department (Including Behar and Benares) 1880–1881*. Calcutta: Department of Revenue.

—— (1883) *Report of a Commission Appointed by the Government of India to Enquire into the Working of the Opium Department of Bengal and the Northwestern Provinces*. Calcutta: Indian Government.

Inglis, Brian (1975) *The Forbidden Game: A Social History of Drugs*. New York: Charles Scribner's Sons.

Jackson, Stanley (1968) *The Sassoons*. London: Heinemann.

Johnson, Bruce D. (1975) "Righteousness before Revenue: The Forgotten Moral Crusade Against the Indo-Chinese Opium Trade." *Journal of Drug Issues*, Fall: 304–26.

Kaempfero, Engelberto D. (1712) *Amoenitatum Exoticarum: Politico-Physico-Medicarum: Quibus continertur Variae Relationes, Observationes & Descriptiones. Rerum Persicarum & Ulterior's Asiae multa attentione in peregrinationibus per universum Orientem, collectae ab auctore Engleberto Kaempfero, D.*, vol. 5 (Fasciculi V). Lemgoviae: Henrici Wilhelmi Meyer I.

Kinkley, Jeffrey C. (1987) *The Odyssey of Shen Congwen*. Stanford, CA: Stanford University Press.

Kramer, John C. M.D. (1979) "Speculations on the Nature and Pattern of Opium Smoking." *Journal of Drug Issues*, Spring: 247–56.

Landes, David S. (1998) *The Wealth and Poverty of Nations: Why Some Are So Rich and Some So Poor*. New York and London: W.W. Norton & Co.

Leary, Timothy (1970) *The Politics of Ecstasy*. London: Paladin.

Le Failler, Philippe (1993) "Le mouvement international anti-opium et l'Indochine, 1906–1940." Ph.D. thesis, Provence, Université de Provence.

Le Fevour, Edward (1968) *Western Enterprise in Late Ch'ing China: A Selective Survey of Jardine, Matheson and Company's Operations 1842–1895*. Cambridge, Mass.: Harvard University Press.

LEGCO, (1883) Straits Settlements. "Straits Settlements Legislative Council Proceedings." Singapore: Government Printing Office.

Lewis, Dianne Nell (1970) "The Dutch East India Company and the Straits of Malacca, 1700–1784: Trade and Politics in the Eighteenth Century." Ph.D. thesis, Canberra, Australian National University.

Lin, Man-huong (1989) "Currency and Society: The Monetary Crisis and Political–Economic Ideology of Early Nineteenth-Century China." Ph.D. thesis, Cambridge, Mass., Harvard University.

—— (1991) "World Recession, Indian Opium, and China's Opium War." Paper delivered at the Second International Symposium on Maritime Studies, Pondicherry, India.

—— (1993a) "Opium Poppy Cultivation, Interregional Migration, and Late Ch'ing China's Population." Paper delivered at the 1993 International Workshop on Historical Demography: Population History of East Asia, Reitaku University, Japan, Jan. 28–Feb. 3.

—— (1993b) "Fluctuations of the Spatial Integration of China with the Asian International Economy, 1850–1949." Paper delivered at the Workshop on "China in Asian International Economic History, c. 1850–1945," Osaka, Japan, May 22–3.

Little, R. Esq. Surgeon (1848) "On the Habitual Use of Opium in Singapore." *Journal of the Indian Archipelago and Eastern Asia*, 2, no. 1: 1–79.

Lo, Yun-yen (1933) *The Opium Problem in the Far East*. Shanghai: Commercial Press.

Lockyer, Charles (1711) *An Account of the Trade in India containing Rules for Good Government in Trade, Prices Courants and Tables: with Descriptions of Ft. St. George, Acheen, Malacca, Condore, Canton, Anjenga, Muskat, Gombroon, Surat, Goa, Carwar, Telichery, Panola, Calicut, the Cape of Good Hope and St. Helena. Their Inhabitants, Customs, Religion, Government, Animals, Fruits, etc, to which is Added an Account of the Management of the Dutch of their Affairs in the Indies*. London: Samuel Crouch.

Lubbock, Basil (1933) *The Opium Clippers*. Glasgow, Scotland: Brown, Son & Ferguson.

Madancy, Joyce A. (1994) "Revolution, Religion and the Poppy: Opium and the Rebellion of the 'Sixteenth Emperor' in Early Republican Fujian." Paper delivered at the Association of Asian Studies, Annual Meeting, Boston, Mass., March 24–7.

Malcolm, Sir John (1823) *A Memoir of Central India Including Malwa and Adjoining Provinces with the History and Copius Illustrations of the Past and Present Condition of that Country*, vol. 2. London: Kingsbury, Parbury & Allen.

Marsden, William (1811) *The History of Sumatra Containing an Account of the Government, Laws, Customs, and Manners of the Native Inhabitants with a Description of the Natural Productions, and a Relation of the Ancient Political State of that Island*, vol. I. London: Orme and Brown. (Third Edition, printed by J. M'Creery, and sold by Longman, Hurst, Rees.)

Marshall, Jonathan (1976) "Opium and the Politics of Gangsterism in Nationalist China, 1927–1945." *Bulletin of Concerned Asian Scholars* 8, no. 3, July–September: 19–48.

Marshall, P.J. (1976) *East Indian Fortunes: The British in Bengal in the Eighteenth Century*. Oxford: Oxford University Press.

Martin, Brian G. (1995) "The Green Gang and the Guomindang State: Du Yuesheng and the Politics of Shanghai, 1927–37." *Journal of Asian Studies* 54, no. 1, February: 64–91.

McCoy, Alfred W. (1991) *The Politics of Heroin: CIA Complicity in the Global Drug Trade*, Brooklyn, NY: Lawrence Hill Books.

—— (1992) "Heroin as a Global Commodity: A History of Southeast Asia's Opium Trade." In *War on Drugs: Studies in the Failure of U.S. Narcotics Policy*, ed. Alfred W. McCoy and Alan A. Block, 237–79. Boulder, San Francisco and Oxford: Westview Press.

McNeill, William H. (1980) *The Human Condition: An Ecological and Historical View*. From the Bland-Lee Lecture Series Delivered at Clark University, Princeton, NJ: Princeton University Press.

Merlin, Mark David (1983) *On the Trail of the Ancient Opium Poppy*. London and Toronto: Rutherford, Madison, Teaneck, Fairleigh Dickinson University Press.

Metcalfe, Barbara (1979) *Land, Landlords and the British Raj*. Berkeley, California: University of California Press.

Mills, L. Scott (1993) "The Keystone-Species Concept in Ecology and Conservations." *Bioscience*, April 1.

Mintz, Sidney W. (1985) *Sweetness and Power: The Place of Sugar in Modern History*, Battleboro, VT: Viking.

Miyazaki, Ichisada (1976) *China's Examination Hell: The Civil Service Examinations of Imperial China*. Translated by Conrad Schirokauer. New Haven and London: Yale University Press.

Morse, Hosea B. (1926–9) *The Chronicles of the East India Company Trading to China*, vol. 1. Oxford: Paragon.

Moser, Thomas C. (1968) *Joseph Conrad, Lord Jim: an Authoritative Text, Backgrounds, Sources, Essays in Criticism*, New York: W.W. Norton & Co.

Nankoe, Hakiem, Jean-Claude Gerlus and Martin J. Murray (1993) "The Origins of the Opium Trade and the Opium Regies in Colonial Indochina." In *The Rise and Fall of Revenue Farming: Business Elites and the Emergence of the Modern State in Southeast Asia*, ed. John Butcher and Howard Dick, 182–95. New York: St. Martin's Press.

Needham, Joseph (1954) *Science and Civilisation in China*. Vol. 1, *Introductory Orientations*. Cambridge: Cambridge University Press.

Nelson, Carl (1972) "The Ironic Allusive Texture of *Lord Jim*: Coleridge, Crane, Milton and Melville." *Conradiana: A Journal of Joseph Conrad* 4, no. 2: 47–59.

Newman, R. K. (1989) "India and the Anglo–Chinese Opium Agreements, 1907–1914." *Modern Asian Studies* 23, no. 3: 525–50.

Nightengale, Pamela (1970) *Trade and Empire in Western India 1784–1806*. Cambridge: Cambridge University Press.

Owen, David Edward (1934) *British Opium Policy in China and India*. New Haven, Conn.: Yale University Press.

Parkinson, C. Northcote (1937) *Trade in the Eastern Seas 1793–1813*. Cambridge: Cambridge University Press.

Parssinen, Terry and Kerner, Karen (1980) "Development of the Disease Model of Drug Addiction in Britain, 1870–1926." *Medical History* 24: 275–96.

—— (1983) *Secret Passions, Secret Remedies: Narcotic Drugs in British Society, 1820–1930*. Philadelphia: Institute for the Study of Human Issues.

Pasquel, J.C. (1895–6) "Chinese Tin Mining in Selangor." *The Selangor Journal: Jottings Past and Present*, IV, no. 2, Oct. 4: 25–9; no. 3, Oct 18: 43–7; no. 6, Nov. 29: 99–103; no. 8, Dec. 27: 136–40; no. 10, Jan. 24. (1896: 168–73).

Perrott, Nadine (1992) *Shanghai: Opium, Jeu, Prostitution*. Translated by Perrott, Nadine. Paris: Editions Philippe Picquier.

Philips, C.H. (1961) *The East India Company 1784–1834*. Manchester, UK: Manchester University Press.

Prakash, Om (1985) *The Dutch East India Company and the Economy of Bengal, 1630–1750*. Princeton, N.J.: Princeton University Press.

—— (1986) "European Trade and the Economy of Bengal in the Seventeenth and Early Eighteenth Century." In *Trading Companies in Asia 1600–1830*, ed. J. van Goor, 19–31. Utrecht: H & S Hes Uitgevers.

Prinsep, George Alexander (1971) "Remarks on the External Commerce and Exchanges of Bengal, with Appendix of Accounts and Estimates (1823)." In *The Economic Development of India under the East India Company 1814–1858: A Selection of Contemporary Writings*, ed. K. N. Chauduri, 51–167. Cambridge: Cambridge University Press.

Pritchard, E. H. (1936) *The Crucial Years of Early Anglo–Chinese Relations 1750–1800*. Washington: Pullman.

Purcell, Victor (1965) *The Chinese in Southeast Asia*. London: Oxford University Press.

Reid, Anthony (1988) *Southeast Asia in the Age of Commerce 1450–1680: The Lands Below the Winds*, vol. 1. New Haven and London: Yale University Press.

Richards, J.F. (1981) "The Indian Empire and the Peasant Production of Opium in the Nineteenth Century." *Modern Asian Studies* 15, no. 1: 62.

Rowe, William T. (1984) *Hankow: Commerce and Society in a Chinese City 1796–1889.* Stanford, California: Stanford University Press.

—— (1989) *Hankow: Conflict and Community in a Chinese City 1796–1895.* Stanford, California: Stanford University Press.

Rowntree, Joshua (1906) *The Imperial Drug Trade: A Restatement of the Opium Question in the Light of Recent Evidence and New Developments in the East*, second edition. London: Methuen & Co.

RoyComm (1895) *First Report of the Royal Commission on Opium: With Minutes of Evidence and Appendices etc.* Seven Volumes. Great Britain: Parliament.

Rush, James R. (1990) *Opium to Java: Revenue Farming and Chinese Enterprise in Colonial Indonesia, 1800–1910.* Ithaca, NY: Cornell University Press.

Sadka, Emily (1968) *The Protected Malay States, 1874–1895.* Kuala Lumpur: University of Malaya Press.

Schoffer, Ivo and F.S. Gaastra (1977) "The Import of Bullion and Coin into Asia by the Dutch East India Company in the Seventeenth and Eighteenth Centuries." In *Dutch Capitalism and World Capitalism, Capitalisme Hollandais et capitalisme mondail*, ed. Maurice Aymard, 215–35. Cambridge/Paris: Cambridge University Press/Editions de la Maison des Sciences de l'Homme.

Scott, J.M. (1969) *The White Poppy: A History of Opium.* London: William Heinemann Ltd.

Shaw, Samuel (1847) *The Journals of Major Samuel Shaw, the First American Consul at Canton with a Life of the Author by Josiah Quincy* (ed. Josiah Quincy). Boston: W. Crosby and H.P. Nichols.

Shen, Congwen (1982) *Recollections of West Hunan.* Translated by Gladys Yang. Beijing: Panda Books.

Singh, Narayan Prasad (1980) *The East India Company's Monopoly Industries in Bihar with Particular Reference to Opium and Saltpetre, 1773–1833.* Muzaffarpur, Bihar: Sarvodaya Vangmaya.

Sinha, Narendra K. (1956) *The Economic History of Bengal: From Plassey to the Permanent Settlement*, vol. 1. Calcutta: Author, (agents, K.L. Mukhopadhyay, Calcutta).

Smyth, H. Warrington (1898a) *Five Years in Siam From 1891–1896*, vol. 1. New York: Charles Scribner's Sons. (1994 Reprint by White Lotus, Bangkok, with an introduction by Tamara Loos.)

—— (1898b) *Five Years in Siam From 1891–1896*, vol. 2. New York: Charles Scribner's Sons, 1898b. (1994 Reprint by White Lotus, Bangkok, with an introduction by Tamara Loos.)

Song, Ong Siang (1923) *One Hundred Years' History of the Chinese in Singapore.* Singapore: University of Malaya Press. (University of Malaya reprint, 1967.)

Spence, Jonathan (1975) "Opium Smoking in Ching China." In *Conflict and Control in Late Imperial China*, ed. Fredric Wakeman, Jr. and Carolyn Grant, 143–73. Berkeley and Los Angeles: University of California Press.

Steinberg, David Joel and David K. Wyatt, John R.W. Smail, Alexander Woodside, William R. Roff and David P. Chandler (1971) *In Search of Southeast Asia: A Modern History.* New York: Praeger Publishers.

Stelle, Charles Clarkson (1938) *Americans and the China Opium Trade in the Nineteenth Century.* Dept of History, New York: Arno Press. (Originally presented as author's Ph.D. thesis, University of Chicago.)

Stoler, Ann Laura (1985) *Capitalism and Confrontation in Sumatra's Plantation Belt, 1870–1979.* New Haven and London: Yale University Press.

Stuart, Rev. G. A. (1979) *Chinese Materia Medica: Vegetable Kingdom.* Taipei, Republic of China: Southern Materials Center.

Tan, Chung (1978) *China and the Brave New World: A Study of the Origins of the Opium War (1840–1842).* Durham, North Carolina: Carolina Academic Press.

Taylor, Chris (1997) "Drugs '8pc of world trade'." *Guardian Weekly,* 4 July 1997.

Taylor, Jean Gelman (1983) *The Social World of Batavia: European and Eurasian in Dutch Asia.* Madison, WI: University of Wisconsin Press.

Terry, Charles and Mildred Pellins (1970) *The Opium Problem.* New Jersey: Montclair.

Tomlinson, B.R. (1993) "The Economy of Modern India 1866–1970." In *The New Cambridge History of India,* Vol. III, part 3, ed. C.A. Bayly, John F. Richards and Gordon Johnson. Cambridge: Cambridge University Press.

Trocki, Carl A. (1979) *Prince of Pirates: The Temenggongs and the Development of Johor and Singapore, 1784–1885.* Singapore: Singapore University Press.

—— (1987) "The Rise of Singapore's Great Opium Syndicate, 1840–1886." *Journal of Southeast Asian Studies* 18, no.1, March: 58–80.

—— (1990) *Opium and Empire: Chinese Society in Colonial Singapore 1800–1910.* Ithaca, New York: Cornell University Press.

—— (1993) "The Collapse of Singapore's Great Syndicate." In *The Rise and Fall of Revenue Farming: Business Elites and the Emergence of the Modern State in Southeast Asia,* ed. John Butcher and Howard Dick, 166–81. New York: St. Martin's Press.

Turnbull, C. M. (1977) *A History of Singapore.* Kuala Lumpur: Oxford University Press.

Verleun, Jan A. (1979) *Patna and Patusan Perspectives: A Study of the Function of the Minor Characters in Joseph Conrad's Lord Jim.* Groningen: Bouma's Boekhuis.

Viraphol, Sarasin (1977) *Tribute and Profit: Sino-Siamese Trade 1652–1853.* Cambridge, Mass.: Harvard University Press.

Vlekke, Bernard H. M. (1946) *The Story of the Dutch East Indies.* Cambridge, Mass.: Harvard University Press.

Vos, Reinout (1993) *Gentle Janus, Merchant Prince: The VOC and the Tightrope of Diplomacy in the Malay World, 1740–1800.* Translated by Beverley Jackson. Leiden, The Netherlands: KITLV Press.

Wakeman, Frederic (1966) *Strangers at the Gate: Social Disorder in South China 1839–1861.* Berkeley: University of California Press.

—— (1975) *The Fall of Imperial China.* New York: The Free Press.

—— (1978) "The Canton Trade and the Opium War," Chapter 4. In *Cambridge History of China,* Volume 10, *Late Ch'ing, 1800–1911,* ed. John King Fairbank, 163–212. Cambridge: Cambridge University Press.

Waley, Arthur (1958) *The Opium War Through Chinese Eyes.* London: Allen & Unwin.

Walling, R.N. (1931) *Singapura Sorrows.* Singapore: Malaya Publishing House.

Walvin, J. (1997) *The Fruits of Empire: Exotic Produce and British Taste 1660–1800.* New York, New York University Press.

Warner, Jessica (1992) *The Notion of 'Addiction.' It's Older than You Think.* Berkeley, California: Alcohol Research Group, submission to The Social History of Alcohol Review.

—— (1993a) "The Life and Times of 'Mother Gin' 1720–1751: Images of Mothers and Alcohol on the Eve of the Industrial Revolution." A paper delivered at the International Congress on the Social History of Alcohol, London, Ontario, May 13–15.

—— (1993b) "The Sanctuary of Sobriety: Images of Women and Alcohol in Seventeenth Century England." A paper delivered at The Social History Society Conference.

—— (1995) "Good Help is Hard to Find: A Few Comments about Alcohol and Work in Preindustrial England." *Addiction Research* 2, no. 3: 259–69.

Warren, James Francis (1981) *The Sulu Zone, 1768–1898: The Dynamics of External Trade, Slavery, and Ethnicity in the Transformation of a Southeast Asian Maritime State.* Singapore: Singapore University Press.

—— (1990) "Trade, Slave Raiding and State Formation in the Sulu Sultanate in the Nineteenth Century." In *Southeast Asian Port and Policy: Rise and Demise,* ed. Jaya Kathirithamby-Wells and John Villiers, 187–212. Singapore: Singapore University Press.

Wasson, R., G. Ruck, A.P. Carl, A. Hoffman (1978) *The Road to Eleusis: Unveiling the Secrets of the Mysteries.* New York: Harcourt, Brace, Jovanovich.

Watt, G. (1893) "Papaver Somniferum." In *Dictionary of the Economic Products of India,* vol. 6, ed. Sir George Allen, 75–105. London: W.H. Allen.

Waung, W.S.K. (1977) *The Controversy: Opium and Sino-British Relations 1858–1887.* Hong Kong: Lung Men Press Ltd.

Wickberg, Edgar (1965) *The Chinese in Philippine Life 1850–1898.* New Haven and London: Yale University Press.

Williams, Samuel Wells (1907) *The Middle Kingdom: A Survey of the Geography, Government, Literature, Social Life, Arts, and History of the Chinese Empire and its Inhabitants,* vol. 2. (Revised edition.) New York: Charles Scribner and Sons.

Williamson, A. R. (1975) *Eastern Traders: Some Men and Ships of Jardine Matheson and Company.* Ipswich: Jardine, Matheson Co. (Private printing.)

Wills, John E., Jr. (1974) *Pepper, Guns and Parleys: The Dutch East India Company and China 1622–1681.* Cambridge, Mass.: Harvard University Press.

—— (1984) *Embassies and Illusions: Dutch and Portuguese Envoys to K'ang- hsi, 1666–1687.* Cambridge, Mass.: Council on East Asian Studies, Harvard University.

Wilson, Constance M. (1993) "Revenue Farming, Economic Development and Government Policy during the Early Bangkok Period, 1830–1892." In *The Rise and Fall of Revenue Farming: Business Elites and the Emergence of the Modern State in Southeast Asia,* ed. John Butcher and Howard Dick, 142–65. New York: St. Martin's Press.

Wong, Lin Ken (1964–5) "The Revenue Farms of Prince of Wales Island." *Journal of the South Seas Society:* 56–127.

Wong, R. Binn (1997) *China Transformed: Historical Change and the Limits of European Experience.* Ithaca and London: Cornell University Press.

Woodruff, Philip (1953) *The Men Who Ruled India: The Founders,* vol. 1. New York: Schocken Books.

Wright, H.R.C. (1961) *East-Indian Economic Problems of the Age of Cornwallis and Raffles.* London: Luzac & Co. Ltd.

Wu, Ching-tzu (1957) *The Scholars (Ju-lin Wai-shih).* Translated by Yang Hsien-yi and Gladys Yang. Peking: Foreign Language Press.

Wyman, Judith (1994) "Opium and the State in Sichuan Province during the Late Qing." A paper delivered at the Association of Asian Studies, Annual Meeting, Boston, MA, March 24–7.

Yamawaki, Teijiro (1976) "The Great Trading Merchants, Cocksinja and His Son," *Acta Asiatica, Bulletin of the Institute of Eastern Culture,* 30: 106–16.

Zhou, Yongming (1999) "Nationalism, Identity, and State-Building: The Anti-Opium Crusade of 1949–52." In *Opium Empires and States in East Asian History,* ed. Timothy Brook and B.T. Wakabayashi. Berkeley, CA: University of California Press.

Index

Acapulco 42
Aceh 34, 51, 170
addiction to opium 25–6, 79, 90–1
Addshead, S.A.M. 130–1
adulteration of opium 62, 68
advances to peasants 63, 83–4
agency houses 101–2
Allen, N. 21
Ambon 54
America 27, 155, 164
American Central Intelligence Agency 171
American Consuls 75–6, 129
American merchants 59, 75–7, 101–2, 164
Andaya, B. 44
Anderson, J. 144–5
Anglo-Chinese War 100
Anglo-Scottish traders 101, 115, 118
anti-drug campaigns 11, 117–18, 128–31
anti-Semitism 115–18
Armenian traders 102, 118
Australia 101, 143

Bangka Islands 43, 44
Bangkok 152, 154
Banhap clique, or kongsi 153
Banjarmasin 51
Batavia 39–42, 44, 76, 101, 152
Benares (Varanasi) 45, 58, 62, 64, 66, 68, 83, 86, 169; opium 2, 34, 45, 96, 102, 110, 118, 164
Benedict, C. 125
Bengal: British control 6–7, 44–5; Council 47; *diwani* of 44; Nawab of 6,
Bengkalis R. 37, 52
Berridge, V. 165
Bihar 45, 58, 62, 64, 66, 68, 74, 83, 86, 110, 169

bills of exchange 73, 98
Blussé, L. 40–1
Bombay 49–52, 80–2, 84–5, 101, 112
Borneo 55, 143
Bowring, J. 164
Braddell, T. 158
Braudel, F. 9, 23–4, 34
British empire xii, 58, 158, 160–4; and capitalism 30; and opium 10
British government 98, 99–100, 162
British merchants 58, 98–103, 111–18, 137
Brown, I. 138
Brunei 51, 56, 170
bubonic plague 125
Buchalter, L. 133
Bugis 43
bullion deficit 8–9, 42–4, 98
Burke, E. 47

Calcutta 36, 46, 49–51,76, 84, 101; auctions (bazaar) 63, 99, 107, 119
Cambay 25, 75, 77
Cameron, J. 141, 154
cannabis 19–20
Canton (Guangzhou) 39–40, 49–52, 76, 80, 91, 98–9, 119
Canton system 97–8, 101–2
Cantonese traders 91–2, 119–21
Cao, Xueqin 90
capital accumulation 46, 62
capitalism and opium 10, 46, 53, 58, 61–2, 77, 83–7; and drug economies 11, 28–32
Chakri dynasty 55
Chandernagore 46
chandu 2, 36, 37, 139
Chang Hsin-pao 100
Chauduri, B.B. 83

Cheefoo 127
Chiang Kai-shek 128, 133–4
China: domestic trade 92–3, 119–22, 125, 165; foreign trade 23, 31, 34, 44, 51, 75–6, 105, 108
Chinatowns in the West 164
Chinese in Batavia 40–1; immigration 44
Chinese Christians 131
Chinese Communist Party 133–4
Chinese coolies 44, 52, 55, 56, 108, 137, 141–8, 156, 157, 165–6
Chinese government 85, 96, 128–9, 165, 167
Chinese merchants 54, 118–22, 134–5, 139–41, 143–9, 156–9, 165–6
Chinese migration 108, 142–4
Chinese planters 55, 143
Chinsura 45
Chongqing 127
Chulalongkorn, King 150, 157
Civil War (American) 110
Clifton, W. 104
clipper ships 104–7, 142
Clive, R. 6, 44–5, 160
coast trade 102–3
Cochinchina 138, 143, 149–52
Cockburn, H. 130
Cohong 97–8, 101–2
Cold War 171
colonial boundaries 158–9
Colonial Office (British) 162
colonialism 137–9, 153–5, 157–9
commodity trade 142–4, 147–9, 156, 167
Conrad, J. xii, 11, 53–4, 118; critique of empire 1, 4–5, 160, 172–3; *Lord Jim* 1–6, 118
Cornwallis, C. 62–4, 160
cotton trade 39, 49, 61, 74, 101, 110
country trade (traders) 40, 48–52, 54, 55, 97, 101–2
country "wallahs" 103
Cox, J.H. 101
Crawfurd, J. 34, 74, 79–80, 85, 93–4, 96, 99, 138, 142
Cushman, J. 156–7

Da Kongsi 133
Damaõ 78
Daoguang Emperor 97–8
Deli 148
Demeter 17
Dent & Co. 102, 105, 107, 114
Descours-Gatin, C. 148
drug cultures xi, 14, 37, 87

drug economies 11, 26–32, 131–4, 166–9
drug epidemics *see* drug plagues
drugs and human society xi–xii; 16, 166
drug plagues xi–xii, 7–8, 26–7, 89–90, 121, 131–4, 165–6, 167–8
drug trade and capitalism xiv, 7–8, 33–4, 59, 86–7, 167, 173
drugs as commodities 8, 27–32, 58, 86–7
drug use: in neolithic and ancient times 16; in Europe 27–32, 165; among Europeans 145; and religion 18; and the state 18; traditional patterns 13–14
Du Yuesheng 133
Dumarest, J. 144–5
Dutch 34, 36, 45, 49, 54, 60, 148; *see also* East India Company, Dutch

East India Company, British (EIC) xii, 6–7, 9, 30, 46–52, 60–1, 83, 96, 119, 133, 162, 171; in Canton 58, 74, 97, 101; Court of Directors 75, 77; opium monopoly 61–73, 85; struggle with VOC 39–42
East India Company, Dutch (VOC) 9, 37–42
Eastern Shipping Company 157
economic problem, the 23
Edkins, J. 35, 124
Empress of China 75
Ethical System 150
Eurasians 41
European drug use 26–32, 88–9, 117–18, 164–5, 167
European empire 11, 22, 33, 56–7, 59, 86–7, 137–9, 160–4, 173
European missionaries 130
European trade 33; with Asia 8–9, 37, 49, 160; with America 26–9
European traders 59, 111–12, 119, 134–6, 157, 165
exotic chemicals 22–3, 160
Ezra, E.D.I. 113

Fairbank, J.K. 162
Farooqui, Amar 77, 83–4
Fay, P.W. 100, 104
Fiengold, D. 68
Fitch, R. 45, 75
Floris, P. 160
Frank, A.G. 59
free trade 29, 47, 56–7, 61, 80, 90, 115, 138, 157
Fujian, 40, 91

Furber, H. 39–40
furs 75–6

Galen, C. 17, 19
gambier 44, 137
Gangadhar, Appa 84
Ganges 107
Ghazipur 64: Council of 46
ginseng 75
Gladstone, W.E. 98
Goa 78, 85
Golden Triangle 134, 171
Great Opium Syndicate 149
Greek fertility cults 17
Green Gang 133
Guangdong 120–1
Guangxi 120
Gubbay, E. 113
Gujerat 78
Gulland, W.G. 117–18, 135
Guomindang 133, 171

Hamilton, A. 37–8, 52, 160
Hamilton, G. 119
Hankou, 92, 123, 127
Hart, R. 90, 118
Hastings, W. 32, 46–7, 51, 62–3, 160
Heilbroner, R. 23
heroin 110
Hobhouse, H. 27
Hobsbawm, E. 27
Holman, J. 93
Hongdengjiao 130
Hong Kong 99, 102–3, 105, 109–10, 120, 140
Hong Xiuquan 92
Hosie, A. 129
Hunan 132
Hunter, W.C. 2

Imperial Maritime Customs 91
Indian government 29, 51, 78, 80, 84–7, 94, 98–9, 129, 162
Indian merchants 46, 48, 61, 77, 84–5
Indochina 150, 153, 171
Indonesia 86
Inglis, B. 18
Innes, J. 102

Jambi 170
Jamesina 103
Jamsetsee Jeejeebhoy & Co. 112
Japan 89, 155
Japanese trade 43

Jardine Matheson Co. 71, 101–5, 107–8, 112–18, 119, 120, 163, 179–80
Jardine Skinner & Co. 112
Jardine, W. 107, 116
Java 43, 60, 79–80, 89, 150–2, 154, 157
Jewish merchants 85, 102, 109, 112, 116–17, 134–5
Johor 54, 89, 147, 149, 170
junk trade, Chinese 40–4, 55, 90

Kaempfer(o), Englebert(o) 25–6, 35–6, 181–2
Kapuas R. 44
Karachi 85
Katsenberg, J. 133
Kedah 51, 171
Kerr, J.D. 147
keystone species 58; modifiers 86–7
Khaw Joo Choe 154, 157
Khaw Sim Bee (Na Ranong) 156–7
Khun Sa 171
Kipling, R. 5, 160
Koeri 66–7
kongsi 55, 143, 149, 156

land tax 73
Landes, D. 59
Lanrick 106
Lansky, M. 133
Laurent, S. 147
Leary, T. 12
Lee Keng Yam 141
Li Mi 134, 171
Lin, Cexu (Lin Tse-hsu) 86, 91, 97–9
Lin, M.H. 61, 96, 98, 121, 123, 124
Lingnan (region) 92, 121, 125
Lintin Islands 102
Little, R. 146
Lo Sing Han 171
Lockyer, C. 34, 53
London 101
long-distance trade 22–5, 160
Lubbock, B. 106–7
Luciano, C. 133
luxury manufactures 22–3

Macau 102
McCoy, A. 134
McNeill, W.H. 62
macroparasitism 62
madat 37
Madya Pradesh 75
Magniac, C. 79

Mahmud Badaruddin, Sultan of
   Palembang 54
Mahratas 80
Malaya 86, 142–5, 149, 154–5, 158
Malays 55
Malay states 56, 143–4,
Malcolm, J. 67, 83, 183
Maluku (Moluccas) 43, 51
Malwa 67, 74–5, 77–86, 135, 169;
   opium 24–5, 66, 78–86, 94, 102, 113,
   164
Malwa Opium Syndicate 112
Mandsaur 84, 113
Manila 42, 101
Marshall, J. 124, 133
Marwari 84, 113
Marx, K. 46
materia medica 20
Matheson, A. 103, 109, 116, 160
Matheson, D. 163
Matheson, J. 115
Medan 148
Melaka 21, 24, 37, 75, 138, 148–9
Melaka Straits 60
Merlin, M.D. 14–17
Mexico 61, 75
Miao Rebellion 121
militias 123
Mindanao 56
miners 52, 144–8
Mintz, S. 27–32, 34, 92
Mission Civilisatrice 150
Miyazaki, Ichisada 92
Moluccas *see* Maluku
Mughal Empire 39, 45–6
Muir, W. 164
Muslim Rebellion 121

Napoleonic Wars 60–1, 78
Needham, J. 20
Negri Sembilan 147
nepenthes 17
Netherlands East Indies 138, 141, 150–1,
   153, 158
Nien Rebellion 121
northeast monsoon 104
Northern Expedition 133

opium: addiction 19, 35, 52, 56, 144–8,
   163, 165–6; balls 68, 70; as cash
   125–6; chests 70; excise 70;
   legalization of 89–90, 100–1, 107–8,
   109–12, 118–19, 134–5, 166–9;
   literature of 174–8; prohibition of 54,
   56–7, 89–90, 126; provision 70;
   recycled 151; quality control 72
Opium Agency 67–8, 74, 110
opium agents 62, 67–8
opium auctions 64, 71–3, 114, 130
Opium Circulars 72, 107, 121, 179–80
opium dens 126–7, 169
opium economy 126–7, 132–4, 166–9,
   171–3
opium exports 73–4, 76, 85–6, 110, 126,
   163
opium farmers 139–42, 147–9, 167
opium firms 85, 109, 111–18
opium imports to China 95–6, 118–19,
   163
opium monopoly 29; by the British 46–7,
   51, 74–5, 80, 86; of the Mughals 45–6;
   in Southeast Asia 150–1, 153–5
opium pipe 36
opium prices 65, 78–80, 111, 129, 147–8
opium production 21; in British India
   61–73, 74–5, 110, 135, 163; in China
   96–7, 109, 119–27, 134–5, 167; and
   famine 123–5; in Malwa 83–6, 183; in
   Mughal India 24–5, 34, 45–6; at
   present 110, 167, 171
opium revenue 66, 73, 82, 128, 135, 155
opium revenue farms 10, 89, 135, 137–42;
   156–9, 170; abolition of 154–5, 161;
   auction of 150, 154; Javanese pattern
   142, 149–52; Malayan pattern 142–9;
   urban 152–4
opium smuggling 90–1
opium trade xii; in Asia 6–7, 20–1, 137;
   and capital accumulation 9, 173; to
   China 25, 32, 49–52, 60–1, 79–82,
   85–7, 93–6, 100–1, 109, 113–14,
   119–21; defenders of 135, 160–4;
   the end 130; in Japan 164;
   long-distance trade 22, 105–7;
   speculation in 99, 110–11, 116–17,
   129–30; studies of 7–8; suppression of
   128–31, 155
opium use: in China 26, 88–92, 94, 96,
   121, 126–7, 165–6; earliest evidence of
   14–15; globally 26; among the Greeks
   18–19; ingestion 25; among Javanese
   35, 79–80, 151; as medicine 20–1;
   among Malays 34–6, 52–4; in
   Melaka 25; among Muslims 19; as a
   pain-killer 91, 144–5; in Persia 25; in
   Roman times 21; smoking of 26, 35–7,
   136, 164–6; in Southeast Asia 88–90,
   144–8; in Taiwan 35; with tobacco 36;

in urban areas 152; by Vietnamese 150; in the west 88–9, 117–18, 136, 164–5; as a work drug 19–20, 52, 55, 144–8, 170–1
Opium War(s) 10, 48, 58, 86, 93, 97–8, 100–1, 108, 109, 121, 135, 162
orientalism 135, 164–5
Outer anchorages 102
Owen, D.E. xi, 6–7, 47, 77, 83, 90

Pahang 89
Palembang 39, 43, 54, 56, 89, 170; Sultan of 43
Pao Shih-ch'en 91
Papaver somniferum 14–16
Paraclesus (Theophrastus Bombastus von Hohenheim) 21
Parkinson, C.N. 42, 48, 59
Parsi merchants 48, 50, 85, 102, 109, 135
pass duty 80, 82, 110
Patani 51
Patna 2, 64; Council 45, opium 2, 25, 45, 96, 102, 110–11, 164
Patna 1–6, 11, 158, 173
patronage 152
peasants: and capitalism 61–2; as opium cultivators 65–70, 83, 86, 163
Penang (Pinang) 36, 105, 138, 140, 145, 152; 154, 156–7
Peninsular and Oriental Steamship Co. (P & O) 112
pepper 43, 44, 75; and gambier 55, 143, 147–8
Perak 54, 89, 143
permanent settlement 62
Persephone 17
Persia 21, 25
Philippine Commission 155
Philippines 5, 89, 128, 143
Pindari 80
Pires, T. 25
plantation system 28–9
Plassey, Battle of 6, 37, 44
Pliny 19
Pontianak 44, 51
poppy cultivation 67–70, 122–5
Portuguese: empire 23–4; ports 78–9
Prince de Neufchatel 104
Prinsep, G.A. 95–6
Prinsep, J. 99
Pritchard, E.H. 49
Purcell, V. 161

Purvis, J. (John Purvis & Son) 115–17
Purvis, J. M. 117

Qing: government 131; literature 90, 91; dynasty 88, 100, 114, 171

rabi 67
Raffles, T.S. 60, 138, 160
Rajahstan 75
Red Army 134
Red River 120
Red Rover 104
régie see opium monopoly
Remington & Co. 112
revenue farmers 83–6; 147–9
Riau 56, 141, 143, 147–9, 152
Riau-Johor 55, 170
Rothschilds, 115
Rowe, W. 92, 131
Rowntree, J. xiv
Royal Commission 130, 144
Ruck, C. 17
Russell & Co. 102, 105, 107

Saigon 145, 153
salt tax 73
Sambas 44, 52
sandalwood 75
Sassoon, D. & Sons 85, 112–16, 120, 135–6, 160
Sassoon, E. 113
Schoffer 42
secret societies 149
Selangor 54, 89, 170
Seventeen Gentlemen 40–2
Shan Plateau 134
Shandong 134
Shanghai 113, 119
Shantou (Swatow) 40
Shanxi 124, 126
Shaw, S. 43, 75–6
Shen, Congwen 131–2
Siak 170
Siam 55, 56, 86, 89, 138, 142–3, 145–6, 156–7, 161, 164
Sichuan 119–21, 125, 129–30
silk trade 108, 114
silver trade 42–4, 58, 61, 97–8, 107
Sind 78, 82
Singapore 104–5, 116–17, 134, 137–8, 140–1, 142, 143, 147–9, 152
Singapore Free Press 154
Singapore Opium Monopoly 161
Singh, N. 62

Sino-British Treaty 128–9
Sixteenth Emperor Rebellion 130
slave system 28
slave trade 23, 29, 56
Smyrna 75–6
Smyth, H.W. 142, 145–7
Society for the Suppression of the Opium
    Trade (SSOT) 117, 128
Song, Ong Siang 140
South China Sea 48–9
Southeast Asia 60, 86, 89–90, 101, 108,
    134, 138–41, 142, 149, 161, 170–1
Spanish dollars 8, 42
Spanish empire 22, 138
Spence, J. 91, 124, 126
spice trade 22, 24–5
steamships 107
Stewart, W. 76
Straits produce 43, 101, 105, 117
Straits Settlements 61, 101, 138, 143, 149,
    154–5, 161
Straits of Singapore 104
Sudder Factory 70–1
sugar 27–32, 56, 87
Sulawesi 51
Sullivan, S. 46
Sulu 55–6, 170
Sumatra 54, 75, 141, 143, 148, 154
Suzhou (Soochow) 91, 127
Swatow Opium Guild 119
Swettenham, F. 161

Taiping Rebellion 92, 99, 108, 121, 142
Taiwan 126
Tan Chung 100
Tausug 55
tea houses 127–8

tea trade 31–32, 39–42, 49, 52, 58, 60,
    87, 108, 114
theriaca 17, 25
tobacco 28, 87
Tokugawa 89
trade balance 42–4, 49, 51, 60, 86
Treaty of Nanking 99–102, 107, 162
Treaty Ports 99
Treaty of Tianjin 109, 112, 162
Trengganu 51, 170
Turkey 21
Turkish opium 75–6, 102

Verleun, J. 3–4
Vietnam 56, 120
Virginia 28–9

Wakeman, F. 99
Waley, Arthur 100
wandering braves 123, 131
warlords 128, 131–4, 171–3
Warner, J. 92
Warren, J. 55–6
Watts, C. 5
Wenchou 127
"White Man's Burden" *see* Kipling
Wickberg, E. 139
Wong, R.B. 59
Wright, H.R.C. 77
Wu, Jingzi 90–1

Yogyakarta 79–80
Yungui (region) 121, 125
Yunnan 119–23, 125

Zhao Erfeng 130
Zhao Erxun 130